TRUTH AND CONSEQUENCES

TRUTH AND *Consequences*

Game Shows in Fiction and Film

MIKE MILEY

University Press of Mississippi • Jackson

The University Press of Mississippi is the scholarly publishing agency of
the Mississippi Institutions of Higher Learning: Alcorn State University,
Delta State University, Jackson State University, Mississippi State University,
Mississippi University for Women, Mississippi Valley State University,
University of Mississippi, and University of Southern Mississippi.

www.upress.state.ms.us

Designed by Peter D. Halverson

The University Press of Mississippi is a member of the Association of University Presses.

Copyright © 2019 by University Press of Mississippi
All rights reserved
Manufactured in the United States of America

First printing 2019
∞

Library of Congress Cataloging-in-Publication Data available
LCCN 2019032097

Hardback ISBN	978-1-4968-2538-4
Trade paperback ISBN	978-1-4968-2539-1
Epub single ISBN	978-1-4968-2540-7
Epub institutional ISBN	978-1-4968-2541-4
PDF single ISBN	978-1-4968-2542-1
PDF institutional ISBN	978-1-4968-2543-8

British Library Cataloging-in-Publication Data available

for my parents,

who let me read and watch whatever I wanted,

and for everyone who has endured the results

CONTENTS

TOSS UP [3]
Trivial Pursuit?

ROUND ONE [34]
What's My Line? Game Shows and the
Quest for an Authentic Self

ROUND TWO [93]
Love Connection: The Game Show's Erogenous Zones

ROUND THREE [130]
Family Feud: The Game-Show Families of
Salinger, Wallace, and Anderson

ROUND FOUR [174]
Fear Factor: Game Shows, State Power, and Death

FINAL JEOPARDY [212]

ACKNOWLEDGMENTS [235]

BIBLIOGRAPHY [237]

INDEX [244]

TRUTH AND CONSEQUENCES

TOSS UP

Trivial Pursuit?

THERE IS SOMETHING PLEASURABLE AND REJUVENATING about studying popular culture. After all, it is what people do among friends: they go over what they have read, they argue (sometimes playfully) about what they have seen (or have not, or should, or refuse to), and they work together to put the film, pop song, or television program of the moment into a broader context, tracing long arcs across era, genre, and media. In the raucous jumble of after-work drinks or the jovial calm of a great dinner party, topics as wide-ranging and far-reaching as these will be introduced, considered, passed along, and evaluated, with some ideas helping those gathered to see culture in a new way, some making them dig their heels in more deeply, and others fading along with their buzz.

The haphazard trek through popular culture that fills one's social time is difficult to replicate in a more sustained academic setting such as this monograph. Academic studies tend to be more concentrated in the topics they will consider, more rigorous in the methods they will employ, and less playful in the tone they will adopt. Further, academic works usually treat media individually, shying away from associative approaches and focusing only on television, or only on film, or subsets thereof. Such work is essential for crafting the most thorough critique, but it does not entirely capture how people encounter pop culture in their daily lives.

The cultural artifacts that stick in people's brains do not come at them as discretely as scholarship suggests. Rather, people often shuffle between music and podcasts in their cars as they drive home to flip channels among game shows, prestige TV, snippets of movies, and as much of the news as they can stand before getting in bed and trying to take in a few pages of the literary work everyone else is claiming to have read as their eyelids grow increasingly heavy. Each of these scraps of pop culture coexists simultaneously with every other scrap. Whether one has time to consume it all or not, these works are all talking to each other, reflecting and molding the zeitgeist in real time while everyone scrambles to keep up. This book strives to capture a sliver of this flow of popular culture by looking carefully at work where several different strands of popular culture suddenly appear together on the same channel. In doing so, I hope to balance a freewheeling conversation among friends with the rigorous analysis of scholarship.

Game shows are an ideal test subject for striking this balance for two reasons: 1) they are too knowingly playful to withstand straight-faced scholarship without making the scholar look humorless, and 2) I love them. Growing up as an only child meant that I had a lot of time to myself, which I spent watching disgusting amounts of television and movies. In the summertime, this meant packing my entire day with game shows, starting with *Family Feud* at 9:00 AM, followed by *The Price Is Right* and *American Gladiators*, then a movie at lunch to dodge the soaps before hitting paydirt: the USA Network's afternoon game-show block, which let me spend the rest of the afternoon gliding through every game show any kid could want to see: *The $25,000 Pyramid*, *Wipeout*, *Hollywood Squares*, *Win, Lose, or Draw*, and my personal favorite, *Press Your Luck*. If I still had not had my fill of big money and fabulous prizes, I could always talk my parents into *Wheel of Fortune* or *Jeopardy!* If not, there were always more movies to watch and books to read before bedtime.

As I got older and snobbier, I started to think of myself as too sophisticated for game shows, which meant I swore them off as trivial, not counting a devotion to *Project Runway* and brief fixations with *The Contender* and—yes, dear reader, I will come clean—*The Apprentice*. But then five years ago I got a nagging sense that something connected J. D. Salinger, David Foster Wallace, and the early work of Paul Thomas Anderson, but I could not place it. I could pair them off no problem, Salinger and Wallace, Wallace and Anderson, but the trio continually resisted coming together. Then game shows buzzed into my mind. All three of them had put family members on game shows. Why would these writers, all of whom are rather obsessed with authenticity, write about game shows? I had to figure it out. The first draft of the fifteen-minute conference talk ran twenty thousand words, and I still had more to say. Were there more works that used game shows like this? Enough for a book?

That is about where you came in.

I share these anecdotes to illustrate why this book desires to blend the sobriety of scholarship with the giddiness of conversation: my scholarship led me back to something I love, and this love permitted me to incorporate something I had sworn off as unsophisticated back into the art that I spend my time overthinking. While this book may not be audacious enough to argue that game shows deserve to be reevaluated as high art (though I will gladly read that book when someone writes it), it does posit that the culture does not grant them the attention that they require to understand the current world. One can glean some of their influence by looking at them directly, but only so much. If one wants to see how much the game show permeates and reflects American culture, look in the spaces it has infiltrated, especially fiction and film, and see how writers and filmmakers use the game show to reflect the world they see. What do they think game shows have to say about where America has been, where it is going, *where it is?*

The game show may not be a hot topic in scholarship, but writers and filmmakers have been toying with these questions for quite some time. Scholars have some catching up to do, and it is worthwhile work because in doing it, they may discover a new lens through which to view and understand the direction of postwar America. This lens may not always present the most favorable picture of the American Project, but it does clarify and unite disparate elements at play in contemporary America whose connections are harder to see otherwise.

Despite all the work that scholars have done to reclaim so much so-called "low" culture from the gulag of bad taste, there are still some programs that have yet to be granted release. Foremost among these is the game show. With its contrived setups, predetermined questions and prizes, and canned chit-chat, the game show can easily be criticized for creating the illusion of answering questions without ever solving any mysteries. In everyday speech, the phrase "game-show host" serves as an insult comparable to "used-car salesman," leading one to wonder why any minor celebrity would aspire to clutch the skinny mic or pastel cue cards, let alone why any academic would consider game shows serious enough to merit scholarly attention. Given the decades of critical writing that exist about game shows (emphasis on "critical") the only matter in question when it comes to game shows is how much to despise them, making the game show a top contender for the dubious honor of Most Consistently Derided Program in television history.

Although nearly every other television form or genre has undergone a massive critical and popular reassessment or resurgence in the past twenty years, the game show's reputation has remained both remarkably stagnant and remarkably low. Even when the game show occasionally enjoys a return to popularity (such as when *Who Wants to Be a Millionaire?* dominated prime time), assessments of its overall cultural worth, quality, or influence pale in comparison even to the most restrained appraisals of "quality" or "golden age" television such as *The Wire*, *Mad Men*, or even *Modern Family*. Most television and media scholars express their disinterest in game-show scholarship by declining to participate at all, tacitly deeming it unworthy of condemnation, let alone critique. Those who do choose to look more closely at the game show frequently seem like they are competing in a game show of their own to deliver the most blistering insult to the format. Some of the most incendiary whammies include the *Sunday Express*'s "chewing gum for the eyes," Fred Allen's "the buzzards of radio," Neil Hickey's "the most primitive and banal form of televised entertainment," and Elayne Rapping's "[the] dregs of American culture and American life itself" (Holmes 3; Holbrook 11). Morris B. Holbrook, who ranks among the least reserved of the game show's denouncers, wagers that he "can imagine no artifacts of popular culture more apparently worthless and more seemingly unredeemed by any vestige of intellectual, esthetic, or moral value than those that constitute the daily spectacle paraded before the public in the form of television game shows," which is to say that he is not exactly what one would call a fan (11).

The most famous condemnation of the game show, however, comes from Federal Communications Commission chair Newton Minow's 1961 speech to the National Association of Broadcasters:

> When television is good, nothing—not the theater, not the magazines or newspapers—nothing is better. But when television is bad, nothing is worse. I invite each of you to sit down in front of your television set when your station goes on the air and stay there, for a day, without a book, without a magazine, without a newspaper, without a profit and loss sheet or a rating book to distract you. Keep your eyes glued to that set until the station signs off. I can assure you that what you will observe is a vast wasteland. You will see a procession of game shows, formula comedies about totally unbelievable families, blood and thunder, mayhem, violence, sadism, murder, western bad men, western good men, private eyes, gangsters, more violence, and cartoons. And endlessly, commercials—many screaming, cajoling, and offending. And most of all, boredom. (398)

The speech, in particular its phrase "vast wasteland," should be quite familiar, and Minow's critique frequently appears in articles attacking television as a "content-free medium" (Ozersky 86). Minow paints all televised content with the same oversized brush; however, his decision to list game shows as the first landmark in that vast wasteland has had a lasting effect on their reputation and legacy. Earlier in the same speech, Minow even uses game-show lingo to attack the NAB, stating that, despite an economic recession, "the price has indeed been right" for network stockholders who have chosen to serve their own interests ahead of the public's as they sowed this televisual wasteland (396). Minow's choice to start his list with game shows should hardly come as a surprise when one recalls that he delivered this speech only a few years after the quiz-show scandals of the late 1950s rocked the integrity of television. Even so, Minow's address granted permission to cultural critics to abuse the game show as television's perennial scapegoat. No matter how much time has passed and regardless of how much television programming has changed, it seems like each new iteration of the game show—from *The Price Is Right* to Chuck Barris's sleazy empire to reality television to electing *The Apprentice* host Donald J. Trump President of the United States—often appears as Exhibit A in *The People vs. Television*.

As prominent as his "vast wasteland" speech may be, this diminished view of the game show did not start with Minow: it has been around as long as the game show itself. Scholars differ on which radio program deserves to be considered the first quiz show. Some argue in favor of *Vox Pop* (1932), others *Major Bowes' Original Amateur Hour* (1934), and still others *Professor Quiz* or *Uncle Jim's Question Bee* (both 1936). Regardless of which show came first, by 1939, one year before Alex Trebek was even born, newspaper critics were discussing whom to "blame" for the "deluge" of quiz shows (Hoerschelmann 20–21). Hand-wringing and finger-pointing did little to affect the quiz show's popularity. By 1955, when quiz shows began to appear on television, their reputation had been rehabilitated to the point that they not only were being used to promote the educational potential of television but were being touted as a decisive force in the battle against the Soviet Union for educational superiority (Hoerschelmann 70). With these raised stakes came larger prizes, which simultaneously increased the shows' popularity—will tonight be the night someone answers the $64,000 question?—and redirected its emphasis to the "pursuit of dollars rather than intelligence" (Holmes 97). The lure of bigger ratings and bigger bucks turned out to be too great and led sponsors and producers to rig these big-money quiz shows to ensure audiences never touched their dials. That scandal led not only to these programs going off the air by 1959 (and to Minow's 1961 speech), but it dealt a blow to the reputation of the game show from which it has yet to recover sixty years later (Hoerschelmann 70).

The big-money quiz show may have gone off the air, but the game show did not lie dormant for long. The prime-time, big-money, highbrow *quiz* show with a simple-yet-serious set such as *Twenty-One* simply became the daytime, low-stakes, lowbrow *game* show, with brighter, more colorful, less dramatic sets.

In the revamped game show, best exemplified by *The Price Is Right*, rather than quizzing contestants on more academic subjects such as literature or opera that could be vulnerable to charges of being rigged, the show would challenge contestants with more commonplace questions such as the price of a tube of toothpaste or a new car, things that the average daytime television viewer would know from their own experience shopping (or watching television). While this rebranding certainly resurrected the game show as a television format, it did little to restore its highbrow cultural reputation or prevent it from accusations of glorifying consumption or belittling the intelligence and social standing of its new daytime audience: women (Hoerschelmann 13–14).

Broadly speaking, the common view that the game show functions as the televised end of capitalism's wedge originates with these post-scandal daytime game shows. Gary Cross, in his book *An All-Consuming Century: Why Commercialism Won in Modern America*, contextualizes the societal changes that allowed game shows to rise to prominence in a culture that also dismissed their cultural value. Cross opens his book by declaring that "the real winner of the [twentieth] century was consumerism," a term Cross defines as "the belief that goods give meaning to individuals and their roles in society" (1). In a consumer society, people no longer identify as an active, engaged political body but as a passive, consuming one "defined and developed by individual acquisition and use of mass-produced goods" (Cross 1). Where Cross discusses how this transformation affects the average American's relationship to society, Jean-François Lyotard shows how it alters our understanding of knowledge itself:

> the relationship of the suppliers and users of knowledge to the knowledge they supply and use is now tending, and will increasingly tend, to assume the form already taken by the relationship of commodity producers and consumers to the commodities they produce and consume—that is, the form of value. Knowledge is and will be produced in order to be sold, it is and will be consumed in order to be valorized in a new production. In both cases, the goal is exchange. Knowledge ceases to be an end in itself, it loses its "use-value." (4–5)

Lyotard characterizes the postmodern era as one in which the relationship between people and knowledge no longer functions as an intellectual endeavor but a commercial one. What one knows only has value insofar as what it can fetch in the marketplace. Knowledge is not something to be prized but rather something used to obtain a prize. Or, as Lyotard bluntly puts it later in *The Postmodern Condition*, "Knowledge is a matter for TV games" (76). Douglas Kellner argues that even though these shows give away prizes for knowledge, it would be a mistake to consider the most knowledgable as winners because the shift to an information-based society, he argues, does not grant knowledge more influence in society. Rather, as I hope to show throughout this book, it works to benefit "hegemonic configurations of corporate and state power" that merge information with entertainment to create a "networked infotainment society" devoted not to "democratic purposes" but to "the accumulation of capital" through the constant delivery of high-end, high-speed spectacle (*Media Spectacle* 12, 14).

This intersection of Kellner, Lyotard, and Cross explains how the game show embodies America's transformation into a country based on consumption and spectacle. The game show tests audiences on their knowledge of commodities and rewards those who "know" the most about these commodities with *more* commodities, thus reinforcing in the viewer the material benefits of "knowing" more about these commodities and giving meaning to the lives of the individuals who know this information. This knowledge, of course, can best be acquired through consuming greater quantities of these commodities and the game shows that promote acquiring them. Game shows in the twenty-first century encourage this feedback loop even more by writing questions about popular media, "rewarding those who have devoted themselves to absorbing the picayune detail of the spectacle culture," which involves consuming large amounts of television and, more importantly, massive doses of advertising (Kellner, *Media Spectacle* 18). Even when a game show "emphasize[s] the tasteful and useful character" of the commodities they give away, it still holds "consumption as a key component of U.S. culture," making the game show "the cheapest television commercial possible," "the delivery of the promises that advertisers make" (Hoerschelmann 56; Fiske 273; Tulloch 9). In this sense, advertisers do not sponsor game shows. Game shows sponsor the real program: capitalism.

Douglas Kellner claims in *Media Spectacle* that promotion forms the essence of commodity spectacle (4). With its prizes, celebrity guests, corporate acts of charity, and on-air voiceovers overflowing with ad copy, the game show folds every conceivable type of promotion into each round of play—advertising, marketing, public relations—making it among the most distilled expressions of commodity spectacle available. Morris Holbrook describes how television, and the game show in particular, serves as

> a vehicle for foisting the values of capitalism on the impressionable masses who uncritically absorb the domestic family-oriented implications of the sitcoms, the patriarchal thrust of the cop shows, the imperialistic ethos of the news programs, and (most of all) the materialistic mania of the commercials en route to being socialized into the prevailing norms

of the consumer culture that serves as a fertile ground exploited by the capitalistic captains of consciousness. (15)

Critics can find no shortage of game shows to fit Holbrook's bill, from *The Price Is Right* or *Supermarket Sweep*'s depiction of shopping as a grand prize in itself to *The Dating Game*'s parade of heteronormativity to nearly every game show's promise that one can get rich quick if one is only willing to play by television's rules.

In devaluing knowledge and elevating the roles of chance and wagering, the game show, according to its critics, contributes to the decline of the Protestant work ethic in America (Hoerschelmann 97). As Su Holmes notes in her book *The Quiz Show*, "There is actually nothing intrinsically 'American' about the idea of giving away money" because receiving material rewards as the result of hard work is the essence of the American Dream (37). However, in the age of the game show, as Gary Cross shows, that ethic has been replaced by "an ethic of consumption" in which people get rich quick, and the game show becomes a crucial force in the reimagining of the American Dream (Hoerschelmann 97).

Where Holmes and Hoerschelmann see a betrayal of the American Dream in the game show, John Fiske sees simply a different part of the dream being emphasized, namely the "rags-to-riches" narrative. This narrative, Fiske argues, takes on a greater importance in a society that describes itself as "both competitive and democratic" (272). Although the American narrative promises that citizens receive the opportunity to improve their station in life, resources and talents are not distributed equally, which explains why luck plays an increasingly large role in post-scandal game shows. Luck, Fiske explains, "mitigates the harshness" of capitalism's inherent inequality while simultaneously strengthening that inequality and "the appeal of gambling, of easy money" among the not-yet-rich (272). The game show, simply put, turns the rags-to-riches narrative into a ritual that contestants and viewers alike can participate in, making their submission to "capitalist and patriarchal ideologies" pleasurable and rewarding (273).

Fiske uses Levi-Strauss's definitions of game and ritual to detail how the game show combines characteristics of the two. Contestants start out as individuals in a ritual who then enter a game that renders their differences insignificant until their unique talents and abilities give them an edge over their competitors in the game, at which point the host, a symbol of the dominant culture's power and influence over events, escorts the victor to the winner's circle, where the ritual returns and leaves the contestant basking in the "fetishistic splendor" of their prizes (267–68). Fiske neatly defines the game show's "ritual-game-ritual" structure as "an enactment of capitalist ideology" (268). Of course, the viewer is unlikely to notice such a "ritualistic celebration" of capitalism amidst all "the trappings of showbiz" that is the game show's carnival aesthetic: bright lights, loud music and busy colors, leaping and screaming contestants, etc. (Fiske 268, 279). The carnivalesque distraction is, of course, by design. Fiske remarks that the game show's combination of the fun and novelty of a carnival with "the knowledge and discipline of the schoolroom" contradicts the nature of the carnivalesque to interrupt the hierarchies and norms that govern everyday life. However, as Hoerschelmann points out in *The Rules of the Game*, the shows' irreverent reversals of so-called American meritocratic norms reinforce the rules they pretend to subvert (Hoerschelmann 61). Fiske's "contradictory" combination of carnival and workplace makes perfect sense as "an enactment of capitalist ideology" in a "networked infotainment society" governed by an ethic of consumption and entertainment (and consumption-as-entertainment). By appearing to represent an escape from the consumer-oriented capitalist everyday, the "excessive and carnivalesque atmosphere" of a game show "naturalize[s] an excess of consumption and normalize[s] consumerism," thus promoting the very thing it presents itself as an escape from more vigorously than the ads that flank each of its segments (Fiske 269; Hoerschelmann 109). Holmes argues that although game shows can still gesture toward a retreat from daily life, "they remain deeply implicated within the politics of the everyday" (Holmes 9).

Holmes states that America deserves to be thought of as the "Land of the Game Show" not only because it has created most of the game shows audiences are familiar with, but also because of America's "association with capitalist greed, commerciality, consumerism and media imperialism" (6, 7). If game shows have been depicted as "institutionalized Monument[s] to Greed," and America is the Land of the Game Show, then it stands to reason that these game shows critics are so eager to dismiss as unworthy of scholarly attention have more to say about American life than critics are inclined to confront (Holbrook 51). The game show may be singled out as offering viewers "something for nothing," but it hardly represents the only voice in contemporary society that makes this promise to its audience. Rather, this promise simply serves as the New American Dream under late capitalism, especially when viewed in light of the fact that America elected a game-show host as the 45th president of the United States in 2016.

While most critics limit their attacks on the game show to accusations of consumerism and capitalist greed, others are willing to go much further. *I Am Not Your Negro*, Raoul Peck's 2017 documentary about James Baldwin, presents Baldwin's argument that responsibility for white America's limited (and bigoted) racial imagination belongs to the entertainment industry, which, according to Baldwin, is compelled, given the way it is built, to present to the American people a self-perpetuating fantasy of American life. Their concept of entertainment is difficult to distinguish from the use of narcotics.... To watch the TV screen for any length of time is to learn some really frightening things about the American sense of reality. We are cruelly trapped between what we would like to be and what we actually are. And we cannot possibly become what we would like to be until we are willing to ask ourselves just why the lives we lead on this continent are mainly so empty, so tame, and so ugly. (Baldwin and Peck 84, 86)

From the nearly endless array of commercial entertainment that Peck could juxtapose with Baldwin's words, he selects game shows almost exclusively. Peck does include brief clips from sensationalistic talk shows such as *The Jerry Springer Show* in this sequence; however, the overwhelming majority of clips feature contestants from game shows wearing absurd costumes, jumping and screaming amidst showers of confetti and smoke. The sequence starts with one of the many moments from *The Gong Show* where Gene Gene the Dancing Machine smiles and dances alone on a garishly lit stage while the audience and the panel applaud and guffaw mindlessly. To allege, as Peck's editing does, that *The Gong Show* exemplifies "the American sense of reality" best is a "really frightening thing" indeed because doing so rebukes the highest ideals that the nation espouses to claim that these ideals have been squandered on displays of excess, objectification, and ignorance in the service of a fantasy of benign comfort and abundance. (*Gong Show* creator Chuck Barris would likely feel incredibly flattered by such a condemnation.) Tellingly, Peck does not distinguish among the different aesthetics of game shows in this sequence. He places clips from daytime game shows with warm, colorful, brightly lit sets such as *The Price Is Right* alongside the cold, monochromatic, cameo-lit style of primetime game shows such as *Deal or No Deal*, thus rendering all game shows equally responsible for informing the American sense of reality.

Peck's editorial decision makes Baldwin's central argument explicit: the American Dream is a drug employed to blind people not only to the suffering of others, but also to the fact that their pursuit of happiness and affluence often depends on denying that same dream to others, even making the inferior status of others into a spectacle. As viewers watch these so-called ordinary people win big bucks from the comfort of their home, they look away from the multitudes (often including viewers like themselves) for whom such a windfall of wealth and success neoliberal American society makes not only improbable but impossible. Peck's sequence continues showing images from game shows as Samuel L. Jackson speaks Baldwin's words: spectacles of entertainment are "designed not to trouble, but to reassure. They also weaken our ability to deal with the world as it is, ourselves as we are" (Baldwin and Peck 86). "When we talk about 'democracy,'" Baldwin declares, "this is what we mean" (Baldwin and Peck 83). These sets might be so brightly lit as to be visible from space, but, as Baldwin and Peck's argument makes abundantly clear, their true goal is invisibility. As long as one keeps watching, they are guaranteed not to see. Baldwin's words speak to the culture industry as a whole, and Peck selects the game show to symbolize the most potent, the most addictive, the most concentrated form of the schedule-1 narcotic known as the American Dream. In *I Am Not Your Negro*, America is indeed the Land of the Game Show: it is hooked on it and all that it represents, powerless to kick the habit.

Despite this seemingly inescapably bad reputation that drowns out any supporters, the game show nevertheless persists, and reports of its demise or irrelevance have been greatly exaggerated. *The Price Is Right*, *Jeopardy!*, and *Wheel of Fortune* are among the longest-running television programs in history, while other shows such as *The Match Game*, *To Tell the Truth*, *The Gong Show*, *Double Dare*, and *Press Your Luck* have recently enjoyed prime-time revivals on major networks. There are also new game shows such as *Who Wants to Be a Millionaire?*, *Deal or No Deal*, and *The Wall* that periodically capture the frantic energy of the culture. Articles as recently as the summer of 2017 are asking, "Are We in the New Golden Age of Game Shows?" (Friedlander). New media has also capitalized on the adaptability of the game show, most notably in the form of the sassy computer game *You Don't Know Jack* (which also briefly appeared as a television show) and the HQ Trivia App, which holds live games twice daily, complete with cash prizes, an obnoxious host, and warnings from critics that it "offers a sign of what the future of propaganda might look like" (Bogost, HQ). And that comes without me even mentioning reality competition programs such as *Survivor*, *Big Brother*, and their spawn that are frequently only "quiz shows in disguise" (Hoerschelmann 150).

As much as one may resist lending any academic attention, credibility, or meaning to a program as seemingly vapid and materialistic as the game show, the truth remains that this television format is one that many people are intimately familiar with, even though they have expended little effort to become intimate with it. The game show is part of the American consciousness: Americans have absorbed its rhythms, its discourse, its worldview. Whether it is the highbrow questions-as-answers format of *Jeopardy!*, the "I'd like to buy a vowel" of *Wheel of Fortune*, the "is that your final answer?" of *Who Wants to Be a Millionaire?* or the "no whammies!" of *Press Your Luck*, people know and use the lingo of the game show. Although it may not be as large in scope or consequence as other media events such as the Super Bowl or the Olympics, the game show nevertheless meets the criteria Kellner ascribes to those other "cultural rituals" in *Media Spectacle* because game shows also "celebrate society's deepest values (i.e. competition, winning, success, and money)" (5). The only difference is that one does not have to wait one year (or four) to see this ritual enacted: it is on nearly every channel, several times a day.

The game show's ability to weather over half a century of critical dismissal and derision earns it a need to be taken more seriously. In diagnosing their detrimental effect on the culture, critical takedowns of game shows avoid examining how they work and function in the culture. Even a harsh critic like Morris Holbrook concedes that "it often seems that the lowliest—the most mundane, trivial, or vulgar—of social artifacts appear the most illuminating in terms of the light they shed on the meanings embedded in human culture" (11). If Holbrook's dire assessment of game shows turns out to be painfully accurate, arriving at such a pronouncement without a full investigation of the game show and its role in the culture deprives everyone of a full understanding of exactly how and why these seemingly vacuous and invincibly popular programs do what their critics say they do.

Thankfully, the reassessment of the game show and its place in American culture is already underway, if in fits and starts. John Fiske concludes his chapter on game shows in his landmark book *Television Culture* with the assertion that a rehabilitation of the game show is "both probable and politically desirable" (282). Fiske's assessment of the political potential of a format as participatory as the game show remains among the most favorable evaluations of the format to date. Although the academic world has been slow to take up Fiske's challenge, two books published in the 2000s constitute important first steps toward examining the social and political implications of America's game-show culture. Olaf Hoerschelmann's 2006 history of the quiz show, *The Rules of the Game: Quiz Shows and American Culture*, encourages readers to view the quiz show not as mindless, lowest-common-denominator entertainment but as "a struggle for the meaning of the objects of everyday life" because it is one of the many forms of popular culture "involved in the organization of understandings of our natural and social world, in the construction of social identities ... and in the validation and invalidation of different forms of knowledge" (155, 4–5). When one abandons the view of the quiz show as being "marginal to social life," Hoerschelmann argues one discovers "unique site[s] ... for the construction of social identities, a place where people can start to negotiate their position in the field of culture, a place where the social subjects can negotiate, challenge, and understand their position in a stratified society" (6). Su Holmes's 2008 book *The Quiz Show* approaches the format with a focus on the form's popularity in the United Kingdom and the aesthetics of the shows themselves, showing how the set design, lighting, and hierarchies within the game replicate "relations of power" in the real world (75, 63). She encourages viewers to ask "to what does its game space 'refer'?" (63). The goal of this book is to discuss Holmes's question by extending her and Hoerschelmann's work beyond the game show itself to its representation across media.

Arguments such as these presented by Fiske, Hoerschelmann, and Holmes are common to many studies of other forms of popular culture, most notably the work scholars such as Ian Bogost have done on video games. Despite being a newer medium, video games have garnered more scholarly attention and critical esteem than the game show, but their similarity to the game show permits one to apply the critical discourse about video games to that of the game show. In his work on the hidden and not-so-hidden rhetoric and ideologies of video games, Bogost argues that the popularity and influence of video games, especially commercial video games, makes critique of them essential. Even though commercial game designers may not create a game (or game show) with a political ideology in mind, games "are not necessarily free from ideological framing" ("Video Games" 175). Kellner concurs that popular media can act as "barometers of contemporary taste, hopes, fears, and fantasies" that can help "appraise the current forms of contemporary society" (*Media Spectacle* 17). To conduct this appraisal, these unconscious texts require an outside party, the critic, to read them carefully and determine what they communicate to their audience beyond the procedural or entertainment aspects of the game itself (Bogost, "Video Games" 175).

Scholars such as Hoerschelmann and Holmes have certainly begun this work with regards to game shows. Their works not only provide valuable history and context for the game show in popular culture throughout the twentieth century and beyond, they also expose readers to the ideologies inherent in the form. However, Holmes herself acknowledges that the game show frequently undermines "the possibility of exploring more complex understandings of consumerism" because its focus remains doggedly fixed on its own context in the immediate present (104). The aesthetics and the narrative format of the game show cannot tease out the game show's latent implications throughout the culture at large. The central argument of this book responds directly to the limits of critique that Holmes identifies. To develop "more complex understandings" of the game show, to understand What We Talk about When We Talk about Game Shows, the view of game shows must extend beyond the game show itself and study the ways in which it has been represented in popular culture. Bogost places the critic at the center of the ability to understand the ideological frames and rhetorical moves of video games, and I include the fiction writer and the filmmaker among the critics who illuminate the hidden values and ideologies of game shows.

In *Understanding Popular Culture*, Fiske argues that "popular forces transform the culture commodity into a cultural resource," meaning that, as Henry Jenkins explains, "mass culture needs to be reworked before it can be consumed, much as raw materials must be processed before they can be used" (Fiske, UPC 28; Jenkins xxx). *Truth and Consequences* adopts Jenkins's assertion and positions writers and filmmakers as figures who "process" the "raw material" of the "cultural commodity" that is the game show and develop it into a "cultural resource" that can be used to understand reality in the Land of the Game Show. In examining how artists have incorporated the game show into their work, one can see the range of the game show's involvement with and infiltration of American culture in a way that watching an episode of *Win, Lose, or Draw* or *Hollywood Game Night* does not provide. Artists use the game show as a narrative device in fiction and film to discuss essential values and social relationships in culture, and in doing so, they reveal how inextricably linked the game show is with the values and relationships in a hypermediated consumer culture. While Peck and Baldwin argue in *I Am Not Your Negro* that quiz shows "weaken our ability to deal with the world as it is, ourselves as we are," game shows have, perhaps in spite of themselves, been able to offer insights into "the world as it is" and "ourselves as we are"; however, these insights become more visible thanks to the interpretive work of artists working in media other than television.

Where one might expect writers and filmmakers to be as univocally dismissive of the game show and what it represents as scholars are, closer examination of texts that employ the game show as a narrative device reveals that, like Peck, they find the game show to be symptomatic of larger cultural issues. Like language, game shows "do not represent the world, but make sense of it, for the world is not already divided up into neat categories" (Fiske 52). Writers and filmmakers show their audiences what larger forces are at play in the game show, and their use of it in their work can be regarded as a form of criticism not only of the game show itself but of the values that the game show performs. Their work broadens the edges of the game show to the world beyond the studio door, revealing that the boundaries between the game world and the real world are not only more fluid than initially thought but barely exist. The game show is the map to consumer society's territory, a hyperreal social space that puts the underlying currents of modern life into sharp relief. The shows are frequently dismissed as crass and tasteless, but the works in *Truth and Consequences* show

how they merely turn up the volume on what is being broadcast at a lower volume in daily life.

Looking at how a television format is represented in print and cinema requires a hybrid approach that does not fit neatly into a single scholarly discourse; however, such a hybrid approach lends itself well to the study of game shows because they themselves are a hybrid form that mixes genres, texts, and media. Nearly every game show combines styles and forms from other game shows, television programs, and cinematic genres, from *The Gong Show*'s parody of a talent competition to *Survivor*'s use of documentary filmmaking and reality television tropes, to *Beat Shazaam*'s revamping of *Name That Tune* for the era of the smartphone. Game shows even invite multimedia approaches in the form of questions (e.g., *Bumper Stumpers*) or gameplay (e.g., *Hollywood Squares* or the video Daily Double on *Jeopardy!*). Some shows even extend play beyond the program itself in the form of home games or activity on social media or other online sites. While many shows often stick to quizzing contestants on one type of knowledge, shows such as *The Wall* are intertextual, incorporating factual questions and tests of human relationships into the gameplay. In fact, game shows are so intertextual, intergenre, and multimedial that scholars disagree over how to categorize game shows themselves. Are they a genre onto themselves, a television format to be licensed and sold, or something entirely different? What makes programs such as *Big Brother* or *American Ninja Warrior* game shows where *The Real World* or *Man vs. Wild* are not? Is *The Bachelor* a game show? Or *Extreme Makeover*? Rather than become mired in this debate, this book prefers to accept that genre definitions are "shifting provisional set[s] of characteristics" that tend to be ill-fitting for individual texts because each text redefines the boundaries and possibilities of the genres in which it participates (Fiske 112–13).

Further, genre-driven approaches to intertextuality do not suffice because intertextuality is more or less inevitable within the flow of television and culture at large (Fiske 116). Fiske advocates for a different hybrid approach in *Television Culture* that he calls "vertical intertextuality," or "a primary text's relations with other texts which refer specifically to it" (118). This approach has much to recommend it; however, he limits this term to secondary texts such as criticism and publicity material of a specific program that contribute to how a viewer reads that program and how producers develop future episodes of that program (Fiske 118–19). The works examined in this book do perform criticism and publicity of sorts on the game show, but that is not their primary mode of discourse, which makes vertical intertextuality an initially appealing but ultimately unsatisfying method of inquiry.

What *Truth and Consequences* is most engaged with is the study of how one form of media, the game show, is represented in another, namely fiction and film. Scholars have named this practice of representing one form of media within a work in another medium intermediality, and an intermedial framework contributes greatly to illuminating the insights that can be gained by studying how writers and filmmakers incorporate game shows into their work. While much scholarship on intermediality devotes itself toward defining the parameters of intermediality, the concept can be broadly understood as "relations between media" or "medial interactions and interferences" (Rajewsky 51). Intermedial works are by their very nature self-referential because this intermingling of different media invites an audience to be aware of the characteristics and nature of each respective medium. This process gives audiences familiar with both forms of media that are interacting "access to different levels of meaning," creating a more dynamic and engaging work because "switching between or among various media not only forces its viewing or, rather, participating, audience to make comparisons among them but also exposes the particularities of the various semiotic systems that each medium embodies" (Ljungberg 83, 90). Despite its clarity in the abstract, Irina Rajewsky notes such a broad definition of intermediality quickly reveals itself wanting because it presumes "tangible borders between individual media" and all of the "dubious essentialist views" that attend such a rigid characterization that assumes, for example, that all novels operate according to the same rules (52). Discussions of different media are even murkier than that because one cannot experience a medium, only the individual works done in that medium (Rajewsky 53).

To clear up such an impending mess, Rajewsky outlines three types of intermediality: "medial transposition" (i.e., literary adaptations), "media combination" (i.e., mixed/multimedia art or performance), and "intermedial references" (i.e., one medium referring to a work from another medium) (55). As useful and clearly delineated as these categories are, they do not adequately capture the works examined in this book that use game shows as narrative devices. Consider the film *Slumdog Millionaire* as a quick test subject. While the film is an adaptation of a novel, it is not an adaptation of *Who Wants to Be a Millionaire?*, which means its use of the novel would be an example of medial transposition, but not its use of the game show because the show is not the material being adapted. The film does combine the game show with a theatrical film narrative, but not in a way that would be classified as mixed media since the film rarely surrenders its cinematic apparatus or aesthetic to that of the game show in any significant way, ruling out media combination. Although *Slumdog Millionaire* refers to the *Millionaire* game show itself, its use of it is so sustained and integral to the film itself that calling it an intermedial reference seems to diminish the show's role in how the film makes meaning. And yet the film is clearly intermedial. Discussing its meaning would be inaccurate if one were to apply Rajewsky's categories and greatly lacking if one were to limit the film's use of the game show to that of a simple plot device.

Axel Englund provides an alternate understanding of intermediality that more precisely captures the work that the texts discussed in this book do. In his essay "Intermedial Topography and Metaphorical Interpretation," Englund describes an intermediality less "geographical" (i.e., concerned with blurring media borders) and more interested in "bring[ing] the 'other' medium into *play*" (69; emphasis added). Englund relates this type of intermediality to Max Black's "interaction view" of metaphor, which describes an author placing two distinct subjects, each with its own set of associations and implications in the mind of the audience, in a relationship that sends the audience "searching for analogies between the ideas associated with the two subjects" and strives to change the audience's conception of both subjects (Englund 69, 70). Such a view does not concern itself with placing a work in one medium or another; rather, this view serves as "a shaping force in our conception of these 'territories'" (Englund 71). The metaphorical approach represents a "strategy" for interpretation of a "system of things" and ideas in which "a definitive distinction between text and interpretation, between internal and external, is neither possible nor desirable" (Englund 70). Since metaphor depends on two things not being alike in order to shine a light on how they resemble each other, one need not become consumed with drawing distinctions between the two media: in order for the metaphor to have any effect at all, Englund explains, "an identity between the arts has to be suggested by the artefacts themselves" (72).

Truth and Consequences proceeds with its analysis of how the game show has been represented in popular culture from Englund's concept of metaphor and intermediality. In their works, writers and filmmakers bring game shows "into play" to find "analogies between the ideas associated with the two subjects" with the goal of changing how a viewer or reader perceives not only the game show or the work of fiction/cinema, but the theme that authors use the game show to interrogate. In the case of *Slumdog Millionaire*, the viewer can gain a greater understanding by viewing its intermediality as metaphorical in nature. As I will discuss in the next round, the film uses the game show as a metaphor for the limitations social class imposes on one's ability to construct a coherent self, and in doing so, prompts the audience to compare game-show knowledge with self-knowledge in a manner that alters their understanding of the game show, the film, and the self.

While the last few paragraphs may seem like an overly complicated and academic way to state the simple claim that writers and filmmakers use the game show as a metaphor, intermediality provides a valuable context in how each medium uses the television program. Despite being intermedial in the sense that one type of media incorporates another into it, each medium's identity remains intact. These films and works of fiction adopt the discourse and aesthetics of the game show without ever becoming indistinguishable from it: the literary works are clearly literary works, and the films go to great lengths to foreground themselves as cinematic works, or, if they do momentarily disappear into the world of the game show, they take great care to provide clear transitions between televisual and cinematic space. This careful sense of being separate from the television game show allows these works to use the game show as a metaphor for cultural ideas that are latent in the game show the works incorporate. Tracking its status as an intermedial metaphor opens up more pathways of meaning than a less nuanced approach would permit.

Jean-François Lyotard would describe this metaphorical approach to intermediality as "imagination" because it displays "the capacity to articulate what used to be separate" by "connect[ing] together series of data that were previously held to be independent"—in this case the game show and the film or work of fiction (52). Such an act of imagination in a language game, in the words of Lyotard, "allows one either to make a new move or change the rules of the game," thus "supply[ing] the system with the increased performativity it forever demands and consumes" (52, 15). Games are of special importance to Lyotard, who calls language games "the minimum relation for society to exist," the "social bond" itself (15). Although he speaks of games in a much broader (and more philosophical sense) than the games of game shows, the game show is, like language games, "the game of inquiry": there is "the person who asks" (the host), "the addressee" (or contestant), and "the referent asked about" (an answer) (15). Game shows transplant "the social bond" of Lyotard's language games to a near-literal level and recast it as an exchange market, rewarding successful communication with cash and prizes. The game show's language game forges a social bond in an era which, as Gary Cross has shown, "Americans have had a strong tendency to define themselves and their relationships with others through the exchange and use of goods," a process which the game show not only reflects but celebrates and encourages audiences to participate in and support (4). If America is, in fact, the Land of the Game Show, then the game show is its language game, its discourse, its social bond. This aspect of reality would not be as visible were it not for the imaginative leap that writers and filmmakers perform when they incorporate a game show as a narrative device in their work.

The game show is but another imitation of life, despite how much its own aesthetics and apparatus may be given over to presenting fantasy or projecting fantasy onto reality. As many critics note, the reality it presents is merely the late-twentieth-century American capitalist ethos made flesh; however, its depiction of that truth goes beyond that of capitalism. While the game show's veneration of capitalism cannot be overstated, it is not the only value at play in a game show. Rather, it is merely the easiest one to spot as it is buried so close to the surface as to be part of it. Game shows present other values that do not become visible until one looks at how they are represented in other, nontelevisual media. Just as game shows take an intermedial approach to their own content, so must scholars take an intermedial approach to game shows. By investigating how they are represented, one can garner a better appreciation for *what* they represent. And even if the truth remains that the game show is but "an institutionalized monument to Greed," these works depict the consequences of that truth in other aspects of daily life. Each game show episode may end and present the audience with a winner or a loser, but its presence and influence over contemporary life always has another round to play.

CATEGORY

NOSTALGIA FOR THE AIR

Even though game shows are tests of memory at their heart, individual episodes appear designed to be decidedly unmemorable. As soon as one episode ends, another version of the same thing appears to replace it; the sheer volume of questions and number of episodes almost ensure that, excepting the occasionally exceptional (or exceptionally wacky and disastrous) contestant, each individual game fades from memory or blurs together over time. Chuck Palahniuk writes in his novel *Invisible Monsters* that "game shows are designed to make us feel better about the random, useless facts that are all we have left of our education" (38). In other words, in attempting to assuage one's fear that their education is trivial, game shows, in their ubiquity and indistinguishability, only confirm it.

Fiske broadly divides quiz-show knowledge into two categories in *Television Culture*: factual knowledge and human knowledge. He subdivides factual knowledge into the "academic knowledge" tested on a show such as *Jeopardy!* and the "everyday knowledge" sought on *The Price Is Right*, and he classifies "human knowledge" as "knowledge of people in general," like what appears on *Family Feud*, or "knowledge of a specific individual," as exhibited on *The Newlywed Game* (271). Because they quizzed people on factual knowledge, the network quiz shows of the 1950s often featured contestants who were either teachers or highly educated instead of the so-called "regular people" who appeared on earlier radio programs such as *Vox Pop* (Hoerschelmann 79). After the scandals initiated the move toward everyday knowledge, what becomes memorable amidst the barrage of questions and episodes are not the questions or the answers but the production values: the Wheel, the Wall, the Center Square, and, most important of all for the sponsors, the prizes. These shifts contributed greatly to the game show's reputation as the most trivial of pursuits.

This view that game show trivia is unmemorable and irrelevant is not universal, however. Woody Allen's 1987 film *Radio Days* employs an intermedial approach that uses the radio quiz show as a metaphor for memory. While it may not be profound to say that Allen's film implies it is "the duty of each generation to pass on its memories to the next," the material that Allen privileges as necessary to pass on is both significant and unexpected (Lee 224). Allen's film encourages an encyclopedic, idiosyncratic, obsessive approach to trivia and memory in which any and all trivia can become a valuable memory under the right circumstances. Since one can never know when or how a moment will imbue a trivial detail with import, they must remember. All of it.

Typically, Allen's approach to memory is one of nostalgia, and one hardly needs to look deeply into scholarship on Allen to encounter discussions of nostalgia and memory. Both have been central to his practice as a filmmaker dating back at least as far as 1979's *Manhattan*. For Allen, cinema functions as the ideal way to preserve, capture, or re-create lost or disappearing moments before they are truly gone, whether the moment is the Brooklyn of his youth, Paris in the 1920s, or the styles of filmmakers he idolizes such as Ingmar Bergman or Federico Fellini (*Radio Days* itself functions an extended homage to Fellini's 1973 film *Amarcord*). In the case of *Radio Days*, however, critics frequently point to Allen's sense of nostalgia to dismiss this ode to his ephemeral childhood. Paul Attanasio (author of the screenplay to *Quiz Show*, which I will get to shortly) claims that *Radio Days* may be nostalgic, "but a kind of aimless nostalgia [that] you peel and peel away at . . . to find, in the end, nothing." He takes his critique of the film even further, closing his review with the assertion that the viewer "get[s] the sense of [Allen] panicking to recover an ever elusive memory—as if his forgetfulness reminds him that he, too, will someday be forgotten. The problem is that Allen's 'radio days' are so immediately forgettable. Without the heft, worrying about oblivion seems merely fussy." Robert Horton and *Variety* agree that Allen's film, although "nice to spend time with," constitutes "an advisedly minor film" in Allen's body of work, something trivial, forgotten as soon as it is over (Horton; Review: "Radio Days").

This reception is not unlike the common reception to game shows discussed earlier, and, like that reception, it overlooks the depth beneath what it dismisses as shallow. Allen's nostalgic treatment of the "radio days" of his youth represents not a warm and fuzzy game of "remember when" but an investigation into what makes the past memorable in the first place and how memory, even trivial memory, can keep the past present in an increasingly disposable culture. Richard A. Blake approaches why the film should stand among Allen's stronger achievements. Like Attanasio, Blake views the film as Allen reflecting on his own aging; however, he positions Allen's aging not as the result of some existential panic over his own relevance but rather a "conundrum" for someone "maturing as an artist in a world that rejects permanence as a matter of principle" (136). Though Allen frequently waxes existential on the impermanence of lived experience, Blake's statement reveals why *Radio Days* may be among the most ambitiously designed of Allen's films and not a minor film of interest only to Allen completists. Allen confronts the real possibility of irrelevance head-on by structuring his film around the most ephemeral of art forms, radio. However, instead of conceding that impermanence is inevitable, Allen uses his film to argue an optimistic, if measured, point: a form of permanence is possible, so long as one can remember, and so long as culture has the means to capture or re-create those memories: cinema.

In his book *Consumed Nostalgia: Memory in the Age of Fast Capitalism*, Gary Cross notes how the accelerated pace of industrial, mediated America creates such an emphasis on the "newest latest" product or trend that it leaves many yearning for "the debris of a modern manufacturing economy" (3). In the face of such rapid change, people attempt "to get the past back as a possession" (8). Because past and present are becoming increasingly dissimilar, Cross claims how people turn to symbolic rituals and totems as a means of slowing their experience of the culture's rate of change. As long as the consumer can collect, they can avoid having to admit that the past is long gone. Ironically, such a practice only hastens the culture's pace because an increased demand for collecting out-of-date or discontinued products only encourages the rapid development of new products that these old goods are intended to fight against (8–9). However, Cross notes that consumed nostalgia's purpose does not stop at collecting the objects themselves. Rather, nostalgia hounds "also master the details, knowledge that many of us might consider 'useless' but that is curiously empowering to those who have it" (5). The trivia surrounding the nostalgia object is not only of equal importance as the object itself, it may in fact be the deeper goal behind the collecting because of the empowerment it provides the collector. This understanding of the empowering elements of nostalgia distinguish it from Fredric Jameson's conception of nostalgia, which he characterizes as a sort of willful amnesia or retreat from the emptiness or harsh realities of the present. Although Cross certainly does not shy away from describing the nostalgic impulse as one that is opposed to the accelerated advance of time, he also makes room for an individual to find agency and mastery in their nostalgia. This action does not merely represent a retreat into the past; it validates the individual and their memory and lived experience.

The nostalgia Allen displays in *Radio Days* aligns more with Cross's expression of it than Jameson's. Even though Allen and cinematographer Carlo DiPalma do not resist imbuing the past with a warm golden tone in every composition, Allen's film does not engage in the naivete and innocence of *American Graffiti* or the "aesthetic colonization" of *Chinatown* or *The Conformist* (Jameson 19). Allen's ethnically, geographically, and personally idiosyncratic portrayal of the past frees the film from accusations of a pastiche that "attempt[s] to appropriate a missing past" through "the random cannibalization of all the styles of the past" (Jameson 19, 18). *Radio Days* seeks not "to lay siege to our own present or immediate past or to a more distant history that escapes existential memory" but rather to stress the value of memory for both preserving the past and constructing meaning in the present (Jameson 19). *Radio Days* does not endorse Susan Stewart's view that nostalgia seeks to "authenticate a past" and "discredit the present" (quoted in *Consumed Nostalgia* 13). Rather than pining for lost time, the film asserts that trivia uses memories of the past to generate a reward in the present that makes the present fuller and more enjoyable, not discredited or obscured.

Radio Days begins as two burglars (Mike Starr and Paul Herman) rummage through the pitch-black apartment of Mr. and Mrs. Needleman, their flashlights haphazardly sweeping across the frame as the telephone rings. The thieves, wishing to silence the phone, answer it, only to discover that the caller is the host of the radio program *Guess That Tune*, where contestants "chosen from the telephone book" win prizes for guessing what song the studio orchestra is playing. The robbers turn on the radio to hear the music and quickly become so absorbed in the game that they forget who they are and what they are doing in the apartment. When they discover they have won the grand prize, they clutch each other and jump for joy, shouting, "We're rich!" The punchline arrives in the following scene, when the Needlemans awake to find a delivery truck unloading a refrigerator and washing machine outside their recently pilfered home.

Such call-in programs were incredibly popular in the early days of the game show because they encouraged listeners to tune in and participate in the show (Hoerschelmann 39). In addition to the financial and interactive entertainment incentives to listen to these programs, the notion that any person could be called on to answer a question at any moment in the broadcast projected a New Deal ideology of all citizens equally having access to and engagement "in a public, mass-mediated forum" (Hoerschelmann 50). The opening scene to *Radio Days* reinforces the New Deal's idealistic vision of broadcasting. Despite occupying a brightly lit and posh performance hall, the host, orchestra, and studio audience are all "in the dark" to the fact that these "common men" guessing the tunes correctly are in fact common crooks. However, the thieves' knowledge of popular music functions as a grand equalizer. Not only do petty crooks win big on the show and make off with $50 and some silverware, their game-show loot goes to Mr. and Mrs. Needleman, suggesting that the prizes of these participatory games are shared beyond the contestants themselves: the crooks get to experience the joy of playing and winning, the Needlemans receive the free prizes, and the neighborhood gets a great story to remember and retell long after the show is off the air.

While opening a film about radio with a scene in the dark certainly conditions the audience to devote greater attention to sound in the film, the aesthetic choices of the scene also support Allen's use of the game show as a metaphor for memory. The first song the band plays for the robbers, "Dancing in the Dark," corresponds exactly with their actions: they, too, are "dancing" to the music in the dark of the Needleman's apartment. With the contrast between the brightly lit game show set and the apartment lit only by flashlights and the orange glow of the radio, Allen portrays the arrival of memory, the intrusion of the moments of the past into the present, as a burst of light in the darkness. The game show calls on the robbers to search through the dark recesses of their memories in the same way that they are searching for loot in the dark of the apartment, hoping to take a prized reward with them into the light. The audience occupies the same position as the robbers because they too are watching light dance in the dark of the movie theater. This light, in the form of the images on the screen, represents moments from the past preserved and viewed in the present, both in the sense that the film re-creates a past time period and that it records the past movements of the actors for posterity. Consequently, audiences watch a memory that then becomes part of their own memory. Even though Allen's visual pun runs the risk of seeming overly clever, the timing can be read as more than mere coincidence and instead as a moment that announces Allen's view of memory in the film: there is an ideal time and place for trivial information to take on profound meaning, and those who can seize upon those moments receive both material rewards and personal validation, just as the robbers receive more joy from winning "Guess That Tune" than they do from ripping off the Needlemans.

By opening a nostalgia-driven film such as *Radio Days* with a quiz show scene, Allen compares the feat of remembering the past to remembering a trivia question on a quiz show and encourages the viewer of *Radio Days* to recognize that remembering small details can retrieve the past from oblivion

Robbers "Dancing in the Dark."

and shepherd it into the present. Such nostalgic notions would appear to conflict with the world of the game show: game shows may be tests of memory, but their questions usually bear little resemblance to the subjective shadings of nostalgic reminiscence. However, when one considers Cross's explanation of the empowering aspects of consumed nostalgia, the game show becomes an ideal way to introduce the themes of Allen's film. "It's all gone now, except for the memories," Allen's voiceover declares at the start of the film, making memory all that remains to defend against the accelerating tide of irrelevance and insignificance. Allen's choice to open *Radio Days* with a game show reveals how the tension between trivia and meaning is the same as the tension between permanence and impermanence. Like radio waves, events disappear into oblivion unless someone or something recalls or records them. By the end of the film, after depicting the rewards of recalling trivial moments from the past, Allen's opening statement that everything from the radio era is gone "except for the memories" becomes a tacit admission that this lost era remains precisely because it is remembered.

The second quiz show appears rather late in the film when Aunt Bea (Dianne Wiest) takes Joe (Seth Green) to New York City. Their trip includes a visit to a live broadcast of a radio quiz show, where Aunt Bea gets selected as a contestant live on the air and must identify different varieties of fish (even though no one listening to the show can see any of the fish). As luck would have it, Bea knows more about fish than most people in the five boroughs because her brother-in-law Abe (Josh Mostel) brings different types of fish home to their cramped Rockaway apartment each day and expounds endlessly on each fish's qualities and defining characteristics. Up to this point in the film, Abe's preoccupation with fish ranges from mildly amusing to mildly annoying, seemingly just another example of Allen's shorthand way of defining an entire character with the broadest of strokes. The film even deems the particulars of Abe's obsession so insignificant as to almost never turn them up in the sound mix; however, the second quiz show scene suggests that remembering knowledge as mind-numbingly dull as Abe's fish monologues can have value in the right situation. The quiz show gives the seemingly irrelevant pool of fish data substance: Bea wins fifty silver dollars and buys Joe his first chemistry set, again showing how more people than the contestant go home winners. The difference between a red snapper and a flounder may not seem like a pressing issue for the average person to retain, but *Radio Days* suggests that, in a certain context, knowing the difference could change someone's life. This trivial knowledge from the past leads to not only wealth (the fifty silver dollars) but to real knowledge (the chemistry set) in the present.

As with the first quiz show scene, Allen again reinforces the New Deal ideology that pervaded game shows of this era in which ordinary people proved to possess extraordinary knowledge. Bea, a woman picked at random from a crowd of everyday Americans, proves that she has esoteric, specialized knowledge bestowed on her by her salt-of-the-earth brother-in-law that earns her attention and a valuable reward that she promptly shares with her nephew. Further, both scenes involving radio quiz shows feature details that relate to vision. The first scene has the robbers literally dancing in the dark in search of loot, and the second results in Joe receiving a microscope in the chemistry set, which will allow him to study the minute details beneath the surface of what he sees every day. In both cases, recalling the past leads to sight in the present.

In the film's final scene, where all the radio celebrities congregate on a rooftop to ring in 1944, Allen appears to suggest that "everything passes." Roger (David Warrilow) and Biff Baxter (Jeff Daniels) express this sentiment when Roger says, "I hope 1944 turns out well. They pass so quickly. Where do they all go?" Biff Baxter replies, "So quickly. Then we get old. And we never knew what any of it was about." Richard A. Blake claims that this exchange, paired with Allen's statement in the voice-over that their voices grow dimmer each year, represents Allen "doubt[ing] the healing power of memories" (*Profane and Sacred* 213). On the surface, this melancholy reading bears out: like the voices on the radio waves, all floats out on the air and drifts slowly into silence, as though it were never there, just as the celebrities themselves, unbeknownst to anyone in the ballroom, gradually leave the party and float upward to the roof and begin 1944 removed from their time and place downstairs. However, to conclude, as Julian Fox does, that "little Joe's life and what his older self

Radio Days' grace note.

remembers of it [is] nothing but vaguely deceptive figments of the airwaves" would overstate the case of this scene and overlook the final seconds of *Radio Days* (Fox 179). Allen certainly voices his reservations about the permanence of radio and expresses his fear that "magical phenomena, like radio, can profoundly affect us and then, in the wink of history's eye, become totally irrelevant" (Schickel 37). But the final moment of the film confirms that Allen does not give in to this kind of existential despair. After each radio celebrity waxes philosophical about the coming year and their place in the universe, each one slowly files back through the rooftop door to return to the party below as 1944 begins. Earlier in the film, Sally White (Mia Farrow) got stranded on the roof, and Allen seems poised to repeat this gag with the entire group of celebrities, dooming them to irrelevance as forgotten figures of nostalgic yesteryear. Only that does not happen. The performers do not get locked out of time on the roof but return to the party and join in its flow. The camera, however, lingers on the rooftop for another moment, panning from the revelers to the bright lights of downtown as a hat-shaped sign rises toward the heavens. While one could read this moment as an existential threat to the audience—the viewer is, in a sense, locked out and does not return to the party—one can also view this extended moment as Allen giving the audience time to savor the details before they float away so that they can remember them later and prevent the moment from disappearing into the air (Wernblad 120). With this grace note to close the film, Allen subtly suggests that, although the performers may fade in his memory over time, they will not be forgotten.

In many respects, everything in *Radio Days* is trivia in one way or another. The bits of gossip that Joe's sister Ruthie (Joy Newman) picks up about their neighbors as she listens in on the party line (her own personal radio soap opera), the true identity of the robust and virile Masked Avenger (the diminutive and nebbish Wallace Shawn), the existence of German U-boats off the coast of Brooklyn, the authentic Judy Holliday Brooklynese speaking voice of refined radio celebrity Sally White, the actual occupation of Joe's father—every element of the film functions as a question on a quiz show, a mystery to be solved. Everything becomes a bit of trivia blended in Joe's adult mind, and all of it is in danger of vanishing unless one can discover a way to harness it, to bring it back from the edge of forgetting. *Radio Days'* episodic, discursive narrative argues that apparently trivial moments early in the film, such as Abe's fish monologues, hold real significance. The thread that holds the film together, apart from the time period, is the sense that it all matters. None of it is a trivial pursuit. No matter how silly or serious, *Radio Days* argues that it all needs to be remembered.

Even though the film adopts radio as its subject, Allen's film privileges cinema as the medium that can capture and preserve the ephemeral moments of radio and ensure that they be remembered. Like the prized Masked Avenger Decoder Ring that Joe covets, memory grants its owner the power to render a moment of insipid trivia into a moment of great significance. In *Radio Days*, that decoder is the camera itself, which captures all the memorable details before they slip away. Carlo DiPalma's cinematography functions as a visual representation of the narrator (Allen) scanning through the warm memories of his childhood and slowly selecting a moment to reminisce on. The soft amber look of the film, the "muted shadows cast by hesitant winter light," "the reds and browns that glow in a golden light from yellow and cream lampshades," the slow zoom-ins that magnify a particular moment in the frame, all create a visual vocabulary for lingering nostalgic memory (Blake, *Street Smart* 131). The trivia of Joe's life is not revealed by the radio: it is revealed on camera because celluloid is more permanent. While the warm hues certainly conjure nostalgic yearnings for the golden days, stopping there would be simplistic. Every memory is golden in the film because the fact that something is still remembered in an ephemeral world is cause for a celebration; the image is warm because the memory is alive. The radio fades and forgets, but Allen's camera remembers. Through this intermedial approach, *Radio Days* presents the game show as a metaphor for memory itself, the very thing that makes game shows possible in the first place.

The way the past interacts with the present in *Radio Days* decides which bits of information remain trivia and which gain the significance of memory. By the end of the film, Joe's memory (and Allen's camera) fills all trivia with import because remembering is the only thing keeping these details not only from being written off as trivial but from ceasing to exist altogether. A person can never know when life will call on them to use any piece of information that they receive. Like the robbers at the Needleman's house and Aunt Bea on the radio program, any moment of one's life could suddenly turn up as a question on a pop quiz. Therefore, nothing can be dismissed; everyone must keep it all in their heads and at the ready. This act of remembering constitutes a magic act that conjures the past out of thin air, just as a radio antenna captures and transmits an invisible signal into private space. Annette Wernblad claims that "the radio (and by implication the younger media) is not just an adventitious piece of furniture or source of entertainment, but a phenomenon which is very much an integral part of our lives, and plays an important role in defining our character" (119–20). *Radio Days* argues that these moments become relevant *because* someone remembers them, thus demonstrating how trivia can bridge the past and the present, keeping the past alive, meaningful. In this sense, recalling the past does not represent nostalgia as a yearning to revisit the past but as a celebration of the past's ability to remain relevant, to give power to the person who can recall the details, who can correctly tune the dial to the right frequency at the right time and pick up the fading signal. That person, it would seem, is a magician bringing the past back from the dead, so long as they can remember. Doing so, it corresponds with Lyotard's description of the knowledge imparted by nursery rhymes, whose rhythms contain "that strange temporalization that jars the golden rule of our knowledge: 'never forget.'" Lyotard characterizes this temporality as "simultaneously evanescent and immemorial," aptly capturing the way *Radio Days* uses the intangibility of radio and the past to revive one's sense of memory through "the act of recitation" (22). Allen beginning *Radio Days* with a game show makes viewers aware of the ways the game show normalizes, structures, and rewards this magical act of remembering, empowering those who buzz in and encouraging those who watch to attend more closely to trivial pursuits.

Just like the trivial details that they quiz people on, the significance of game shows is not to be overlooked. They are perfect examples of a trivial artifact with unexpected importance, urging one to reflect on how they have informed their sense of self, of love, of family, of politics. Game shows are not trivial but conduits for genuine and generative meaning not only within the programs themselves, as Fiske, Hoerschelmann, and Holmes argue, but in the hands of artists who use their forms metaphorically. They form and mold memory in the media age, and, as it is in *Radio Days*, one's past and one's identity cannot be constructed or remembered without them. This book accepts that as a truth and wishes to investigate the consequences that stem from that truth.

CATEGORY

GROUND RULES

Truth and Consequences interrogates the ways in which over two dozen works of fiction and film—bestsellers, blockbusters, disasters, modern legends, forgotten gems, award-winners, self-published curios, and everything in between—find meaning in the game show. Writers and filmmakers use the game show intermedially as a metaphor for what it means to be a person, a lover, a child, a citizen in the media age. Despite media culture's promises of global equality and connectivity (and one's efforts to realize that promise), individuals wind up isolated by market-driven deception, wealth, or ethnicity. People use media to achieve greater intimacy with others, but the market nudges them to keep their distance from each other in the name of exploring options. Other networks can still assert themselves, such as the family, but can only sustain themselves if they openly defy and rewrite the rules of the media culture they inhabit. Although America espouses a commitment to democratic freedom, the state partners with imagemakers to make one's lack of choice entertaining and resistance self-defeating. Amidst these obstacles, Americans still feel called on to remember, to connect, to buzz in, to answer, hoping that an escape awaits in the next round, behind the next door.

This study is a far cry from comprehensive; game shows are everywhere in fiction and film, and there are many more works that merit closer scrutiny, creating space for other scholars to continue the work begun in this book. This study also does not account for intermedial instances of the game show in other television programs, where "[Character] Goes on a Game Show" is a stock episode arc that nearly every show employs if it lasts long enough, from *The Andy Griffith Show* to *L. A. Law* to *The Fresh Prince of Bel-Air* to *That 70s Show* to *It's Always Sunny in Philadelphia*. There are so many that one could write a companion volume (or two) to this one and still not cover every instance.

To mimic the rhetoric of game shows, the chapters in this book will be called rounds, with each section labelled as a category. The rounds are arranged thematically based on what writers and filmmakers use the game show to represent metaphorically. Each round broadens in scope, starting with how writers and filmmakers use the game show as a metaphor for the self, followed by love, then family, culminating in the ways that the game show serves as an apt metaphor for state power.

Round 1 explores works that use (and abuse) trivia to reveal how the hypermediated consumer culture of late capitalism traps individuals in a metaphorical isolation booth, unable to establish a stable sense of self. Just as the quiz-show scandals of the 1950s nearly killed the quiz show, works such as Robert Redford's film *Quiz Show*, Jonathan Demme's film *Melvin and Howard*, Danny Boyle's film *Slumdog Millionaire*, and Chuck Barris's "unauthorized autobiography" *Confessions of a Dangerous Mind* (and George Clooney's film adaptation) suggest that a rigged game presents an existential threat to the self. Amidst the pressure to conform to the norms of the community of television, individuals betray themselves to get ahead in America, often finding themselves trapped in the isolation booth of their social class. Further, Philip Roth's novel *Zuckerman Unbound*, Kiese Laymon's novel *Long Division*, and Robert Olen Butler's story "The American Couple," show how these questions of selfhood in the age of the game show can be exacerbated when the protagonist is an outsider to game-show culture.

A game show seems to be the last place where one would find love; however, many artists have seen a deeper quest hidden inside the game show's pursuit of trivial knowledge: the desire to know another person completely. Round 2 argues that game-show discourse and romantic discourse are not as dissimilar as one would initially think. Films such as Ron Shelton's *White Men Can't Jump* and Jim Sharman's *Shock Treatment*, works of fiction such as Alexandra Kleeman's *You Too Can Have a Body Like Mine* and Helen De Witt's *Lightning Rods*, and the unexpected-but-nevertheless-real subgenre of game-show erotica demonstrate the ways in which the game show can help lovers navigate the romantic hypermarket.

Round 3 features a detailed study of three works by three major American authors who not only make game shows central plot devices but also create familial relationships among the game show producers and contestants, transforming all conflicts over the game show into family conflicts. These "quiz-show families" blend the most intimate relationship, the family, with the least intimate kind of human interaction, the game show, in order to interrogate how people connect with each other (or not) in an image culture. J. D. Salinger's Glass Family saga, David Foster Wallace's story "Little Expressionless Animals," and Paul Thomas Anderson's film *Magnolia* exploit the insincere nature of the game show to make sincere assertions about everyone's similarities as wounded humans. Where one might expect these prophets of sincerity to find nothing but cynical grins and cheesy puns, they instead use game shows to affirm their commitment to radical authenticity by finding moments of compassion and transcendence in the emptiest of places, offering a glimpse of a new way of living in the Land of the Game Show.

Whether in the service of sharp-edged satire or stonefaced social commentary, each generation has responded to an increasingly commodified and mediated landscape by imagining a world in which life and death become stakes on a game show. The works discussed in Round 4 transpose the conceit of "The Most Dangerous Game" to the world of commercial broadcast entertainment, pitting characters against each other in competition for the ultimate prize: their own lives. Stephen King's novella *The Running Man*, Suzanne Collins's *The Hunger Games* series, and their respective film adaptations lead this discussion of how the game show has come to represent the political and personal dangers of citizenship in the Land of the Game Show. Each work envisions an America governed by a late-capitalist consumerism that has morphed into a new brand of totalitarianism that turns people into trivial objects and trivial objects into subjects of the highest importance. The "reality" of these games and their rules represent a simulated and heavily mediated environment posing as real to conceal a sinister truth, and the narratives of these stories turn on the protagonists using their knowledge rather than their bodies to discern the truth (i.e., the "answer") of their environment and present that answer to a populace that has been kept oblivious by mass media. In order to challenge the dominance of this inverted world order, the protagonists must first defeat totalitarianism's synecdoche: the game show.

Before November 8, 2016, the game show and its influence appeared to be nearing the end of its time in the spotlight. Then America elected someone who is, among many other things, a game show host, to become the 45th president of the United States. The game show's involvement with and influence on American culture has only begun to be apprehended since then. Such a stark fact makes one wonder whether there is a possible future world that does not live under the shadow of the game show and what it represents. This final round will examine works by Chuck Barris, Donald Barthelme, Max Apple, Philip K. Dick, and Jonathan Lethem to explore whether America will ever be free from the game show's grasp, and how citizens can take control of the Land of the Game Show if escape is impossible.

CATEGORY

A NOTE ON THE TEXT

This book recognizes that gender is non-binary, so, unless referring specifically to a character or author, this book will use "they," "them," "their," and "themselves" as third-person singular pronouns.

Unless otherwise noted, all emphasis in quoted text is original.

Round One

WHAT'S MY LINE?

Game Shows and the Quest for an Authentic Self

IF ONE MUST BEGIN A DISCUSSION OF GAME SHOWS BY RE-viewing how much scholars and critics revile them, the next topic one must address is the only aspect of the game show's identity and history that has merited sustained scholarly attention: the quiz-show scandals of the late 1950s. The big-money quiz show's ability to spark water-cooler conversation and anticipation for the next broadcast fueled the rising popularity of live television. Their success would not have been possible without the 1954 Supreme Court case *The Federal Communications Commission v. American Broadcasting Co., Inc.*, which legalized game shows by ruling that jackpot prizes did not constitute gambling. Networks capitalized on this ruling instantly: the $64 grand prize question on CBS radio's *Take It or Leave It* mushroomed into CBS television's *The $64,000 Question*. The audience for quiz shows increased proportionate to the size of the jackpots. At the quiz show's height, during the 1957–1958 season, viewers had twenty-two game shows to choose from across the three networks, with quiz shows alone constituting 18 percent of NBC's entire slate of programming (Anderson 104–5).

Facing pressure from their sponsors to garner higher ratings from an ever-growing television audience in an increasingly competitive field, the producers of *The $64,000 Question*, *Tic-Tac-Dough*, *Twenty-One*, and other quiz shows kept audiences hooked on their programs by rigging the outcomes of their contests, usually by giving contestants the questions and answers in advance and arranging for a contestant's defeat when their ratings stagnated. Allegations of fixing surfaced as early as 1957 but did not garner traction until a year later when contestants from several shows came forward with similar allegations. While a congressional subcommittee would not investigate quiz shows until 1959, the networks responded promptly and began cancelling shows after the allegations, assisted by a glut of too-similar programming, decimated ratings. By the end of 1958, quiz shows occupied just three hours of airtime across all three networks, making "quiz," as *Time* suggested, "television's own four-letter word" (Anderson 132, 133).

The effect that these scandals had on game shows is easy enough to see. For starters, quiz shows were renamed "game shows" to distance the new programming from that other four-letter word that smacked of scandal, and game shows moved out of the networks' primetime lineups to daytime slots, where they generally remain today. However, more substantive changes fell into place as well: prize money on a television show could not exceed $75,000, and the FCC made it a crime to broadcast a contest with intent to deceive the audience (Holmes 49). But the fallout from the quiz show scandals was not limited to the game show format: it molded the history and identity of television itself. As Kent Anderson puts it in his history of the quiz-show scandals, networks, especially CBS, "attempted to institutionalize honesty" in an attempt to regain the public's trust, going so far as to prohibit laugh tracks or fake applause from all shows and to announce to the audience whenever any material had been previously recorded or scripted (159–160). The most significant change to television that the scandals aided in was the end of "sponsor-controlled programming" (Hoerschelmann 70). Rather than one company sponsoring an entire program and thus having a disproportionate influence over that program's content (e.g., Geritol's sponsorship of *Twenty-One*), several sponsors bought time during specifically scheduled blocks of the broadcast called commercial breaks (Holmes 49). Thus, the scandals contributed greatly to the identity broadcast television enjoyed until the arrival of cable.

Television's transition from its pre-scandal identity of uninterrupted, single-sponsor programming to its fragmented, multiple-sponsor programming identity post-scandal resembles the shift in American culture's understanding and presentation of the self from the modern to the postmodern era. Douglas Kellner outlines this shift in "Popular Culture and the Construction of Postmodern Identities," arguing that although identity in the modern era becomes more pliable and fluid, its boundaries remain relatively fixed, dependent on a person's social roles (mother, worker, etc.) and what aspects of one's identity society deems worthy of recognition (141). This situation produces the modernist senses of self-consciousness, anxiety, and alienation: once one becomes aware of possessing a self, "one can choose and make—and then remake—one's identity"; however, "one is never certain that one has made the right choice" or discovered one's "true" self, and even if one were, one can become anxious over or alienated by that identity not being "socially validated" (142). As modernity gives way to postmodernity and social relations become faster and increasingly complicated and ambiguous, the self becomes more "fragmented and disconnected" and "no longer possesses the depth, substantiality, and coherence that was the ideal and occasional achievement of the modern self" (144). In the face of such instability, "the postmodern self accepts and affirms multiple and shifting identities" in what amounts to "a theatrical presentation" of an ambiguous self that is constantly in flux, dependent less on one's social role than on one's idealized conception of their identity at any given moment (158, 156). The postmodern self embraces the notion that identity is artificial, "a *game* that one plays" wherein players adopt and shed identities at will as they jockey for the "admiration and respect of other *players*" (153; emphasis added). For Kellner, the postmodern sense of self serves as "a function of leisure and is grounded in play, in gamesmanship" and "center[s] on looks, images, and consumption," with players turning to popular culture, especially the visual rhetoric of advertising and television, to provide the looks they choose from to construct their identities (153). The postmodern self that Kellner describes is but another, smaller-scale spectacle in an age of media megaspectacle.

Like Kellner, Jean-François Lyotard sees the presentation of the self as a game one plays within the postmodern social realm, alleging that "no self is an island," stable, autonomous, and unmoving, but rather a "post" or "nodal point" in "a fabric of relations ... through which various kinds of message pass" (15). The transfer of these messages back and forth occurs at the level of language, which, for Kellner, includes the language of images and media as a whole. Lyotard modifies Wittgenstein's concept of "language games" to describe these transfers of information, stating, "Each of the various categories of evidence can be defined in terms of rules specifying their properties and the uses to which they can be put" (10). Given that it constitutes a structured social interaction with rules that declare only certain moves, answers, and behaviors acceptable, a game show is but another language "game of inquiry"; however, Lyotard explains that performativity (or play) in social relationships "contributes to elevating all language games to self-knowledge ... jolt[ing] everyday discourse into a kind of metadiscourse," with "ordinary statements" increasingly indulging in "self-citation" (62). Each "ordinary statement" of inquiry eventually winds up addressing the self, making the language games of social interaction, even those on a game show, into quests for greater self-awareness and presentation.

Twenty-One's isolation booth.

Therefore, while all these images, narratives, and games that make up the social bond appear concerned solely with things outside the self, engagement in and among these elements of culture winds up increasingly illuminating one's interior, as players use these artifacts to discover, construct, and present a self in the hope that their self will be rewarded, that they will not be isolated from the social bond but rather become prominent "nodal points" in the network of social relationships.

The intermedial texts that incorporate game shows into their narratives position the game show and its scandalous origins as a metaphor for how individuals construct, manipulate, and broadcast a self to others in a media age. The rigged quiz show *Twenty-One* featured a production element that illustrates this postmodern sense of self: the isolation booth. Contestants stood in these soundproof booths for the length of the game, unable to see the other contestant's score or hear their answers. The players were totally alone, yet fully on display. These isolation booths, along with the questions locked in a Manhattan bank vault until moments before broadcast, sold audiences on the show's authenticity, isolating and displaying integrity as prominently as the contestants' bodies. Of course, that sense of authenticity turned out to be a façade, part of a rigged and scripted spectacle. What a contestant can or cannot hear through their studio headphones becomes irrelevant when that contestant already knows all the questions and the answers they will be asked. In the place of actual authenticity and knowledge, *Twenty-One* delivered the performance of authenticity and knowledge; as Kent Anderson put it, "showmanship would have to take precedence over honesty" (46).

The fact that both the display of integrity and the contestants' display of knowledge were all part of a rigged performance aligns with the transition from a modernist concern with authenticity to a postmodernist preference for performativity. Like the reality shows that followed in the Land of the Game Show, the big-money quiz shows were "all about the simulation rather than the representation" of identity (Morreale 104). The films and books that use the game show intermedially as a metaphor for the self follow suit, depicting American life as a rigged game in which one must betray themselves in order to succeed, making themselves over into a ready-for-primetime persona, an inauthentic self in a rigged world. In doing so, these works "make visible the ways that identity is created through rehearsal and performance of already fabricated images. It naturalizes the idea that identity is fluid and mobile, a commodity sign that we circulate in an endless attempt to make meaning" (Morreale 104).

Works such as Robert Redford's *Quiz Show* and Chuck Barris's *Confessions of a Dangerous Mind* (and George Clooney's film adaptation) declare "there is no coherent core, no deep interior behind the surface appearance of a social self" because media culture cannot represent it, comprehend it, or sell it (Morreale 104). The deeper, more authentic self touted by modernists and Romantics cannot be broadcast or reduced to an image commodity, which makes it a casualty in a hypermediated consumer society. In entering the "community" of television, players must change something about themselves, which could be as innocuous as capping their teeth or as monumental as denying what they know or where they come from—their identity. However, in the world of these works, contrary to Kellner's assessment of postmodern identity, authors portray these alterations to identity as betrayals. Just like the isolation of single-sponsored programming gives way to the fragmented chorus of commercial breaks, these works show how television ushers in a postmodern sense of identity for the individual: players betray the fixed self of the modernists for a fluid postmodern identity in order to escape isolation and join the "community" of the televisual landscape.

The works in this round use the isolation booth metaphorically to represent how the self functions in a mediated world where people are simultaneously isolated and visible. Isolation booths of all stripes, both literal and figurative, appear in fiction and films that use the game show as a narrative device, be it the literal isolation booth on a game show set, the isolation booth of a police interrogation room, the isolation of social class, ethnicity, and nationality, or the isolation that comes from one who hides who they are from the world at large, even from themselves. In presenting the illusion of authenticity, the game show isolates the self from itself in favor of a more telegenic, performative persona.

Past writers and thinkers endorse an unmediated self as the more authentic, coherent, and desirable self, but writers and filmmakers in the Land of the Game Show, after Kellner, concede that such a self no longer exists because one either exists inside the sphere of media or does not exist at all. After all, as Kellner shows, one cannot construct a self if one does not play the game. The bulk of this round on authenticity and the self deals with works that view the self through a lens of deception and subterfuge: rigged games, false testimony, duplicitous identities, from the quiz show scandals to Chuck Barris's alleged double life as a CIA hitman to racially and economically motivated exploitation and discrimination. In their depiction of liars, cheaters, and killers masquerading as average Americans, these works illustrate the number of different selves and masks citizens have on hand to present to others.

While one might expect American stories and films to result in triumph for the individual, instead these works present a world with everyone's roles and outcomes already defined. These works illuminate how the logic of game shows and consumer culture at large promise a ticket out of the trappings of one's social class but actually keep players trapped in their social position by imposing limits on what a person can know—and how much they can achieve—based on socioeconomic standing and ethnicity. The American meritocratic narrative holds up one's knowledge as a method to transcend the confines of race- and class-based stereotypes and limitations; these works call knowledge's power to topple prejudice and oppression into question and, by extension, the American narrative of achievement itself. Any advancements outside one's position in the rigged game of American life constitutes an infraction of the social order, and these gains must be repossessed by the dominant culture. The game show becomes more than a willing tool in this process but an instigator, co-conspirator, or microcosm, transforming the presentation of self into a spectacle for audience consumption. The mechanics of television become the arbiter of the true self, deciding what will "play" as a marketable identity. As such, the game show as depicted in these texts becomes a totalizing entity that comes to represent the totalizing entity of media culture at large, with the spectacle becoming the only thing that is real, stable, and true. Fiction and films featuring successful depictions of resistance to television's postmodernist conception of the self eschew realism in favor of fantasy-based happy endings, coincidences, and musical numbers that tacitly acknowledge the impossibility of a return to a modernist or even Romantic sense of self occurring in reality, or at least not in a reality that media can imagine.

CATEGORY

TO TELL THE TRUTH

> "An educated man, then, and a quiz show contestant are moving rather rapidly in opposite directions. The world of the educated man is full of mysteries. It is foggy and dark; with lots of unlighted passages leading off to no one knows where. The more educated he is the more passages he discovers. . . . Opposed to the dim uncertainty of the world of the educated man is the bright little circle of light in which the quiz show contestant basks in his isolation booth. All is certainty there. One need not worry or be distressed. Only those questions are asked which have answers. And then only if the answers are available, on a card held in the M.C.'s hand. Probably fireflies, flitting about in the spring twilight, are as sure of their little circles of luminescence as the contestant is of his."
>
> —CHARLES VAN DOREN (QUOTED IN ANDERSON 100)

Columbia University professor Charles Van Doren wrote this seemingly humble and self-effacing passage in *Life Magazine* in 1957, shortly after his success as a contestant on the quiz show *Twenty-One* had catapulted him to a level of stardom that earned him comparisons to Elvis Presley (Anderson 70). Van Doren, approaching his new status as a national role model with the utmost gravity, sought to steer his many admirers toward the "dim uncertainty" a meaningful education provides rather than the "bright little circle" of big money and fame that television promises. Less than two years later, his assertion that "all is certainty" in the isolation booth would acquire a bitter irony after he testified to a congressional subcommittee that his quiz-show success resulted from the producers of *Twenty-One* feeding him his questions and their answers in advance. However, rather than damning Van Doren as a charlatan, his statement predicts the televisual reality that big-money quiz shows inaugurated. The world is now the "bright little circle" of television, and viewers the "fireflies" avoiding the "unlighted passages" outside its "little circle of luminescence."

Dieter Hoffmann-Axthelm describes identity as "one of the grand promises of the modern, . . . the paradise of a secularized promise" where "one need not be torn apart, or identify with any rival power—but could remain true to oneself" (200). Robert Redford's 1994 film *Quiz Show*, which dramatizes the rigging of *Twenty-One*, challenges Hoffmann-Axthelm's assertion. In *Quiz Show*, the arrival of the age of mass media, best represented by television, constitutes a "rival power" that threatens to tear apart the "educated man" or woman naïve enough to refuse to "identify with" television and attempt to "remain true to oneself" in the "bright little circle" of one's isolation booth.

The film wastes little time in establishing the menace of broadcasting. The opening scene contains the first appearance of mass media in the film, when protagonist Richard Goodwin (Rob Morrow) flips on the radio of an immaculate Chrysler in a car dealership. The car's shiny chrome antenna rises gracefully upward, only to pick up the signal of a far more significant launch: Sputnik. While this scene's juxtaposition of the Chrysler with Sputnik may appear to correspond with the big-money quiz show's endorsement of "knowledge and education" as "an important counterbalance to consumerism," the opening credits montage that follows the car dealership scene shows how such notions are like the Chrysler's chrome antenna: shiny luxury objects that distract from the threat lurking in the airwaves (Hoerschelmann 73). In a cruel twist of irony, one needs the appurtenances of mass media to pick up the media's nefarious signal, and by then it is too late. Overtures to intellectual advancement over consumption are just that in *Quiz Show*: camouflage for media's (and its sponsors') infiltration of every aspect of American life. While everything looks good and clean and top-of-the-line, these elements function as window dressing for a hostile, unapologetic takeover of the American narrative and the individualism that so often symbolizes its beating heart.

The opening montage of *Quiz Show* features the only period song cue in the film, Bobby Darin's 1959 rendition of the Weill-Brecht standard "Mack the Knife." Stephen J. Whitfield notes that Redford plays fast and loose with history in these opening scenes: the Sputnik launch happened six months *after* Charles Van Doren first appeared on *Twenty-One*, and Darin's recording of "Mack the Knife" was not released until 1959, the same year as Van Doren's testimony before Congress. Redford makes these events simultaneous to allege that America's fascination with media and consumer goods creates embarrassments such as Sputnik and the quiz-show scandals. As the song plays, the camera follows the sealed envelope containing the questions for a night's broadcast of *Twenty-One* as its makes its way from a safety deposit box in a Manhattan bank vault to an armored car with a police escort to NBC studios to host Jack Barry's hand seconds before the live broadcast begins. The film has yet to introduce a contestant or showcase a sponsor, suggesting, much like *Twenty-One* did, that the questions—and their sterling authenticity—are the stars of the show. The questions even walk the red carpet as photographers and adoring fans look on and "Mack the Knife" swells to its climax. At first glance, a murder ballad such as "Mack the Knife" seems an odd choice for this sequence; however, including the song at the beginning of the film encourages the viewer to read *Quiz Show*'s

The questions are ready for their close-up.

narrative as a tale of violence and mass murder that exposes the "hypocrisies and injustices of capitalism" (Whitfield). A cursory read of the film would lead one to conclude that television is Mack and the truth is what falls victim to his shiny knife, with the performance of authenticity surrounding the questions acting as the shiny façade that distracts the viewer from the sharp knife producing the shine. The truth, however, is but one of the many fatalities in *Quiz Show*, and the film adeptly shows how the shenanigans behind the production of *Twenty-One* symbolize the slaughter of the individualist narrative at the heart of the American Dream. In prearranging the outcome of its quiz shows, television producers seduce contestants into betraying their intellects and integrity, then discard the contestants when they are no longer of use. It is literal character assassination posing as the rags-to-riches fantasy more commonly known as the American Dream.

Each of the characters *Quiz Show* assassinates is a man trying to make a name for himself in an increasingly competitive and unequal country. Herbert Stempel (John Turturro), Charles Van Doren (Ralph Fiennes), and Goodwin all seek to use television to isolate attention on themselves and gain admission into a more affluent and privileged world, but television's corporate sponsors have designs of their own. Another game takes place behind the scenes of *Twenty-One*, a game in which the producers coax the contestants into trading their identities for instant fame and the promise of a future in television. The figure standing in the isolation booth during the broadcast represents the new postmodern self: a hypervisible individual sculpted by television, which is itself the creation of advertisers and corporate interests.

The film starts with Stempel at his peak as the seemingly unbeatable champion. Television, Stempel brags to his wife, "is the biggest thing since Gutenberg invented the printing press, and I'm the biggest thing on it." Appearing on *Twenty-One* catapults him from anonymity to national fame; however, regardless of how many right answers he provides, the producers of *Twenty-One* treat Stempel like a wrong answer. As producer Al Freedman (Hank Azaria) asks Charles Van Doren, "if you were a kid, would you want to be an annoying Jewish guy with a sidewall haircut?" Host Jack Barry (Christopher McDonald) foregrounds Stempel as an outsider to the Manhattan world of broadcasting when he begins a game by asking Stempel, "How are things in Queens," identifying him not by who he is or what he knows but where he is from. When it comes to trivia, Stempel seems invincible, but his ratings are not; they have "plateaued," which makes both the network and the sponsors question his appropriateness. When told that Stempel is the kind of underdog that New Yorkers like to root for, Geritol president Martin Rittenhome (Martin Scorsese) quickly retorts, "Queens is not New York." Another executive (Griffin Dunne) echoes Rittenhome by saying Geritol "wants a guy on *Twenty-One* who looks like he can get a table at '21.'" Instead of presenting a populist talent search devoted to showcasing "the cop who knew Shakespeare," *Quiz Show* depicts a world in which only those who look successful succeed because their triumph bolsters an image of success that sells the advertiser's product. In fact, Stempel's shameless and unscripted endorsements of Geritol at the start of one show may be what motivates Rittenhome to replace him: he is unwilling to have his product associated with someone as "common" as Stempel.

To ensure Stempel's quick departure from the show, the producers talk him into "taking a dive," or getting a question wrong on purpose. This performance of ignorance requires Stempel to betray himself by denying what he knows; however, the betrayal goes deeper than the factual. The producers ask Stempel to state that *On the Waterfront*, not *Marty*, won the Academy Award for Best Picture in 1955. Stempel objects vehemently because *Marty* is his favorite movie, but when Dan Enright (David Paymer) and Al Freedman promise to put him in consideration for a panel show, he agrees, denying himself and throwing away his identity as an intellectual powerhouse for the chance to be a television personality—not a mind but a face with capped teeth. In the isolation booth, Stempel betrays himself and answers "*On the Waterfront*," remaking himself into the Herbert Stempel that television wants him to be.

The choice of question and (wrong) answer are so thematically appropriate that one has a hard time believing that they are not scripted by a poet. *Marty*, Stempel's favorite film, chronicles the yearnings of a blue-collar butcher from one of the outer boroughs, while *On the Waterfront* tells the story of a has-been boxer who threw away his title shot by "taking a dive" for the easy money. In answering "*On the Waterfront*," Herbert Stempel rejects his identity as Ernest Borgnine's Marty and instead becomes Marlon Brando's Terry Molloy. The fact that Stempel does not in fact land the panel show he thought the network would give him in return for his loss only confirms his affinity with Molloy's identity further: he too "could have been a contender," he too "could have had class," he too "could have been somebody," instead of the nobody he becomes once he goes off the air. Like Molloy, Stempel turns stool pigeon, but the similarities to *On the Waterfront* stop there because Stempel's testimony is not enough to bring down television. *Quiz Show* reveals *On the Waterfront*'s gritty realism masks some magical thinking: in the rigged game of American life, the truth is seldom the right answer.

Stempel is not the only character the producers of *Twenty-One* ask to be ignorant of his love. Although only featured in two scenes, artist James Snodgrass (Douglas McGrath) shoulders many of the film's central ideas about selfhood. The producers wanted him to lose on a question about American poets by misattributing a quote by Emily Dickinson to Walt Whitman. Snodgrass refuses to play along and instead gives the right answer, not because he was after more money, but rather because Emily Dickinson was his favorite poet and he, unlike Stempel, refuses to deny his personal tastes to win the approval of the sponsors (Anderson 75). Like Stempel's scripted incorrect answer, Snodgrass's unscripted response is not without its poetic undertones. His expected wrong answer, "Walt Whitman," aligns with television's fluid, public, expansive sense of broadcasted identity, a visible isolation booth that can "contradict [it]self" because "it contain[s] multitudes"; while the correct answer, "Emily Dickinson," represents the impervious, compact self, a true isolation booth, a "nobody" sequestered from the "admiring bog" of the "public" (Whitman 76; Dickinson 1, 8, 6). In choosing Dickinson over Whitman, Snodgrass opts out of the mediated world and retains his modernist sense of self.

Ultimately, Stempel gets his panel show in the form of testimony before the congressional subcommittee, and he milks the spotlight from his newfound isolation booth, delivering manic one-liners that eclipse the stilted stage presence he exhibits on *Twenty-One*. For a moment, Stempel appears to be both emcee and returning champion on his own game show, *Are You Smarter Than Herbert Stempel?*; however, television quickly cancels his program when he dares to implicate Charles Van Doren in the scandal. After he names Van Doren, the congressmen grill him with questions about his mental and financial instability, reducing him once again to the sweaty, inarticulate dullard that he was in the isolation booth of *Twenty-One*. The film handles Stempel's testimony as another of his desperate attempts to get back in the spotlight, depicting his testimony, like his intellect and identity, as tainted by television's allure. Stempel begins the film on top and falls to the bottom, but the film does not portray his arc as the tragedy its form suggests; instead, his obsession with fame and willingness to betray everything about himself to secure it rewards him with the anonymity and infamy the film and the executives seem to believe he deserves. He suffers a fall from a grace that he never possessed. The real tragic hero of the film is Charles Van Doren, the prince who tumbles from the highest perch. His desire to make a name for himself distinct from that of his famous father Mark Van Doren (Paul Scofield) motivates him to partner with television, a "rival power" to his father's academia, and he is "torn apart" as a result. Paul Attanasio's script subtly positions Van Doren as an obscured, isolated figure searching for a notoriety that he believes he is entitled to. The film introduces him by having a woman ask him, "Are you the son?" confirming that his identity is contingent on the identity of another. Van Doren himself explains his career to *Twenty-One*'s producers as a series of failed attempts at stardom. He states that he missed his chance at greatness in astrophysics (the stars), so he wrote a novel about a boy who kills his father (a star poet-intellectual), and now he hopes to become a star himself in the isolation booth of *Twenty-One*. Van Doren's identity is empty, a void waiting to be filled, a substance in search of a form.

Ironically, Van Doren trades on the name recognition of his father to make a name for himself. His family name gets the attention of everyone who hears it; even before they meet him, everyone asks, "*Van Doren* Van Doren?" on hearing Charles's name. Tellingly, Van Doren's father connects appearing on television to losing a sense of self. After finally watching his son perform on *Twenty-One*, he expresses his amazement over what Charles recalls under the pressure of live television. If he were on the program, he claims, he would not be able to remember *his own name*. Television annihilates Mark Van Doren's sense of self-knowledge, where Charles uses the show to make his name; however, Charles's resulting self is just like the knowledge he presents on the show: inauthentic, predetermined, and ultimately out of his control, a parody of the intellectual he professes to be. When he confesses his involvement in the scandal to his father, he calls it "an ill-favored thing" but argues that "it was mine," to which his father responds, "Your name is mine." With this statement, his father reveals that Van Doren's quest for individuality has been doomed from the start. He is trapped in his family, isolated by the shadow of his successful father, and his attempt to break out, although it works for a time, only serves to isolate him further in the end when he becomes television's sacrificial offering to Congress.

Redford turns to vertiginous compositions to depict the way television seduces (and finally discards) Charles Van Doren. As Van Doren deliberates answering the rigged question that will deliver him his first victory, the camera booms up and tilts down, dwarfing Van Doren in the limited space of his isolation booth. The film cuts to a view from the control room where Van Doren's face is visible on an even smaller studio monitor. These shots place him amidst the apparatuses of television production until he appears as but one more prop in television's operation. After he wins the first rigged appearance, he opts to take the stairs rather than the elevator, and Redford cuts to a shot near the bottom of the stairwell looking up at Van Doren as he descends the dizzying staircase. The camera performs a series of 360-degree pans as Van Doren makes his way down the stairs. The dizzying composition appears to establish the stairwell as the setting for a private, moral struggle where Van Doren can reflect honestly on his betrayal of himself; however, when he steps into the isolation of his closeup, he stops and ecstatically exclaims, "Twenty thousand dollars!" From there, he continues his descent, an "educated man" thoroughly seduced by the "bright little circle" of television. Redford cuts to the reverse angle, looking down at Van Doren as he ventures into the maw of television. This time, however, the camera remains wide and locked in place, suggesting the finality of Van Doren's decision. When he gives the wrong answer that releases him from the show, Redford and cinematographer Michael Ballhaus dolly in to Van Doren's back while simultaneously zooming out, stretching the space around Van Doren so that he becomes increasingly separated from the *Twenty-One* set and the studio audience. This move illustrates how giving the wrong answer cuts Van Doren off from television's "bright little circle" and thrusts him back into the "dim uncertainty of the world" outside the screen. Collectively, these shots suggest that Van Doren's involvement with *Twenty-One* does not transform him into a star. Rather, it diminishes him to a small detail in a larger system that consumes and then forgets him.

Two additional scenes in the film demonstrate television's influence on Van Doren and his sense of self. The first begins as an NBC driver drops Van Doren off at Columbia. Van Doren notices how tranquil and empty campus seems. He checks his watch, then tells the driver he needs to tie his shoes. Van Doren bends down but does not tie his shoes. He waits until students begin exiting the building, and then he emerges from the limo to greet an astonished audience. The moment represents the peak of Van Doren's quest for a distinct self because these students recognize him not as "the son" but as "Charles Van Doren." Further, he achieves this feat on Columbia's campus, where he has frequently languished in his father's shadow. Television bestows on Van Doren the identity that he seeks, with the studio limo ushering him out of the isolation of his father's shadow into the "bright little circle" of fame; however, he cannot achieve it honestly. He must fabricate it. To succeed in an image-based culture, Van Doren submits himself to it, and this submission

GAME SHOWS AND THE QUEST FOR AN AUTHENTIC SELF 47

Van Doren in the isolation booth.

Van Doren as a creature of television.

Van Doren descends into television's maw.

Van Doren in another isolation booth.

requires that he deny his integrity at the expense of his image, right down to lying about the state of his shoelaces. The end of this scene foreshadows that Van Doren's glowing moment in the spotlight will be short-lived. Once Van Doren gets through the crowd of onlookers he manufactured, he enters his office to find Richard Goodwin waiting to ask him about his awareness of unusual practices on *Twenty-One*. The scene as Redford constructs it captures Van Doren's entire arc in one scene: Van Doren wishes to be the center of attention, so he tells a small lie that garners him an intense, instant following, which he coasts through until he meets his biggest fan, Goodwin, who, despite his affection for Van Doren, takes him down.

After his encounter with Goodwin, Van Doren, rightly, feels the heat and enters a phone booth to place a frightened call to Dan Enright. As Van Doren grows more worried that Goodwin will expose the scandal, a passerby (Mario Cantone) recognizes him and begins alternately praising, quizzing, and taunting Van Doren, pointing him out to other pedestrians, who crowd around the phone booth. Redford and cinematographer Michael Ballhaus place Van Doren on the far right side of the screen and use a long lens to pen him in shallow focus. A shallow depth of field reduces the bustling Manhattan streets in the background to a blur to illustrate Van Doren's hypervisibility: he is the only object of attention. This composition transforms the phone booth into a real-world iteration of the isolation booth in *Twenty-One*, with the scene operating as a reenactment of Van Doren's performance on the show. Outside the booth, he appears to be a bright, charismatic figure that charms America; inside the booth, however, he is helplessly dependent on his producers for answers. He betrays his identity as a private intellectual in his attempt to make a name for himself as a public (and postmodern) intellectual, but this notoriety is outer-directed, malleable, and dictated by mass media.

Van Doren's statement before the congressional subcommittee, much of which *Quiz Show* reproduces verbatim, exhibits a remarkably postmodern view of selfhood. "I was involved, deeply involved, in a deception," Van Doren states. "The fact that I, too, was very much deceived cannot keep me from being the principal victim of that deception, because I was its principal symbol" (Anderson 142). Van Doren concedes "Charles Van Doren" is not a coherent, fixed self but a "symbol" manipulated by others in support of their agendas. Despite acknowledging that his celebrity and achievement were all based on an elaborate deception, Van Doren chooses to view the spoils of that deception as genuine, claiming, "I have deceived my friends," and adding "and I had millions of them" (Anderson 142). These "millions" figure as the other "players" who admire and respect how Van Doren plays the postmodern game of the self Kellner describes. Van Doren admits to presenting a false self in more places than *Twenty-One*. He claims that he has "been acting a role for 10 or 15 years, maybe all [his] life. It's a role of thinking that [he has] done far more than [he has] done, accomplished more than [he's] accomplished, produced more than [he has] produced" (Anderson 149). Van Doren views his self as a persona, as performative, an empty symbol of intellect and privilege masking a lack of genuine achievement. And like symbols in the postmodern landscape, the meaning of "Charles Van Doren" is fluid.

Because he shuns the limelight at every opportunity, it would appear that *Quiz Show* intends to exalt Richard Goodwin (on whose memoir the script is partly based) as immune to television's seductions and thus in possession of a fixed, stable sense of self (Whitfield). However, Goodwin's failed prosecution of television proves his valiant pursuit of integrity futile because the culture has moved beyond the modernist vision of the self he subscribes to. Redford plays on the difference between cinematic language and televisual language to illustrate this distinction, elevating the former as a greater arbiter of fixed truth while condemning the latter as a "philistine" purveyor of manufactured, fragmented truth (Whitfield). Goodwin discovers Snodgrass's act of defiance by watching a 16mm film transfer of his appearance on *Twenty-One*. Unlike the isolation booth of *Twenty-One*, the projection room Goodwin constructs in his hotel room is a truly private space obscured (literally) by the bright light of the moving image. In the isolation booth of a projection room, Goodwin can expose NBC's lies by replaying and scrutinizing the television image, and, through film, capture the moment when Snodgrass goes off-script and delivers the correct answer. In this private space, Goodwin, not television, is in control of the image; however, television remains the brightest part of the frame, and

Goodwin's private projection room.

Goodwin's attempt to transfer his control of television from his hotel room into the public sphere of a congressional subcommittee hearing gives television an opportunity to reassert its authority over public life. The truth, it seems, can only survive in private spaces, which wield little influence over public life.

Goodwin's refusal to put himself in the public eye results in him being ignored. In the same way that Mack the Knife's victims cannot see his weapon because they are distracted by the shine of his blade, those in power cannot see Goodwin when they are entranced by the "bright little circle" of television. Unlike Mack, however, Goodwin's invisibility renders him ineffectual, not fatal. These hearings ought to be Goodwin's star turn. Instead, Redford shoves him to the margins of the frame in the chamber, both visually and narratively, placing him beneath and to the side of the congressmen and those testifying to demonstrate how the spectacle dwarfs both him and his pursuit of the truth. By the time Van Doren appears to testify, Goodwin has been moved behind the congressmen, far from the action. Like Stempel, he has "plateaued," and the producers decide to make a change. Television co-opts his exposure of their wrongdoing and alters the outcome of the narrative, turning him into an audience member at his own hearing, which, perhaps is what he has always been. He may be able to spot a liar in a poker game or correctly answer all the questions when he watches *Twenty-One* at home, but he cannot win because he refuses to play the game himself, deeming it "too rich for [his] blood." While this act may preserve his integrity, it also renders him powerless to create change. Through Goodwin, Redford subtly suggests that one cannot remain detached from image culture and hope to make a name for themselves or effect change. In *Quiz Show*, television has divided

Split focus diopter shots.

the country into players and audience members, with the audience members receiving a fixed, powerless identity and the players enjoying a fluid identity that enables them to enact change, but only through betraying that fixed self and constructing a new self to present to the world.

Redford's film ends on its most damning note: the rigged game is not in broadcasting but in every aspect of American life, where the corporations have all the answers. NBC and Geritol rig Goodwin's hearings the same way that they rigged *Twenty-One*. "The public has a very short memory," Martin Rittenhome tells Goodwin, "corporations, they never forget," which explains why the congressmen conduct their hearing the way the corporations want them to: the corporations are their real constituents. The congressmen alternately joke with the NBC president about his golf game and grill Herbert Stempel with scripted questions about his mental and financial stability and castigate him for implicating someone as distinguished as Charles Van Doren in the scandal. In pitting Stempel against Van Doren, they produce a legal version of *Twenty-One* (or, more accurately, *To Tell the Truth*), brought to you by NBC and Geritol. Redford accentuates the hearings' similarity to *Twenty-One* by shooting several exchanges between Goodwin and Stempel with the same split focus diopter filter he uses when Jack Barry asks Stempel and Van Doren questions.

Although it may be shot similarly to *Twenty-One*, this congressional game show serves a larger function than mere entertainment. In making the hearings into a Stempel-Van Doren rematch, NBC, with the assistance of Congress, distracts the public from the real scandal and silently slips into the background where it can manipulate the spectacle. Just like on the quiz show, they give all the contestants the questions in advance, controlling what comes in and out of

Split focus diopter shots.

the isolation booth and gets shared with the public. Any answer they broadcast then, in effect, is the correct one. While Dan Enright allows all the blame for the scandal to fall on his shoulders, his admission of guilt is not portrayed as any sort of punishment. Just like Stempel did on *Twenty-One*, Enright takes a dive for NBC; however, unlike Stempel, Enright's submission secures his future in television, and he returns with *The Joker's Wild* in 1972. This scheme is, as Enright unironically says to Charles Van Doren, "so pure it floats." In echoing the slogan for Ivory Soap, Enright shows how even the most basic truth claim becomes postmodern and fluid, bathed in the language of advertising.

"We're not going to get television," Goodwin warns at the end of the film, "Television is gonna get us." While this line runs the risk of being too on the nose, portraying television as some kind of crazed spree killer, the closing moments of Redford's film introduce a complexity that dwarfs this trite one-liner. As Goodwin leaves the Capitol, the camera cranes up and pans right to a wide shot of Washington, DC. Audio of testimony from other characters play on the soundtrack and gentle music rises underneath as the image dissolves to a shot of an audience in a theater looking up at a screen and laughing uproariously. The shot of the laughing crowd at the end marks Redford's most subversive turn: the crowd simultaneously represents America's obliviousness to the rigged games it watches and participates in and represents the film watching America and finding its obliviousness hilarious. Like the contestants on the show, America too betrays itself and its commitment to the truth in exchange for being part of the "community" of television, banishing those who care about authenticity and integrity to the isolation booth of the world outside the screen. The ending of the film agrees with Goodwin that "TV is gonna get us"; however, Redford

The audience laughs, but at what? At whom?

suggests that TV will not come in the guise of some slasher movie villain. Instead, TV will slay its victims as they are transfixed by its "pearly white" glow. Redford's choice to end the film with another rendition of "Mack the Knife," a downtempo, dreamy version by Lyle Lovett produced specifically for the film, confirms that not only is Mack "back in town" to slay yet again, he never left. In fact, he runs the town. In 1960, immediately after the scandals, two-thirds of people told the *New York Daily News* that they would have no qualms about appearing on a rigged quiz show (Anderson 156). The song remains the same for 1960, 1994, and today. Television remains on the loose, carving up the selves of innocents naïve enough to believe in its shiny promises.

CATEGORY

WHO GETS TO BE A MILLIONAIRE?

Quiz Show demonstrates that making a name for oneself through achievement is a fantasy because American culture is as rigged as *Twenty-One*. The film offers a brutal take on the way that television has shaped America's understanding of its own meritocratic narrative, changing the emblematic game from baseball to the rigged quiz show. The NBC President in *Quiz Show* (Allan Rich) may argue that "Stempel has an everyman quality. You know, that American Dream thing? You too can be rich." However, before he can finish halfheartedly rattling off such platitudes, an executive cuts him off, saying "if the ratings stay high."

Redford contrasts the cynical, superficial world of NBC with Stempel's Queens neighborhood when he includes a scene featuring Stempel's triumphant return following his last victory. As he exits the NBC limo, he receives a hero's welcome from his neighbors (and one of his only tracking shots), who view success for Herb as success for them all. This scene operates as the antithesis to Van Doren's shoe-tying and phone booth scenes because Stempel does not have to wait for a crowd to form. However, the success of a guy from Queens winning big is not entertaining to a broad enough audience. In the cynical world that *Quiz Show* presents, the "everyman" can get rich provided their achievement generates profit for the sponsors; American ideals of selfhood and individualism represent nothing more than a ratings ploy. The fact that Stempel's success is entirely rigged strengthens this sense: his achievement is, like Van Doren's, sponsored entertainment, a paid program. Stempel rejects the American Dream's concept of achievement through honesty when he defends his lies to his wife, saying, "My father used to tell me, 'Work hard and you'll get ahead.' Was that honest?" In the free interplay of signs that constitutes *Quiz Show*'s postmodern world, whether or not accomplishments come as the result of actual merit is irrelevant: the image of merit suffices.

Richard Goodwin's character becomes the conduit through which all these ideas pass, transposing his disenchantment with Charles Van Doren to a disenchantment with America. Goodwin occupies a liminal space between Herbert Stempel and Charles Van Doren socioeconomically: he is a middle-class Jew who made it to the top of his class at Harvard Law School and now works in Washington. His ambitious nature can be read as an attempt to escape the world of Herbert Stempel and enter the world of Charles Van Doren, which he believes he can do on merit alone. One of Goodwin's co-workers quips that "Dick hopes someday to be confused with an important person," and clearly, that person Goodwin longs to be confused with is someone resembling Charles Van Doren; Goodwin naively believes that his Harvard education means that he and Van Doren "speak the same language." Stempel calls Goodwin out over these class pretensions, implying that his education paradoxically makes him more naïve: "Just because you went to Harvard you think you have some stake in the system." Van Doren takes advantage of Goodwin's hunger to be accepted by him, seducing him via invitations to lunch at the Athenaeum and invitations to family birthday parties in Connecticut with Edmund Wilson and Thomas Merton. Similarly, Van Doren falls back on the privileges of his class when cornered, treating it as the shibboleth that will absolve him of all suspicion. When Goodwin begs him to confess to cheating, Van Doren asks Goodwin if he would participate in a rigged quiz show. When Goodwin says he would not, Van Doren simply asks, "And I would?" Van Doren's answer does not satisfy Goodwin, but he also does not challenge him further, accepting it as representative of the impassable distance between them.

In many respects, the Goodwin-Van Doren relationship is the love story in the film, and it turns *Quiz Show* into a story of heartbreak, rejection, and betrayal. Goodwin becomes the jilted admirer who is simultaneously rejected because of his social status and disgusted by what he desires. Although the film may share in Goodwin's disgust with the system by the end of the film, in positioning Van Doren as the lost love object, *Quiz Show* shares Goodwin's investment in the class structure as it stands, no matter how inauthentic or performative it may be. The film may be highly critical of Charles Van Doren and the fraud he participated in, but it rejects nothing about his life or aspirations apart from his deception, which suggests the film advocates for an authentic version of the class structure presented on *Twenty-One*, not for reorganizing American life. The film yearns for a time when the ruling elite came by their power and privilege honestly (whenever that was), if only to justify both America's admiration of them and the average American's exile from their world.

In this way, *Quiz Show* becomes a drama about class in America, using the game show intermedially as a metaphor to depict the ways in which American culture promises a postmodern fluidity of class but fails, perhaps even refuses, to deliver. Despite the promises that the postmodern self offers to those wishing to shape themselves into a new and better self, the films and novels that use the game show as a metaphor for the self show that the privileges of a fluid identity are not available to all. The "named" already exist and operate like a closed club. One cannot transcend the confines of their social standing; rather, they must remain in their lane or suffer the consequences for wanting what America promises. Ironically, works such as *Quiz Show*, Jonathan Demme's *Melvin and Howard* (1980), and Danny Boyle's *Slumdog Millionaire* (2008) demonstrate that when true upward mobility rears its head, it must be put down while still preserving the image of merit at all costs. Thus, the egalitarian narrative found in game shows actively negate the ideals it promotes. Instead of being contradictory, these opposing forces reinforce each other, promising viewers that anyone can make it in the Land of the Game Show, just not you. At least, not yet. Keep playing. Tune in tomorrow and it might be you.

John Fiske outlines the connections between the format of a quiz show and the American narrative of advancement through achievement. For Fiske, the "ritual-game-ritual" structure of a typical quiz show "is an enactment of capitalist ideology": players begin the game as individuals with equal opportunity, and the game brings their innate differences to the surface, rewarding those who naturally rise to the top of the game with "upward mobility into the realm of social power" and all of its "material and economic benefits" (268). Fiske also describes how this model mirrors the education system, the very institution that the big-money quiz shows wanted to emulate and support in America's post-Sputnik panic. Much like a quiz show, "all students (supposedly) start equal" in the education system: as in a game, "those with natural ability pass successively more discriminating tests (examinations) and emerge as the highly qualified few who are fitted (by nature, so the story goes) for the high-income jobs, and positions with high degrees of social power and influence," a.k.a. prizes (268). Fiske shows how this game show/education model "naturalizes the class system" by using knowledge "to separate out winners from losers and to ground the classification [of being a winner or a loser] in individual or natural differences" (268, 269). Any class difference or inequality is therefore the result of "natural" differences between people that the game merely draws out, not the machinations of an inherently unfair or biased system. The ideology persists even when the show is revealed to be rigged.

The makeover that quiz shows underwent as they transitioned into game shows mimics the transition from a modern sensibility grounded in coherence to a postmodern one based on fragmentation, and not just because of the interruptions that commercial breaks introduced. The game show's new, postmodern identity "positions its viewers to identify with and desire an affluent, up-scale lifestyle via its projection of images of a high-tech, high-consumption affluent society" in which they can "live out the fantasy of unbridled capitalism" (Kellner, "Popular Culture" 150). As Joanne Morreale writes in her essay on makeover shows, which harken back to earlier game shows such as *Strike It Rich* and *Queen for a Day*, these shows assert that "transformation is attainable, given the participant's continued motivation and effort (i.e. willingness to play the game)" (100). Such a transformation of the contestant "present[s] the illusion of a unified self who is 'better' than what was there before" to the audience, suggesting to the audience that one can "begin from a position of lack and inadequacy" and can arrive at a dramatic reimagining of the self "through the purchase of products," where "our becoming, our transformational potential becomes confined to image consumption and production" (Morreale 100, 105). This fairy tale narrative reinforces the American fairy tale of upward mobility based on merit, with a twist: the mobility and the merit derive from "learning how to select and consume goods and services appropriately" (Redden 150). During this postmodern era, personal transformation in the American fairy tale results from consumption, not achievement.

Filmmakers use the forced inequality of the rigged game show intermedially to represent the inequality of America and the ways that fairy tale traps people in a fixed identity by dangling the promise of fluidity before them. These films adeptly depict social class as an isolation booth: each person remains confined to their own social status, with television facilitating the rigged game, controlling what information passes in or out of each booth, ensuring that anyone who does manage to escape the isolation booth of social class and attempt to enter another, higher booth, will have their gains seized by representatives of the ruling order.

The motif of repossession runs throughout Jonathan Demme's *Melvin and Howard*, "a comic picaresque" about the ups and (mostly) downs of a "middle-American Everyman" who meets an extraordinarily rich man and, briefly, makes a name for himself (Fischer 33). The Everyman is Melvin Dummar (Paul Le Mat), and the enigmatic tycoon Howard Hughes (Jason Robards) is the rich man whom Melvin claims to have rescued from certain death in the desert after Hughes crashed his motorcycle. Melvin also claims Hughes rewarded him by naming him a beneficiary in his will, and Melvin must go to court to prove not only that Hughes's will is legitimate but that he, Melvin Dummar, is not a loser with souped-up dreams. Lucy Fischer describes this narrative, which is based on actual events, as "a modern-day fairy tale, or an American wish-fulfillment fantasy" in which a working-class dreamer wins the grand prize of instant wealth (in the form of being included in Howard Hughes's will) as a reward for simply being himself (33). Fischer could just as easily be describing the narrative of most game shows, where people win big bucks for small achievements. Unlike Charles Van Doren or Herbert Stempel, Melvin does not betray himself in exchange for success because his values and the values of consumerist America align perfectly. Instead, Demme shows how the America Melvin believes in with religious fervor is rigged against him to keep him in the isolation booth of economic and personal stagnation. In staying true to himself and his dream, he betrays himself and ensures he will never achieve it. The only name Melvin makes for himself is "loser" because the instant wealth he claims to inherit from Hughes's, like most things he acquires in the film, gets taken away from him, repossessed, making *Melvin and Howard* the story of a man who dreams the American dream of upward mobility only to spin around in endless circles, ultimately going nowhere.

From the start, *Melvin and Howard* is preoccupied with movement, and this movement—or lack thereof—represents Melvin's inability to move out of his social standing into another, more prosperous one. Tak Fujimoto's gritty cinematography and fast-moving camera makes the rest of the film feel continuously on the run, as though it is afraid of being apprehended. The opening scene of the film features Hughes recklessly racing his motorcycle and crashing it in the desert. Melvin's encounter with Hughes takes place entirely in Melvin's truck, where he sings his original song about Santa's souped-up sleigh. Melvin first lives in a mobile home, whose exterior is riddled with carcasses of old cars, hubcaps, and tires. After they split up the first time, Melvin's wife Lynda (Mary

Steenburgen) sends their daughter to Melvin via Greyhound. Lynda appears on a game show called *Easy Street*, which features cars and trips to Hawaii as prizes. Melvin drives a dairy truck that frequently breaks down on him, and later he operates an automotive service station, working to keep other people moving while himself remaining physically and economically immobile.

But the most ubiquitous reference to movement and the ways in which upward mobility is denied to Melvin comes from the series of repossessions that run throughout the film. Melvin's trucks, cars, and boat get taken from him, isolating him in the blue-collar world he longs to escape. The abundance of these literal repossessions lead one to view other events in the film as repossessions as well. For instance, Lynda leaves Melvin several times, repossessing herself and their children, and Melvin's boss at the Rockwood Dairy attempts to repossess Melvin's "Milkman of the Month" award. Most importantly, the trial regarding the authenticity of Hughes's will represents the legal system's attempt to repossess millions from Melvin, an attempt which, like most of the others, ultimately succeeds. These repossessions keep Melvin exiled from Easy Street, trapped in his social class, still dreaming the (impossible) American Dream.

Melvin, however, refuses to view his status in terms of class. When Lynda says, "We're poor," Melvin corrects her, "We're *broke*, maybe" portraying himself as part of a fluid group, one of the not-yet-rich, rather than someone trapped in the isolation booth of class. Melvin's mindset mimics what Guy Redden sees on display in makeover shows, where "learning to adopt the right signs of identity is depicted as an investment that will yield social power in the workplace" and elsewhere (154). Redden explains how a makeover's investment in individualization works to perpetuate the existing power structure. In a makeover, the individual does not engage in self-determination; rather, one "monitor[s] and change[s] oneself" by "learn[ing] to apply the discourses of industry experts" (162). The person does not want to change the system, only their place in it. The "rightness" of one's makeover "involves channeling one's agency towards consumption consistent with what is deemed socially acceptable and productive" (Redden 164). *Melvin and Howard* can be read as a makeover show in which the contestant (Melvin) competes for a prize by continually "adopt[ing] the right signs of identity" for an affluent American but never receives the prize of "social power" in return (154). Melvin's pursuit of his dreams by consuming beyond his means does not constitute an investment but rather a trap that keeps him from achieving anything. In trying to empower himself, Melvin only works to better the system that keeps him isolated from the spot on Easy Street he seeks (and the system promises).

Demme's film demonstrates how Melvin's overinvestment in the superficial aspects of the American Dream make him a tool of capital in which other

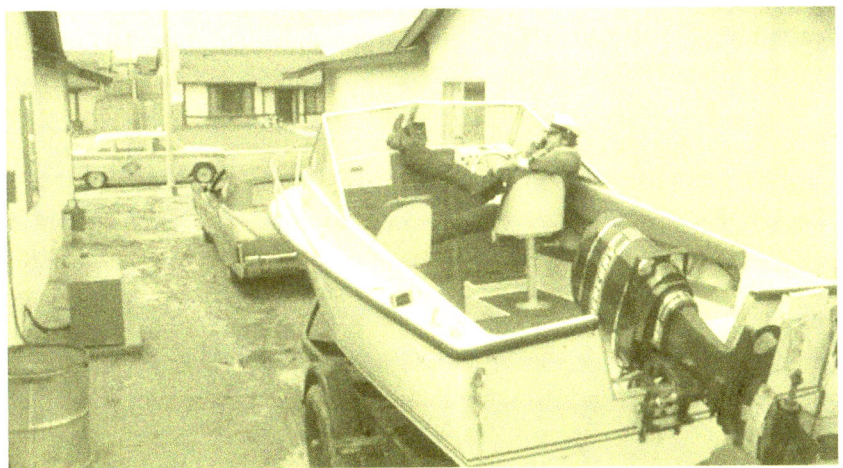
Melvin docked far from Easy Street.

people profit from his failures. Melvin's pursuit follows what Douglas Kellner calls "the logic of capital," which uses "advertising, fashion, consumption, television, and popular culture [to] destabilize identity" so that it can market "new products and identifications" as stabilizing solutions to "restructure one's identity" ("Popular Culture" 172, 174). Instead of revolting against his boss at the dairy for attempting to repossess his Milkman of the Month award, Melvin allows him to deduct his pay so long as he gets to keep the title and the Zenith television set that accompanies it. Melvin trades real money that could help him achieve the upward mobility he seeks for the superficial material that gives him the appearance of having already achieved it. Melvin's title "Milkman of the Month" therefore becomes ironic: it creates the image of someone delivering sustenance when he cannot pay his bills.

Despite his inability to keep most of the things he buys—or perhaps because of it—Melvin is depicted as the ultimate consumer, "an over-achieving student in the American cultural school" who is wholeheartedly invested in a fluid postmodern identity defined by high-end products and advertising jingles, always trying to buy his way out of his problems (Fischer 36). Melvin views consumption as an investment in the self that will one day pay off when his potential matures. When Lynda discovers he blew much of her *Easy Street* winnings on a car and a boat, Melvin tells her, "That's not just a car, it's *our* car. I used to see cars like that. I used to want one; now I got one," implying that the purchase makes him into the person that he dreams of becoming. Melvin's attitude confirms Kellner's assertion that "capital itself [acts as] the demiurge of the allegedly postmodern fragmentation, dispersal of identity, change, and mobility," or, in Melvin's case, immobility (172). Melvin consoles himself by pretending to be captain of his boat on the open water, ignoring that this boat remains firmly "docked" on his driveway.

If Easy Street exists in *Melvin and Howard*'s America, it is nowhere on display in Demme's film, which "paints a picture of consumer culture as a wasteland filled with objects unworthy of desire" where the comfort and glamour of Hughes's riches remain as elusive and sequestered as Hughes himself (Fischer 35). Demme's depiction of the game show becomes playfully subversive in this regard. On *Easy Street*, which Fischer dubs "a cross between 'The Gong Show' and 'The New Treasure Hunt,'" contestants perform in a talent competition, and the performer the audience "loves" the most gets to pick a "gate," behind which could await their prize, or nothing at all (34). As far as game shows go, *Easy Street* may be among the sleaziest and the cheapest, making it a perfect representation of success in the Dummars' "world of material kitsch" (Fischer 35). Like Redford does in *Quiz Show*, Demme privileges cinematic language by stripping any television gloss from the look of *Easy Street*. The main colors of the set are black, gray, and gold, and the program's host, Wally "Mr. Love" Williams (Robert Ridgeley), speaks almost entirely in sexual innuendo, even referring to himself as "Uncle Wally" when coming on to Lynda. Demme's framing of the scene shows the flimsy wooden backs of the flats that constitute *Easy Street*'s set, along with frequent glimpses of the boom mic and the host's cue cards. Every aspect of the scene effaces any expectations of glitz viewers may bring to the show, continually deflating it as less than it purports to be to show how the dream the Dummars chase is a cheap imitation of the real thing, a sideshow distracting them from how far they actually are from Easy Street.

Demme's film shows that the Dummars do not have many options other than to dream of winning it big because they are locked in the isolation booth of social class. According to Fischer, Melvin shirks the Protestant work ethic because it is not a game that he can win. The only area where he does win is when he watches *Easy Street* on television. Su Holmes details the promotional strategy of game shows to call attention to its contestants also being viewers of the show by asking them "how they 'do when playing along at home'" (121). Such a question "foreground[s] 'ordinary' people" such as the viewers at home "temporarily touching the media world," inviting viewers to keep their dreams as outsized and fantastic as those the show fulfills because one day the televised fantasy could happen to them (Holmes 121). Watching at home, Melvin picks the gate that holds, appropriately, a new car, which leads him to convince his wife Lynda (Mary Steenburgen) to go on the show. Even though the stakes are much higher and the odds of success much less in his favor on a game show, Melvin can "put [his] faith in more chancy, get-rich-quick schemes" such as *Easy Street* because he has had success with it, if only as a viewer (Fischer 34).

Besides, a car that Melvin works for the old-fashioned way can get repossessed if his fortunes change and he falls behind on his payments; a car won on *Easy Street* cannot be repossessed. The Dummars do win big on *Easy Street*, but only because Lynda ignores Melvin's advice and chooses another door. When the stakes are real, Melvin remains a loser, and the prizes Lynda wins cement Melvin's stasis. A living room set and a piano cannot transport Melvin to a new station in life but rather are bulky objects that make moving more strenuous, which may explain why Melvin spends the $10,000 that Lynda wins on not one but two forms of transportation, a car and a boat.

If *Easy Street* is the only place in the film where success is permanent once achieved, then *Melvin and Howard*'s vision of America is quite dark indeed. Kent Anderson sees the quiz show as an "instantaneous demonstration of American savvy translated into dollars" that did not foster greed but mimicked the competitive drive for money and material goods already on vivid display in American culture (176, 177). Lucy Fischer sees the film presenting the game show "as a metaphor for the dynamics of achievement in American society, where success is frequently a capricious matter of luck, accident, or chance—a consummate gamble" (34). Not surprisingly, many of the locations in *Melvin and Howard* are centered around gambling: Reno, Vegas, and low-rent casinos (Fischer 34). Melvin's advice to Lynda to prepare for her appearance on *Easy Street*, "keep betting up," essentially serves as his motto for life. Most of Melvin's actions in the film can be read as a form of gambling, where he keeps raising his bet with each roll of the dice until he craps out and the house repossesses what remains of his chips. Game shows might not qualify as gambling under the law, but Demme's blending of casinos, game shows, and the American institution of upward mobility suggests that they are all manifestations of the same drive that only vary (if at all) in degrees of vulgarity.

Easy Street is not the only game show in *Melvin and Howard*, though it may be the only one that is not rigged. The "Milkman of the Month" competition can be read as a real-life game show competition that Melvin "wins" at great cost to himself, but the ultimate game show in *Melvin and Howard* is also the most rigged: the probate trial over Hughes's "Mormon Will." Melvin's attempt to achieve the all-American rags-to-riches story promised by both the larger American narrative and the game show itself becomes a legal matter, and he must enter the isolation booth of the witness stand to demonstrate why he should be allowed to transcend his blue-collar status. Who Wants to Be a Millionaire? indeed. Demme connects the trial to a game show such as *Easy Street* with his sound design and shot composition. The voice on the phone that notifies Melvin about the will sounds like a studio announcer telling a contestant what prize they have won, subtly suggesting that the inheritance is

Melvin and Howard's "Mormon Will" trial.

a prize on *Easy Street*, "just another form of cultural sweepstakes, of the societal game show" (Fischer 35). The cutaways to the audience in the courtroom are even shot from a similar angle as the cutaways to *Easy Street*'s studio audience. Demme's handling of the probate trial, which features attorneys angrily speaking directly into the camera when questioning Melvin, embodies the logic of Redden's argument that "the moralizing tone of the makeover show derives from the operation of symbolic violence" (154). This trial, like a makeover show, reinforces "the symbolic power of the elite group" who, like the audience of *Easy Street*, must decide whether they "love" Melvin enough to let him win (154). Turns out, they do not, and in the final cruel twist, this game show probate trial ends without a winner: the judge would prefer giving the grand prize to no one rather than let Melvin take it home.

The only thing that never gets repossessed from Melvin is his dream, a fact the film portrays with a withering ambiguity. While the film does not explicitly deny Melvin's account of meeting Hughes, it adopts a fatalistic view that, no matter what Melvin does, he will remain trapped in a rigged game, so he might as well hold tight to his souped-up dream. Melvin seems aware of it, telling his attorney he "knew they weren't going to let Melvin Dummar have $156 million." But Melvin seems less interested in the lost money than in the fact that he got Howard Hughes to sing his song "Santa's Souped-Up Sleigh" in his truck. This memory, if it is in fact true, cannot be repossessed from him, and even if it is a fabrication, Melvin can still keep it because it holds no value for anyone else. This "memory" becomes Melvin's consolation prize for being a losing a contestant on the American game show, "a social farce" that offers him "limited and paltry goals"—and then repossesses them (Fischer 39, 35).

Dreams and fatalism also take center stage in Danny Boyle's 2008 film *Slumdog Millionaire*. Like *Melvin and Howard*, the film operates as a makeover show about "a kind of postmodern Everyman" who "confronts the game show of life" and, unlike Melvin, triumphs over it (Courtright). While it may seem odd to be talking about American values in a film set in India and directed by an Englishman, *Slumdog Millionaire* wants its audience to believe that the possibilities offered by The Land of the Game Show have colonized the whole world. Thus, a British film employs a British game show as a narrative device for a Dickensian rags-to-riches narrative set in "the India [that] Westerners, starting with its former British masters, heartily dream, an India where everything is possible," so long as these postcolonial subjects embrace the values of their former colonizers (Koehler 77). However, to present this India of limitless possibilities and reify the dreams of its main character rather than repossess them, the film escapes reality and enters a dreamscape divorced from the real world, as if tacitly admitting that what it depicts can only be written, not actualized. In doing so, the film inadvertently depicts image culture as a force trapping the disenfranchised in the isolation booth of their abject social class.

Slumdog Millionaire incorporates the quiz show into its narrative structure more than any other film in this book. In fact, the quiz show's structure *is* its narrative structure because a question on the quiz show initiates each flashback sequence in the film. (The same is true of Vikas Swarup's novel *Q & A*, on which *Slumdog Millionaire* is based.) Further, the questions on the quiz show and events in the main character's life align chronologically, conveniently allowing each to propel the other along without any confusion for the audience (Tyree 35).

The first thing to appear onscreen is a multiple-choice question:

Jamal Malik is one question away from winning 20 million rupees. How did he do it?
  A) He cheated
  B) He's lucky
  C) He's a genius
  D) It is written

This opening positions the film as a quiz question for the audience to answer; however, "it is written" is so obviously the right answer that it immediately releases the audience from having to use any of its lifelines. Like the questions on *Who Wants to Be a Millionaire?*, *Slumdog Millionaire* reduces the world to simple, discrete categories, especially when it comes to identity. The quiz show structure of the film echoes the probate trial from *Melvin and Howard* and the congressional subcommittee hearings in *Quiz Show* in that it operates like a trial or interrogation that places Jamal Malik (Dev Patel) on trial for who he is, asking him to prove his identity and thus prove himself worthy of life-changing wealth. Structuring the film this way asks viewers to share the suspicion of those interrogating him, if only to reward the viewers' trust that his success is "written" and thus authorized by some higher authority with whom they have been aligned all along.

The interrogator's question "what the hell can a slumdog possibly know?" echoes the film's opening question by linking identity to knowledge, implying that Jamal's position in the social hierarchy prohibits him from knowing more (and thus winning more money) than a college professor. Although the show purports to discover who "wants" to be a millionaire, the film shows how the real question is who "deserves" to be a millionaire. The film's question-and-answer format and its correlation to events in Jamal's life makes the film into an interrogation of his worth, an extended verification scene that confirms the relationship between Jamal's knowledge and his experience. When viewed in this light, *Slumdog Millionaire* differs little from charity shows that devote most of their time to chronicling the hardships of the about-to-be-transformed person or family before giving them rewards, as if to assure the audience that these people deserve nice things because their lives are worse than theirs.

Dieter Hoffmann-Axthelm describes the inspection of a passport as "the paradigmatic scene of the modern era" that is "both obvious and fathomless" (196). For Hoffmann-Axthelm, this act of "being forced to prove one's identity" represents "an alliance" of "public and private interests" that enforces "the coupling of name and form" for "an era which no longer trusted its eyes" (196, 198). Jamal's backstage interrogation by the police and onstage interrogation by the host of *Millionaire* operate in much the same fashion as Hoffmann Axthelm's passport examination. The entire conflict of *Slumdog Millionaire* turns upon public interests—the game show and the police—rejecting the name and form of a private interest—Jamal—because he conflicts with the names and forms—slumdog, phone basher, chai walla (tea server)—that they have already applied to him. The more correct answers Jamal gives (and thus the more money he wins), the more suspicious and specious his identity appears because, as Hoffmann-Axthelm states, "the identity of the person is called more radically into question the more exact the certified verification becomes" (197). The film portrays the show's attempts to impose a fixed, modernist identity on a person in a postmodern, fluid world, striving to isolate characters into discrete categories the same way that the game show offers only four possible answers to every question. As with a fixed identity, only one of these choices is the "correct" one that is determined by the show in advance. Jamal can be a slumdog, a hustler, a chai-walla, or a millionaire, but not all of the above.

The contrast between the aesthetics of the game show and the rest of the film reinforces Boyle's sense that the rigid worldview of the ruling powers cannot contain the dynamism of real life. *Slumdog Millionaire* contains few circles in it; rather, it is an angular film that continually moves forward, even if its directions are uncertain. The set of the game show in the film is much like its real-world counterpart: cold, metallic, an inert and precise environment with isolated beams of light shooting across the darkness. Like the game itself, this world is a machine run by a computer, antiseptic, cold, composed, smooth, continually scanned by searchlights. The world of the street is the lively antithesis to the set of *Millionaire*, rugged, jittery, glitchy, saturated and warm, always shifting. Boyle and cinematographer Anthony Dodd Mantle destabilize the image in ways that no computer could predict, frequently crossing the 180-degree line and framing shots at oblique angles, even tilting some shots completely sideways. These nontraditional techniques favor the dynamic and ever-changing world of postmodern identity that cannot be reduced to the show's multiple-choice format or classical cinematographic traditions. Other options and possibilities always exist for those willing to hustle. A slumdog can become a millionaire as rapidly as Bombay can become Mumbai, no matter how much the precision and sterility of the *Millionaire* set attempt to prevent such dramatic reversals of fortune. As will be clear later, for all its apparent sympathy for the slumdog, this gaze is imperial in its patronizing sentimentality.

The two styles of the film, that of *Millionaire* and that of Mumbai, merge in the backstage interrogations where police, in cahoots with the producers of the game show, torture and question Jamal to compel him to confess to cheating at the game. The scene features the orange glow and oblique angles of the Mumbai streets, but the more precise compositions and less erratic handheld camerawork suggest the exactitude of the *Millionaire* set. This merger of styles effectively characterizes the interrogation room as the real-world quiz show for the underclass where the winners go home with bruises and the losers go to jail or the morgue. The interrogation room is itself an isolation booth that features a host (the interrogator) who asks questions of a contestant (Jamal). The set even includes a buzzer in the form of the electric shocks Jamal receives during his questioning. The film makes the connection even more explicit in the editing of the opening sequence, which starts in the interrogation room and only cuts to the game show when the interrogator slaps Jamal for failing to answer his questions. To blend matters further, the police play a videocassette of the first few rounds of the game show as "evidence" for their interrogation, literally making the show and the interrogation part of the same investigation. If Jamal does not "win" the interrogation round by proving that he is not cheating, he cannot advance to the next "round" of questioning that is the final round of the game show.

Each strata of society that Jamal works his way through in the film, from the abject brutality of child trafficking to the mechanized glamour of *Millionaire*, operates as a rigged game in which the corrupt keep themselves on top through exploiting the needs of those beneath them, accusing anyone who wants to break out of that cycle as a cheater or a fraud. The film draws parallels between the gangsters and game show hosts by having Pram (Anil Kapoor) turn out to be both a former slum kid and a nefarious, corrupt figure. Pram claims to identify with Jamal as a fellow slumdog, telling him, "Do the right thing, and you'll be as rich as me," but he frequently encourages Jamal to quit while he is ahead and, when Jamal persists, attempts to sabotage him by giving him a wrong answer under the guise of being charitable. The convention in *Millionaire* that gives contestants the chance to walk away with what they have won so far becomes representative of a culture's message to those trying to elevate themselves: they are advised to accept modest gains because, like a game show contestant, they could lose it all with one wrong answer and return to their life of crushing poverty (Courtright). Thus, the precarity of the poor and that of a game show contestant become synonymous, but only one of them even stands a chance at winning big.

Through Jamal's victory and the abundant opposition to it, *Slumdog Millionaire* shows how threatening it is for the exploited to suddenly gain agency and control over their own destiny (and income). Although Jamal frequently finds himself thrust into situations of someone else's design, his knowledge provides him with an escape route that others around him do not have access to. Jamal's intelligence, derived from his authentic experience rather than from traditional schooling, is a question the host and the police cannot answer, and their inability to account for his uncanny knowledge stands in for an inability to comprehend or control a person who breaks out of the isolation booth of social class that the culture has set up for them. Jamal uses the tools of materialistic culture to get what he wants—an autograph, a relative's address, etc.—rather than being controlled by these materials. Such a situation makes Jamal's success a threat to the established order. The film portrays Jamal's life and success as a rebellion against the culture that produces him: like Melvin, he immerses himself in a system that oppresses him; however, unlike Melvin and Jamal's brother Salim (Madhur Mittal), he transcends it because he does not pursue monetary wealth.

Jamal's refusal to accept the answer that he's been given by those in power, gives him the knowledge he needs not only to break the show but the entire system (at least for himself). Jamal's first correct answer operates as a metaphor for how he makes his way through the world. The question—"Who was the star

Jamal awash in his better life.

of the 1973 hit film *Zanjeer?*"—prompts a flashback to when Jamal got Amitabh Bachchan's autograph. When Bachchan's helicopter lands in Jamal's village, a crowd gathers to see him, but not Jamal because Salim has locked him in an outhouse. Not to be denied, Jamal bypasses the locked door by plunging into the shit below and making his way to the crowd, all of whom quickly move from the excrement-covered Jamal, giving him full access to Bachchan and allowing him to get his autograph. Ironically, Jamal's abjection allows him to get closer to success than anyone else, just as his life of poverty advances him further on *Millionaire* than college professors competing on the show. As the Amitabh Bachchan scene demonstrates, Jamal triumphs because he is willing to leap into the shit in order to rise above it. Salim promptly sells the autograph, which initiates a cycle in their lives where Salim pursues profit and Jamal pursues love. Like Melvin, anything Jamal gains is promptly repossessed and sold off, especially his love Latika, who allows herself to be bought and sold in exchange for an illusory stability. The climax of the film echoes this dynamic in order to invert it: Salim dies in a bathroom in a pile of money that he will never be able to spend, whereas Jamal thrives in a shower of confetti (or trash) and Latika waits at a train station for a man (Jamal) to take her away to a truly better, more stable life.

Slumdog Millionaire characterizes money as a tool of exploitation and death. While his appearance on a game show such as *Millionaire* may appear to contradict that, one must remember that Jamal's goal in going on the show is not to win money but rather to attract the attention of Latika (Freida Pinto), a girl whom he has been infatuated with since childhood and with whom he hopes to reunite. Even though Jamal is the one who wins the money, we never see him awash in it. Challenging the show and the outcome it wishes to rig for him becomes an assertion of self for Jamal, and the film depicts his path as the only one toward a coherent self uncorrupted by the materialistic, hypercapitalist culture that surrounds him. By going on the game show, Jamal may be commodifying himself and his experience; however, it is for his benefit rather than someone else's, which, in the world *Slumdog Millionaire* imagines, constitutes a radical act because it subverts the exploitative cycle of capital. The film's structure becomes an extended justification for why his existence deserves to be rewarded monetarily amidst the suffering masses around him. Unlike them, Jamal's motives are "pure" because they are motivated by love rather than a desire for money, as though simply wishing for a life above the poverty line is a desire to unseemly to entertain.

J. M. Tyree sees the film as "searching ... for a sense of coherence in which the accumulated experience of life will add up after all to a unified whole, everything falling into the right place" (35). The film positions Jamal's defiance of the television quiz show as the "final answer" to transcending the limits of the social class, insisting that a slumdog can, in fact, become a millionaire. This assertion is where the film's ideas become open to Tyree's accusation of "trying to have it both ways by allowing images of actual horror to seep into a Bollywood-like dream and then letting us off the hook by suggesting not only that true love conquers all, but also that personal decency might well result in a multimillion-dollar payday" (Tyree 36). Because the film blends Jamal's life events with quiz show questions that are in turn used as evidence in a police interrogation, the film, as Robert Koehler argues, "reinforces the myths of reality game show TV as actual rather than manufactured suspense and as a machine for getting rich quick, while—in total contradiction—suggests that TV can also be a partner with the police in torture" (76). For *Slumdog Millionaire*, *Who Wants to Be a Millionaire?* is simultaneously Jamal's ticket to a new self, an affirmation of his current (and past) self, and the state's means of keeping him from escaping his social class.

Despite everything the viewers' eyes and ears tell them to the contrary, the film asserts that such an achievement is possible solely because "it is written." However transformative *Slumdog Millionaire* wishes Jamal's victory to be, the game show in the film reinforces the existing unequal class structure. Jamal's success unconsciously justifies the abject status of every other poor character in the film. After all, Jamal only arrives at his fortune through the unbelievable coincidence that every question he is asked just so happens to correspond perfectly to a pivotal event in his life, making the notion that such an opportunity remains available to anyone else impossible to believe. Simultaneously, the film encourages audiences to dream that the possibility of them changing their station in life also "is written." As with Melvin, such a dream requires them to buy into the vision of success and upward mobility that the ruling culture presents to them. Consequently, their dream perpetuates their inability to attain it, just like the gangsters rig the game of begging by offering street kids the promise of food and family only to (literally) rob them blind.

The film engages in some rigging and determinism of its own with its emphasis on everything being "written." Jamal becomes a lucky contestant on the show whose existence is smiled upon by some cosmic host while all the other slumdogs, phone bashers, and chai-wallas continue to wallow in squalor. As Robert Koehler states in his review of the film, the notion that "a little Muslim boy raised in Mumbai's worst hellholes can become rich and famous" is "ridiculous" because "the sheer impulse to push the story into a frothy romance functions as a betrayal of its fundamental material" (76). The film "endorses a wish-fulfillment view of temporality in which disasters can be undone ... as though nothing bad had ever happened," making *Slumdog Millionaire* as rigged as any quiz show (Tyree 38). The sheer fact that his "written" destiny also follows the "written" script of a game show suggests that the two are not as incongruous as the movie would have viewers believe. After all, how can the film object to rigged games when an answer such as "it is written" endorses predetermined outcomes?

Slumdog Millionaire follows Dieter Hoffmann-Axthelm's logic by suggesting that "self-possession and self-perception can only be attained outside the social production process on the level of signs" that are "continuously subject to decay, emptiness and the necessity of replacement" (215). This shift in emphasis to perception becomes "an instrument of labor" because of "its indispensable relation to concrete objects" (215). As much as the film asserts that Jamal stands apart from the corrupt, materialistic world represented by *Millionaire* and gangsters because of his faith in the undying powers of love and fate, the structure of the film tethers his entire sense of self to the world of a game show which ratifies his experience and thus solidifies its cultural authority as verifier of identity and the arbiter of upward mobility and success. As fluid and autonomous as Jamal's sense of identity may seem, each important stage of his life is tied to a game-show question, which articulates a culture's values surrounding knowledge and education. Further, these questions connect him to moments in his life where he encounters objects of that culture such as cricket, celebrity autographs, European literature, and American currency and weapons. In this regard, his "escape" at the end into a Bollywood dance extravaganza does not represent the radical break from the world of *Millionaire*; it reifies it, functioning as another facet of the same machine that "packages misperceptions about India" and works to "support the dominant Western view of the Subcontinent" (Koehler 75). This unfortunate result reinforces Douglas Kellner's contention that identity "has been problematized anew in the contemporary orgy of commodification, fragmentation, image production, and societal, political, and cultural transformation

Slumdog Millionaire's escape to Bollywood fantasy.

that is the work of contemporary capitalism" ("Popular Culture" 174). Although Jamal may narrowly slip through the grasp of every "host" who chases after him, he cannot escape the bankrupt film that hosts his story, which takes his pursuit and acquisition of "new possibilities, styles, models, and forms" of identity in the rapidly changing and globalized landscape of Mumbai and flattens him into a symbol (174). His destiny may thrive in such a destabilized environment because it is "written," but a closer look at *Slumdog Millionaire* suggests that it is "written" not by Jamal or some higher spiritual power but according to "the logic of capital" (172).

In using the game show as an intermedial text that represents the attempt to construct a self unburdened by the isolation booth of social class, *Quiz Show*, *Melvin and Howard*, and *Slumdog Millionaire* illustrate the "attempts of capital to colonize the totality of life, from desire to satisfaction" (Kellner, "Popular Culture" 173). As Joanne Morreale explains, "the self may be fluid and mobile" as these films suggest, "but it is still constrained by the capitalist ideology of individualism: with will-power, determination, and role models (and the right hair and clothes), people can re-incarnate themselves as particular social types" (98). That makeover ideology, however, depends on that promise of reincarnation remaining unfulfilled, leaving believers and consumers alike trapped in the isolation booth of their social class, hoping that Easy Street is lurking behind the curtain of another purchase.

CATEGORY

WHO GETS TO BE AN AMERICAN?

Game show questions may be different in each episode, but what they seek remains constant: not information about empirical facts but about people, what they know, what they do not, and whether they are willing to play a language game that reveals an individual's entire relationship to the outside world. As *Slumdog Millionaire* shows in its structure, the question-and-answer format invites players to validate their conception of themselves by demonstrating what they know and how well that knowledge conforms to the knowledge valued by the show or that the show expects them to have based on the stereotypes ascribed to their social class. Game shows project limits on the knowledge of the contestants that the contestants must transcend, lest they prove that the game makers have judged them correctly. Passing judgment on what someone knows functions as judging their identity, which demonstrates how game shows express the values and impose the limits of the culture that produces them.

These values and limits, however, are not limited to education but extend to all areas of culture and identity. Game shows may avoid explicitly addressing the thorny topic of identity politics, but that hardly means they do not enact and validate cultural prejudices and stereotypes. Olaf Hoerschelmann describes how the knowledge game shows value works to "articulate forms of knowledge closely connected with dominant groups to specific cultural practices" (85). In the case of American game shows, this knowledge is "rooted culturally in European high culture" and aligned with whiteness (Hoerschelmann 85). *Slumdog Millionaire* dramatizes the lowered expectations that society places on people from the lower class, and *Saturday Night Live*'s recurring *Black Jeopardy!* sketch has repeatedly exploited the game show as a platform for awkward comedic conversations about race and ethnicity. Other works of fiction employ the game show intermedially as a metaphor to illustrate the ways race and ethnicity function as isolation booths for the individual in America. As an expression of the "specific cultural practices" of the dominant group, game shows operate as citizenship tests in American culture that determine whether a non-white Other is "allowed" to identify as an American. These works illustrate how contestants, in the attempt to be seen, become invisible as individuals. Instead, the show isolates them as non-white Others who must either star in a patronizing aspirational narrative that benefits white culture or remain unseen and unknown because of white culture's own historical and cultural blindness.

Considering that *Quiz Show* occurs during a time period when, according to Stephen J. Whitfield, "Jews were largely invisible" in popular culture, such a preponderance of Jewish characters in leading roles—Herbert Stempel, Al Freedman, Dan Enright, Dick Goodwin, and more—is unusual for a film that is not explicitly about Jewish identity. But "Jews," as Stephen J. Whitfield puts it, "are everywhere" in *Quiz Show* as both "perpetrators and victims of television fraud" who are "sucked into the vortex or a scandal that mixed duplicity with unchecked avarice and ambition." Whitfield's observation offers another way to read *Quiz Show*: as a story about invisibility, about television moving visible Jews into the isolation booth in favor of the "homogeneity" of WASP identity (Whitfield). Whitfield describes ethnicity as "a mere quirk that prosperity was expected to erase" and that television promoted such a "disintegration of ethnicity" by broadcasting "the American Way of Life itself," encouraging ethnic viewers to "exorci[ze] the rancors of the past" and transfer "loyalty to ancestral traditions" to loyalty to the televisual melting pot.

Whitfield states Stempel "could not be mistaken" for anything other than "Jewish lower middle class." While his social class may be unappealing to the suits at NBC, what really damns Stempel in their eyes is his unescapable Jewishness. Stempel's ethnicity is his greatest flaw, something that capped teeth cannot conceal. Even though Dan Enright promises to get him on a panel show in exchange for taking a dive, Stempel's invisibility remains the real goal. Therefore, he must be replaced with a more palatable, white contestant, thus cementing the image of success as something available only to WASPs (Whitfield). These Jewish producers reject a fellow Jew in favor of promoting an image of an idealized America that implicitly excludes them. The film portrays Stempel as near-paranoiac in his sense of anti-Semitic persecution. He calls his loss to the "uncircumcised putz" Charles Van Doren Van Doren's "first kosher meal," and he considers his situation as another entry in the annals of white exploitation of ethnic others. He even compares himself to the Native Americans who sold Manhattan for $24 and reminds his son that the only reason people call them Indians is "because some white guy got lost." But his most biting claim is that the quiz shows "always follow a Jew with a Gentile, and the Gentile makes more money." Stempel may sound paranoid, but Goodwin discovers that his claim is true, and the film shows how this pattern repeats itself elsewhere in life: Stempel gets replaced by the Gentile Van Doren again at the House Subcommittee hearings, and Van Doren's testimony overshadows his own.

Unlike Stempel, Richard Goodwin's Jewish identity is not readily visible. He and his wife (Mira Sorvino) are the only people who bring it up apart from the secretaries and salesmen who mistakenly call him Goldwyn and Goodman. He is far more likely to mention that he attended Harvard Law School, and this detail may represent his attempt to pass in the WASP world. Goodwin's identity exists in a liminal state, allowing him to "move up and down the social ladder with ease," passing for a hungry climber in every space he enters (Whitfield). In fact, Goodwin's ethnicity appears most around food. He stuns Stempel when he tells him he knows what rugelach is, which suggests that even Stempel, perhaps blinded by Goodwin's Harvard pedigree, does not identify him as Jewish. Goodwin also calls attention to his Jewishness when he lunches with Van Doren at the Athenaeum, boldly ordering a Reuben and then making the joke, "I don't see any Reubens."

Goodwin keeps his identity in an isolation booth because he hopes to pass, as his co-workers joke, for "an important person," which, in this context, means not Jewish. Goodwin's loyalty to his ethnic background does not take precedence over his allegiance to the elite class whose approval he desperately craves. In the same way that Stempel goes along with NBC's scheme in the hope of appearing on a future television show, Goodwin shields Van Doren from scrutiny and testimony to secure him as a friend and confidante, as though keeping Van Doren's name far from the taint of the scandal will somehow be rewarded with membership into Van Doren's club. Goodwin goes to such lengths to protect Van Doren at the expense of Stempel that his wife calls him "the Uncle Tom of the Jews." The film may not entirely endorse her characterization of Goodwin's betrayal, but the events of the film prevent it from being read as anything other than a repression of his Jewish identity to ascend in American culture. Goodwin experiences more success in passing than Stempel and gains admittance to a larger, decidedly WASP community, but such gains among intellectuals and politicians cannot be won without accusations of betrayal from those still isolated by ethnicity, and Stempel serves as a reminder to Goodwin both of what he is betraying and the danger in remaining too closely identified by one's heritage.

Goodwin is not the only Jew in fiction or film to betray Herbert Stempel in order to advance in American culture: Nathan Zuckerman, the protagonist of Philip Roth's 1981 novel *Zuckerman Unbound*, also projects his fears of being isolated by his Jewishness onto the disgraced quiz show contestant. Stempel inspires Roth's paranoiac Alvin Pepler, who haunts Nathan Zuckerman as he attempts to manage the success and scorn coming at him from all directions after the publication of his novel *Carnovsky*. Roth's novel does not feature a quiz show in it, but Pepler's appearance in the first scene of the novel positions the post-*Carnovsky* Zuckerman in the cultural role previously held by Pepler: famous Jew. Through Zuckerman's antagonistic relationship to Pepler, Roth demonstrates how rising in American culture pushes Jews to make a choice: hold fast to their Jewishness and become invisible in American culture, or betray their heritage and become hypervisible. However, the ending to Roth's novel reveals both paths end with the invisibility of dissolution: in his self-destructive rise to fame, Zuckerman isolates himself to such a degree that the world he once knew vanishes around him, leaving him even more isolated than ever.

Even more than Stempel, Pepler sees his fame as elevating Jews in America. "I made no bones about my religion," he says, because "it did the Jewish people [no] harm having a Marine veteran of two wars representing them on prime-time national television for three consecutive weeks" (Roth 19). Of course, Pepler's involvement in the quiz-show scandals quickly destroys his identity as "Pepler Man of the People" and turns him into "Pepler the human garbage can," "a pariah" with a "dirty name" worse off than "a McCarthy victim" (17, 28, 18). Like the question Stempel takes a dive on, Pepler's losing question humiliates him; however, this humiliation comes not from missing a question that would equate him with an Average Joe but one that would identify him as an American. First, Roth names Pepler's Gentile opponent Hewlett Lincoln, which carries with it the suggestion that, in defeating Pepler, Lincoln preserves the Union from a violent internal threat. Second, the category Pepler must feign ignorance of is "Americana." His loss "let[s] the Jewish people go down on prime-time TV as not knowing their Americana," and consequently not appearing fully American to an audience that already harbors prejudice against them (37). Pepler betrays himself because he, like Stempel, believes he will be rewarded with a job "broadcasting the Yankee home games," only to discover that no such offer could be made to him in earnest because broadcasters do not view him as a "Yankee" or at "home" in America (34). Television spurns Pepler, leaving his anger and paranoia to fester until he becomes the stereotypical unhinged Jewish paranoiac who can only do harm to the Jewish people.

Pepler may state the he "wouldn't dream...of comparing" himself to Zuckerman, but Roth makes no such protest, continually juxtaposing Zuckerman and Pepler until Pepler represents the future self Zuckerman must avoid even if it means denying his ethnicity (19). Zuckerman's success as the "arch-assmiliated-Jew-writer" stems from a similar betrayal of the Jews as Pepler's (Cooper 179). His *Carnovsky*, clearly based on Roth's *Portnoy's Complaint*, makes him a literary celebrity but also earns him accusations of betraying the Jewish people by parading (and perhaps validating) negative stereotypes about them to gain success in what Zuckerman calls "Johnny Carson America" (Roth 159). Zuckerman may be more famous and successful than Pepler, but he is also a bigger target for hatred. He receives letters from readers addressed to "The Enemy of the Jews" or "Kike, Apt. 2B" written "in memory of those who suffered the horror of the Concentration Camps" telling him that "it is hardly possible to write of Jews with more bile and contempt and hatred" than he has done (58,

176, 59). Roth suggests Zuckerman's novel constitutes an act of self-denial, an attempt to escape from the isolation booth of Jewishness by destroying or at least denigrating his connection to his ethnicity. Mary, his agent's wife, aptly accuses him of "cloud[ing] the issue" of his ethnicity "with Jewish jokes," as though he can ensure "nobody will mistake [him] for a Newark Yid" if he disparages Jews savagely enough (46). However, Zuckerman's novel associates him with his Jewish identity more than ever, especially in the eyes of his family and fellow Jews, who will not allow him to erase them from his life. His brother Henry berates him for betraying where he came from in exchange for success:

> What does self-denial mean, *restraint*—anything at all? To you everything is disposable! Everything is *ex*posable! Jewish morality, Jewish endurance, Jewish wisdom, Jewish families—everything is grist for your fun machine. Even your shiksas go down the drain when they don't tickle your fancy anymore. Love, marriage, children, what the hell do you care? To you it's all fun and games. *But that isn't the way it is to the rest of us.* (217)

Like so many of the characters examined in this round, Zuckerman's quest to enter the media community represented by television and quiz show success compels him to reduce the struggles of his community as "disposable" "fun and games" that he can pick up and discard at will, erroneously believing "he can betray benignly and escape behind the walls of his art" (Cooper 180). Doing so may free him from the isolation booth of Jewishness temporarily, but it creates a permanent division between those on television in "Johnny Carson America" and "the rest of us" Jews, who, like Pepler, "go down the drain" once they cease to "tickle [the] fancy" of the "fun machine."

As *Zuckerman Unbound* develops, Roth blurs the distinction between Pepler and Zuckerman until Zuckerman fears that Pepler is a walking-and-talking manifestation of his imagination, a sequel to *Carnovsky* that stalks Zuckerman in the real world, and threatens to eclipse him. Pepler's desire to, with the help of Zuckerman, "write a publishable book" to clear his name threatens to absorb Zuckerman's identity into his own, tainting Zuckerman's success until it is indistinguishable from Pepler's disgrace (20). Zuckerman literally runs from Pepler after their first encounter as though his condition and his "dirty name" are contagious. The novel's scenes revolving around Zuckerman's half-eaten (by Pepler) pastrami sandwich and the semen-stained handkerchief Pepler sends to Zuckerman reinforce the notion that Pepler's Jewishness could contaminate or be transmitted to Zuckerman and his work. Zuckerman thinks that fleeing Pepler physically and fleeing his Jewishness figuratively in his writing will inoculate him from Pepler's pathetic shame, but in the passage where Zuckerman boards a plane to return to Newark, Roth suggests that Zuckerman's paranoia about his ethnicity contains both his success and his undoing:

> Had [Pepler's] *landsman* spent into Zuckerman's handkerchief the last of his enraged and hate-filled adoration? Was that the end of this barrage? Or would Zuckerman's imagination beget still other Peplers conjuring up novels out of his—novels disguising themselves as actuality itself, as nothing less than real? Zuckerman the stupendous sublimator spawning Zuckermaniacs! A book, a piece of fiction bound between two covers, breeding living fiction exempt from all the subjugations of the page, breeding fiction unwritten, unreadable, unaccountable and uncontainable. (198)

The repetition of words such as "breeding," "beget," "spawning," and "conjuring" emphasize that, in conceiving this novel that places his Jewish identity in the isolation booth of fiction, Zuckerman's work instead broadcasts his unwanted seed so far that it will obscure him. In making the furtive onanism of Gilbert Carnovsky into a public spectacle, Zuckerman gives birth to the very things he wishes to isolate himself from. Rather than be separated from them, he will be replaced by his creation. People already call him Carnovsky on the street, so in many ways the damage has already been done: the more famous Zuckerman gets, the more unbound he becomes from his identity.

Zuckerman's desire to make his own Jewishness invisible erases his community from the world he inhabits. The novels ends as Zuckerman stares at a Newark he no longer recognizes as his own; unlike him, it has moved on without much concern or room for him and his anxieties. Zuckerman ends his nostalgic trip home abruptly, realizing, "You are no longer any man's son, you are no longer some good woman's husband, you are no longer your brother's brother, and you don't come from anywhere anymore either" (224–25). Zuckerman achieves the obscurity he desires, but it is an obscurity in which one cannot recognize themselves and where they come from (Cooper 187). One could read the ending as demonstrating the effects of extreme solipsism, where the rest of one's world simply vanishes, leaving the self as the center of an empty universe; however, another viable reading would be that Zuckerman's self-denial in fiction and in life successfully represses his Jewish identity to the point that it is invisible to everyone, including himself, making the novel a tragic representation of assimilation or shame. Rather than pretending not to know anything about Americana as Pepler did, Zuckerman pretends not to know the worth of his roots, leaving him with "just his fame," publicly known to everyone except himself (Cooper 187). Betraying his roots in pursuit of fame "disconnects him from the mass of his kind," making him truly unbound, absorbed by his fiction and dissolving into the culture (Cooper 187). Unfortunately, the novel makes this point by engaging in some race-based fearmongering of its own, depicting Nathan's now-African American neighborhood as evidence of nightmarish decay and alienation.

Kiese Laymon's 2013 novel *Long Division* offers a strong corrective to both the erasure of *Zuckerman Unbound* and the fatalism of *Slumdog Millionaire*. Identity in *Long Division* is not determined by the quizmaster or ruling culture but by the player, who defines and redefines the self with each question and situation. The main characters' refusal to allow white culture to dictate their identities to them illustrates Jonathan Friedman's description of how "in conditions of empire, or stable hegemony and a clear hierarchy of identities" force the Other "to speak through our *categories*" but that the Other's "self-identification interferes" with the authority of the empire's discourse (332; emphasis added).

In Laymon's novel, the game show in question is *Can You Use That Word in a Sentence*, which replaces the Scripps Spelling Bee after people complain that its questions were "geographically biased" against children from the South, Midwest, and Southwest (Laymon 7). Rather than modify the Bee to be more inclusive and equitable, officials choose to create a new game entirely for those children being discriminated against. The competition perpetuates bias, and the adjusted standards are only the start of how officials use the show to isolate people by their race, "trying to decorate the contest with a little color" to convince themselves that they are not racist (28). The novel opens with City Coldson and his frenemy LaVander Peeler squaring off against two Mexican Americans from Arizona in the finals. While City assumes the contest and their standing in it is legitimate, LaVander removes the blinders from City's eyes about their role in the contest, asserting that the game is racially biased to ensure people of color do not fail. He cites as evidence the word City got in the regional finals: "chitterlings." "You get them black words every time the championship is on the line" (32). City refuses to believe LaVander or accept that his success has been rigged by others who doubt his linguistic prowess. However, when City gets his first word at nationals, "niggardly," he knows LaVander's accusation was accurate and that, despite all his pride in his abilities, he has never had authority over his own narrative (McCall). At first, City attempts to avoid the question, telling the judges, "I know the word, but it's just that my insides hurt when you say that word"; however, when the judges insist he answer them, he confuses the word's meaning with the adjectival form of the racial epithet it sounds like (38). City does not take a seat after being told he is wrong. Instead, he remains at the microphone and begins a tirade that ends with him shouting, "*And fuck white folks!*" (40). The contest only deteriorates from there when LaVander receives the word that could win the championship for him: "chitterlings" again. They quickly realize that the contest has been rigged in their favor and that the absence of white contestants further proves that "they didn't believe any of us could really compete" against white children and that they were "all decoration" used to make white people "feel good about themselves" (43, 33).

Where City strikes back at the contest by "mak[ing] a speech about why the contest wasn't fair after [he] lost," LaVander sabotages their cynical display of affirmative action (43). He appears to finish his "chitterlings" sentence correctly, prompting the judges to blast the "Harlem Shake" and joyously declare that LaVander has "done the unbelievable" and is an "exceptional young Mississippian," "a symbol of American progress" who shows "the past is the past and today can be tomorrow" (43). However, LaVander adds another clause to his sentence that invalidates his correct answer, leaving the judges' plan to let either City or LaVander win in tatters. Both City and LaVander recognize the double-bind that the show places them in: they cannot lose, but they also cannot win because "even if [they] used the word right, [they] still would've lost" by affirming the judges' low estimation of them and their abilities (38). According to his family members, City's outburst reinforces negative stereotypes whites have about African Americans and gives whites "a reason to take away the rights we done worked so hard for" (92). Their statements invite comparisons between City and a post-*Carnovsky* Nathan Zuckerman, both of whom launch attacks against the stereotypes of white culture only to strengthen these stereotypes. Even though their responses may make Nathan and City famous, they do little to alter the paternalistic course of race relations. LaVander may not win as a result of his actions, but then again, neither do the judges attempting to award themselves a prize for racial progress that they did not earn.

In their refusal to play by the white man's rules, the young characters in *Long Division* display an innate desire to write their own story and thus inscribe an America in which they are allowed to play any game they choose. City tells Coach Stroud, "Y'all are too old to care about [whites] so much. They can only do as much harm as you let them, and all y'all oldheads are letting them do way too much" (93). Similarly, in the novel-within-the-novel, also called *Long Division*, a character named Baize rejects the approval of white judges and institutions: "I do not need to win the Spell-Off to know I'm special. This is Baize Against the World, not that *Akeelah and the Bee* life" (186). These characters reject the game as it has been laid out for them by white culture, deeming it too small and ineffectual to give them the kind of control they want over their lives. Rather than subjecting themselves to the white's gaze by appearing on their television show, City suggests that "their eyes ain't gotta be everywhere [we] are" (93). The novel's quest becomes a search for an alternative space for African Americans to craft a narrative for themselves free from the meddling of whites.

That answer, Laymon suggests, comes not from a focus on answers, endpoints, or prizes but on the spaces between such terminal points where the direction of a narrative or life are still subject to change and revision. The novel's title becomes integral in advancing this concept. Shalaya Crump asks City "why you gotta be so long division," meaning he is "busy trying to show all [his] work." City claims that he "hate[s] the answer" in long division and prefers the work, but Shalaya tells him that hating the answer is not enough: one must reject "mastering the smaller steps" in favor of "linger[ing] in the smaller steps." Shalaya wants to "really pause at each step in long division and talk about it" (56). Shalaya's description of long division suggests that it lacks freedom, and Laymon's choice of the word "mastering" reinforces this notion and gives it an additional charge within the novel's civil rights narrative. For Shalaya, the traditional form of long division limits one's options and understanding by placing all the control and emphasis on the final answer: there is but one path to the truth and only certain steps are allowed and only in a certain order that one must "master" to be "correct." "Mastering" every small step in the process more closely resembles "serving" in that it requires the person solving the problem to submit to someone else's way of doing things, leaving that person or institution in control and thus limiting the solver's freedom. Individuals are not "mastering the smaller steps" but being mastered by a larger institution that merely wants them to arrive at a predetermined answer in a rigidly predetermined manner by solving an already-solved problem.

In lingering on each step of the work, however, one does more than show that they can do it and fully understand each step: one initiates a conversation that reveals how and why each step came to be. A focus on the big answer accepts the outcome as inevitable, predetermined, and natural. Such a rush to the answer may work fine in elementary mathematics, but Laymon shows that when it comes to selfhood for a person of color in America, this rushing becomes an act of submission that allows people in power to determine the value and ability of another. *Can You Use That Word in a Sentence*, of course, exemplifies this kind of long division: the white judges make City and LaVander show their work to arrive at a predetermined outcome, "mastering" them while pretending that they are being allowed to act and create freely. City and LaVander's resistance to the show's plan "lingers" on the steps leading to the rigged result and exposes the racist ideology that guides it. They may not be aware of it at the time, but their actions illustrate Laymon's claim that lingering on the steps in life will expose the master narratives that produce the "big answer," and that becoming aware of and understanding those narratives gives the disenfranchised the knowledge they need to change not just the steps, but the "big answer" itself.

Jason McCall eloquently explains how the novel's ellipses motif advances Laymon's concept of lingering and helps situate it into a historical context. Near the novel's end, Baize tells City that if she could be any punctuation mark, she would be an ellipsis because "the ellipsis always knows something more came before it and something more is coming after it" (245). McCall argues that *Long Division* "embodies the ellipsis, the idea of an understood but unspoken beginning and ending." Laymon applies this idea about punctuation to theories about history when characters repeatedly remind City of his place within a continuum of the African American struggle for freedom, telling him that his behavior "impacts not only black folks today, but black folks yet to be born" (17). This view prevents one from viewing oneself as an isolated, standalone figure but part of an ever-developing, ever-shifting sentence, an emerging thought not yet fully expressed. The novel's time travel plot only underscores these notions. According to this logic, characters—and the people in the real world that they represent—compose themselves like narratives, undergoing "edits and revisions" in an eternal drive forward (McCall). The ellipsis becomes the symbol marking the space a person has to revise themselves, the world they inhabit, and the course of time itself. Thus, lingering over that ellipsis rather than the fixed points that border it frees a person from being an isolated self who can be acted on by those in power and calls on them to reimagine themselves as not only someone with a history but as a player in history itself. Just as City is a character, a reader, and an author in *Long Division*, so is each person a character, a reader, and an author in the ongoing American story. The novel, then, is the anti-*Slumdog Millionaire*. For Laymon, events do not occur because "it is written" but because the world is always being written. The novel refuses to hide behind destiny and other fatalistic clichés that rely on coincidence and circumstance to redeem characters. In *Long Division*, everything, even time itself, is in the character's control, making the self not something that is written but something that is always in the act of writing.

Laymon's novel demands immersion in and ownership of America's story to free oneself from the isolation booth white culture creates. Robert Olen Butler's 1992 story "The American Couple" suggests that Laymon's solution may not be so universal. For Butler, immersion in American culture, which he uses the game show to exemplify, isolates immigrants from their identities, relatives, and traditions because it compels them to adopt the identity created for them by American culture, and no matter how much they succeed in the Land of the Game Show, they cannot rise above it and remain connected to America. Their success will always lead them back to America's imperialist impulses. Scholars such as Mats Tegmark read Butler's collection as "depict[ing] characters who manage to cross these borders [of ethnicity and nation] in order to construct new hybrid identities," challenging "the very idea of fixed identity-formations based on nationalism and ethnicity" (94). Butler's brave, risky decision to write the stories in this collection from the point of view of non-white characters (and his success in doing so) lends more credence to this idea; however, the border crossings and hybrid identities depicted in "The American Couple" represent failed attempts in which characters wind up either alienated from their present or lost in "the excesses of the empty-headed culture around [them]" (Butler 233).

Gabrielle Tran's name itself tells a story of isolation. She alters her real name, Tran Nam Thanh, to secure an audition for *Let's Make a Deal*, muting her foreignness so as to be admitted into the community of television. Her acceptance only goes so far. Even though Gabrielle believes her intellect and keen powers of observation make her a better fit for "answering questions or solving puzzles or guessing prices," she winds up on *Let's Make a Deal* dressed as a duck because the trivia-based shows "stay away from people who have an accent," and no matter how assimilated into American culture Gabrielle Tran might be, one "can hear [her] foreignness in [her] pronunciation" (158, 159). This decision counts as the first deal she makes in being on the show, and she ultimately receives a reward for it. That reward, at least to her, is not the trip to Mexico she wins but the "long sigh of envy" she gets from the crowd after the prize trip is revealed. Even though the audience sighs on cue, the sigh tells her that "they were playing this wonderful game in this wonderful world where these things can make people happy." She proudly declares, "The trip was really worth a sigh, and I won that" (160). The sigh is the prize signifying her acceptance into the "wonderful world" known as America, the Land of the Game Show.

To prove that acceptance even further, the hotel where the game show sends Gabrielle and Vinh has at least three other winners from other game shows as guests. Gabrielle quickly figures out that all the women in the hotel are American and game-show contestants, but the other women see Gabrielle as neither. In fact, they do not seem to see her at all, remarking to each other in front of her that they "look like [they're] from the same side of the border," refusing to acknowledge the possibility that Gabrielle could also hail from their "side of the border" (165). Gabrielle "feel[s] invisible" at the hotel until Frank, the Vietnam vet husband of one of the game-show women, asks her whether she is from America. Gabrielle compares the moment to the 1933 film *The Invisible Man*: "When I first saw the movie ... it got me to thinking about what it would be like to be invisible. And the scary part was always getting yourself into a place where you shouldn't be and then suddenly becoming visible again" (174). She does not necessarily desire visibility because according to her statement, she is in "a place where [she] shouldn't be," which makes becoming visible dangerous. Butler keeps the name of "the place [she] shouldn't be" deliberately vague, but one can infer that she means "among white Americans." Gabrielle and Vinh eventually do become visible and accepted into the group of Americans; however, it does not occur until Frank, the veteran and representative of America's military, scopes them out and determines whether they are friend or foe. When the couples discover their "game-show equality," one woman exclaims, "Four winners. What a hoot" (175). Her status as a game-show winner proves her American citizenship. Similarly, Frank connects the notion of being a "winner" to being an American when he implies that not "winning" the Vietnam War is a blemish on his character. He introduces his wife as "the winner in the family" and says he "wish[es] [he'd] been part of a winner for you folks" in Vietnam (177). The Tran's presence threatens to invalidate Frank's fragile masculinity as well as the American story propped up by both nationalistic and game show narratives. His fixation on steering every moment toward his experience in Vietnam culminates in him engaging Vinh in a childish war game to capture a small bathroom structure at the top of a hill, a clear attempt to reenact the War so that, this time, Frank can be a "winner." The Trans' participation in the game show initially promises to grant them inclusion into the American experience, but their enjoyment of that experience makes them visible, which leads the other American couples around them to isolate them as Other, and their thoughts slowly turn toward war.

Butler crafts a series of isolated settings in which to trap his characters, each one more stripped down and alienating than the last. To start, the story takes place at a resort in Puerto Vallarta, Mexico, whose only guests appear to be winners on seemingly every game show televised in America. The resort, which ought to signify an escape from the Land of the Game Show, only isolates "winners" more deeply in it. From there, Gabrielle and Eileen, Frank's wife, drag their husbands to see the remains of the set of the film *The Night of the Iguana*, which put Puerto Vallarta on the map when Richard Burton and Elizabeth Taylor cavorted about the area during the film's production. After the disappointment of seeing remnants of the movie set, Frank and Vinh discover the small bathroom building and engage in the war game on the hilltop that even Gabrielle remarks "remind[s] her of Vietnam" (211). The spoils of a game show lead to the ruins of a romance, which lead to the ruins of a movie set, which lead to the ruins of war. This progression shows how entertainment culture obscures America's violence and acts as the source of Gabrielle and Vinh's isolation from America, not their ticket to acceptance. As Gabrielle sits "on a crumbling boat dock at the foot of the set of one of [her] favorite movies," she realizes that "all of the things that [she has] a sweet tooth for" in American culture, "the light and lively and less filing and soft as a cloud and reach out and touch someone culture that America had to offer," what she calls elsewhere "the feel-good culture," conceals the horrors of war that her husband and Frank have seen and trivializes their suffering (214, 213). Here Butler reveals that violence lies at the core of American escapism, a desire to make all that does not comfort and entertain disappear, or, if that fails, turn making those things disappear into entertainment. Gabrielle seems to be ascending to the heights of American culture on this trip—game show riches, celebrity romances, movie sets, luxury resorts, etc.—but when she reaches this peak, she and Vinh find themselves where they have always been: isolated as invisible others who, if they become visible, must disappear in order to comfort white America.

Bridges carry symbolic weight in Butler's story as well, but where bridges often act as symbols of connection, Butler uses them to emphasize separation. Gabrielle and Eileen gaze at the small walkway connecting Burton and Taylor's houses just as "the whole world watched that bridge for months to see [Liz and Dick] go back and forth" (202). Gabrielle comments that "the bridge between the two houses [makes] her feel bad" because "it seemed so empty. It arched there against the blue sky and it cried out for some lover to come across and take his woman in his arms. But it was empty" (202–3). Bridges then call attention to separation; despite working as conduits, most of the time they are empty, a space between two objects reminding people that these objects are and remain separate. The attempts in the story to bridge cultures fails. The movie set that the Trans visit with Eileen and Frank has "balconies that didn't connect to anything at all" and the top of the hill contains "just wreckage and weeds and silence" (212, 218). Rather than forging a connection, this trip alienates Gabrielle from her husband and American culture, until she becomes alienated even from herself. As her husband and Frank stalk each other, she "step[s] out of [her]self" and sees "all that was in [her] mind." "The romance was gone right away," she says, and "all the things that [her] mind knew were beautiful seemed flat" (223). The game show, which is supposed to reward her for her knowledge, instead gives her a different kind of prize, revealing to her how little she understands about her husband and American culture and how even fewer bridges exist to connect her to it. The reality around her is "a distant event, farther from [her] even than the Hollywood studio-set wars [she] watched from under the covers" (228).

Gabrielle and Vinh do connect and "return to earth" at the end of the story when Vinh parasails past Gabrielle's hotel window in an act of reconciliation (234). This "return to earth" goes beyond Vinh's return to the ground from parasailing or the couple's return to "the real world": it seems to hint that returning to earth involves leaving the culture that has distracted them from their real-world situation. Gabrielle comments that this moment plays out "just like in the movies," but it echoes earlier statements she makes about her ideal way of living in which she imagines that her and Vinh's powers of observation would place them together "on a hill above it all" or in the sky "where you can fly and everything is peaceful" and one can be "separated from [their] body" and "won't have to worry about anything on the planet Earth anymore" (234, 165, 192). Butler's Hollywood ending to the story may seem to express the redemptive power of American culture, but when coupled with Gabrielle's earlier statement, the dilapidated movie set, and the violent confrontation on the hilltop, this moment reads as a flight from the sentiments of American entertainment and ideology, not an immersion in it. The fact that the "red and yellow" parachute matches the colors of the flag of South Vietnam also suggests that escaping American culture will give them the lift they need to "glide in the long angle of this sun and feel at peace" (234).

American culture is contradictory for Gabrielle, "sometimes tolerant and sometimes intolerant" but claims that "improvisation" makes America different and great because "when things get strained, you don't fall back on tradition [in America] but you make up something new"; however, the opposite happens in the story itself (187, 158). When the other American couple, Frank and Eileen, encounter "something new" in the Trans, Frank "fall[s] back on tradition" in the form of reliving his Vietnam experience, bonding with Vinh by eventually turning him into his enemy, burning the very bridge that joins them. Butler's story shows how American media projects the illusion of improvisation when in fact American culture is trapped in a rerun of its own past.

The isolation of pop culture reinstates the isolation of history, and the story offers little hint that the culture will change. Early in the story, Gabrielle remarks that even though she views the game-show women "too flatly" and that they were in fact "complicated human beings" who "worked at making their surfaces simple," "they have no control" over "the forces that make [them] speak and dress and act the way they do" and could not "change any of those things even if they were conscious of them and wanted to" (167). Unlike these women, Gabrielle views her choices as causing her predicament. She says she "had embraced this culture with such intensity that it isolated [her] from [Vinh], made it impossible for him to find a way to touch [her] anymore" (233). This embrace of the Land of the Game Show traps her into betraying herself, and she views her attempts to fit in to her adoptive culture by changing her name and dressing up like a duck on a game show amount to a "disappointment of dignity" (174). Gabrielle may admit that "things have to change from the inside," but when, in the midst of reproaching herself for embracing American culture, she compares her skin to "the skin of the leper beggars," she indicates that her sickness derives from an external infection that has disappointed her dignity, which she associates with her skin, the very thing that marks her as Other in America. After all, leprosy does not come "from the inside" (168, 233). The events of "The American Couple" present characters beginning and ending trapped in isolation booths constructed for them by history, race, and culture.

When it comes to race and ethnicity, these works use the game show to argue that American media culture does not form bridges between people, countries, or time periods. The game show may have moved on from rigging the game itself, but as these works demonstrate, the identity of the ethnic other is still subject to the "contradictory overdeterminations and contextual constraints" that Kellner speaks of in his book *Media Spectacle* (113). The way to create and maintain an authentic self comes through renouncing America's game-show narrative, either by writing one's own story or flying away, unconnected from everything. This disconnection represents an escape from the isolation booth, but not from isolation, whereas engaging fully with the game show and playing by its rules leads to self-betrayal.

CATEGORY

THE JOKER'S WILD

The films and works of fiction discussed in this round depict characters attempting to carve out space for themselves in the Land of the Game Show by escaping the isolation booth circumstances have put them in without betraying themselves in the process. These figures often fail to construct authentic, unmediated selves because, as Kellner has shown, the self has become but another spectacle presented to the audience within a media landscape. Chuck Barris's *Confessions of a Dangerous Mind* (1984) and George Clooney's 2002 film adaptation mock such efforts to stay true to oneself in the hypermediated postmodern world as alarmingly naïve. Barris's story and Clooney's film depict what Morreale calls "the contemporary production of the self as commodity-sign," or the "cultural shift from the notion of *having* a product to *being* a product as a route to personal fulfilment" (95). One cannot betray the self in Barris's cosmology because there is no self left to betray.

Chuck Barris occupies the center square of the transition from the authenticity-focused early days of television to the spectacle of today's reality-based programming. *Quiz Show* depicts television as a well-orchestrated lie standing in for the lies that course throughout American institutions. By the time Chuck Barris comes along, these lies are the only truths that remain, making television the ultimate truthteller. One may not be able to find many Barris programs on television today, "but his legacy is all around the dial" (Doherty, "Sex, Half-Truths and Videotape" 13). Thomas Doherty credits Barris with "facilitat[ing] the late twentieth-century breakdown of public and private spheres in American culture," effectively dissolving the boundary between television and the real world ("Sex, Half-Truths and Videotape" 13). The isolation booth, then, disappears and the private self becomes absorbed into the "community" of television.

In his "unauthorized autobiography," Barris alleges that while he was creating hit game shows such as *The Dating Game*, *The Newlywed Game*, and *The Gong Show* he worked as a contract killer for the CIA. This alleged double life isolates Barris from himself, though it is an exile that he gleefully welcomes. In *Confesssions*, rather than, as one of his critics would claim, "[reveal] his passion for self-debasement," Barris reveals his passion for the debasement of self, fashioning a self so dissolute that it does not even possess the authority to authorize its own account of itself (Barris 180). Barris's "confession" of his "secret" life as a hitman is so patently absurd that it plays as a sendup of confessional memoirs in the same way that *The Newlywed Game* mocks intimate relationships and *The Gong Show* defames talent.

The memoir genre is too small a target for Barris's hitjob. Assassination acts as a metaphor in *Confessions* for the "highly tenuous and fragile" nature of "identity construction" in the postmodern world (Kellner, "Popular Culture" 153). In mocking both authority and autobiography in his "unauthorized" personal account, Barris slays the impulse to imbue life with depth, presenting a parody of identity as an unending depthless spectacle, a $1.98 Beauty Pageant of emptiness. The fact that it is all for show becomes, for Barris, the only truth there is. As Joanne Morreale writes of makeover shows, *Confessions of a Dangerous Mind* treats identity as "a kind of staged performativity that obliterates the line between reality and fabrication" (104). Barris portrays himself as a contestant on a game show continually "learning to play a new version" of himself (Morreale 104). Barris establishes himself by "renouncing relationships and memberships," even his relationship with himself, essentially proving identity, or what Dieter Hoffmann-Axthelm calls "the modern object of desire," to be "empty" (205).

George Clooney and cinematographer Newton Thomas Siegel create this fragmented sense of identity visually through camera movement and *mise-en-scène* in adapting Barris's book. An early sequence in the film chronicles how Barris (Sam Rockwell) gets hired at NBC, beginning as he tours NBC studios and concluding with him, now employed as a page, asking for an application to be a management trainee. Where most filmmakers would cover such a series of events in a montage, Clooney and Siegel capture the entire sequence in one continuous tracking shot. Barris begins the shot in the entrance of NBC as a tourist, then suddenly appears at the rear of the lobby as an NBC page leading a different tour, only to reappear again sipping coffee in the break room, each time wearing different clothing and interacting with a different group of people. Clooney performs a similar stunt when Barris gets his idea for *The Dating Game*. The camera pushes in on his face until his eyes fill the frame. As viewers stare at his eyes and he describes his idea for the show, the set behind Barris rotates from the bathroom set to an NBC boardroom so that when the camera pulls out from Barris's eyes, viewers find him, props in hand, in the midst of pitching *The Dating Game* to a conference table full of television executives.

This fluid blending of scenes within one shot establishes the antic pace of the film and the unexpected turns of its plot. Everything happens fast in *Confessions of a Dangerous Mind*: one moment a person is on a tour, the next moment one is leading the tour, the next one is a game show host, the next one is a contract killer for the CIA. The dots simultaneously appear out of nowhere and connect seamlessly. This technique portrays Barris's unstable self as a moving target, one that must transform continuously, becoming a different self with every appearance, as though he were afraid of being pinned down. Barris presents the same rationale in his book when he describes surviving his first assassination attempt. The "brilliant fireflash" of the paparazzi in his fantasies becomes the flash of a gun firing at him (Barris 165). The only reason Barris survives, he claims, is "because [he] moved" at the same moment the aspiring assassin pulled the trigger (Barris 165). This juxtaposition equates stasis with death, photography with murder, and portrays the adoption of a new identity as a hit on a previous one. Therefore, identity must be both fluid and fragmented: Barris must always keep moving and shifting who he is, or the next "brilliant fireflash" he sees will be his last.

Such a predicament ought to require one to lie low, but privacy and secrets represent "agony" for Barris (Barris 77). As a creature of television, Barris exhibits the urge to broadcast, to avoid isolation from the community of television at all costs. Rather than use his secrets to pursue an authentic existence, Barris, paradoxically, wishes to be known as a fraud, essentially making himself the real target of his hits. The most telling line in the film captures this paradox well. Barris tells Patricia (Julia Roberts) "all the information I have about myself is from forged documents." He delivers this line as an original statement revealing the deepest truth about himself. Patricia, however, identifies it as a quote from Vladimir Nabokov, thus identifying Barris as a fraud. Yet this fact also makes the line completely truthful: Barris's life does resemble a collection of forged documents and identities—songwriter, game-show producer and host, sex addict, possible contract killer—and passing this quote about himself off as original confirms the truth of his patchwork identity even more.

David LaRocca describes autobiography as a site "where [the truth] is made" rather than a report of already established and understood facts (90). If this is the case, then Barris's story has the opposite effect because it only "reinforce[s] our disbelief in the worldly truth of his account," perhaps even of truth itself (LaRocca 91). "With Barris," LaRocca writes, "we don't get closer to anything—certainly not the 'real' Barris" (91). However, according to Stanley Fish, "The autobiographer can do nothing to be inauthentic" because everything they say, true or false, reveals a truth about them (LaRocca 92). The fact that someone else wrote the "forged document" line only confirms the truth of his claim that "forged documents" hold the key to his identity. Even more appropriately, the Nabokov quote comes from his novel *Despair*, which also concerns a man who forges his identity when he encounters a man he believes to be his doppelganger. Similarly, Barris wishes for his audience to believe that the host of *The Gong Show* is the same man as a CIA hitman, or that they are at least the same program playing on "two channels" even though there is little chance that it is true (Doherty, "Sex, Half-Truths and Videotape" 12). The notion that the two identities bear no resemblance to each other does not affect Barris's plan because, much like Nabokov's protagonist, Barris creates one identity to kill the other.

Not surprisingly for a story about spies and hucksters, forged documents are legion in *Confessions of a Dangerous Mind*. Toward the end of Clooney's film, Patricia forges a suicide note for Barris that reads, "I'm not the person you took me for." Similar to the "forged" Nabokov quote, this ersatz "suicide note" acts as an authentic epitaph for Barris's real life and what *Confessions* wishes to tell the world. The veracity of Barris's claims ceases to be relevant: either way, he emerges fraudulent and truthful, but never the person everyone took him for. In this respect, *Confessions of a Dangerous Mind* is itself a forged document, a rigged game where "identity exists next to [us] as a status object which can be shown to [ourselves] and can be changed, modified, and reproduced" at will (Hoffmann-Axthelm 206).

Barris exhibits few qualms about how rigged his own shows are. In fact, if they were not rigged, no one would have ever heard of Chuck Barris. When the contestants on *The Dating Game* prove too sordid for television, he hires an actor to pose as a representative of the FCC to scare them away from making "lewd or licentious remarks" on-air that would jeopardize the show (Barris 63). Barris even dares to tout *The Gong Show* as an authentic display of America's talent in *Confessions*: it is the other talent shows that are rigged, he says. According to Barris, *The Gong Show* initially set out to be a bona-fide talent show; the problem was "there weren't tons of exceptionally talented people roaming the streets. What were roaming the streets were tons of exceptionally *un*talented people" (155). With such claims, Barris deflects blame for the bleak picture he paints of the world by alleging that the other, more flattering pictures are fabrications. He is not a depraved bullshit artist; he stands alone as a brave truth-teller in a world of deceit.

Barris's rigged assaults on conventional notions of truth extend to the theological as well. Barris cast a *Gong Show* stagehand as Father Ed, whom Barris would ask theological questions. To ensure that this stagehand could not accidentally provide a profound answer to life's big questions, Barris would put his cue cards out of order and load them "with twenty-five dollar words that weren't there in rehearsal, and some highly creative pornographic expressions" that Ed would refuse to speak on-air (Barris 190). This satire of belief and certainty has the same effect as the dreadful "talent" on *The Gong Show*: to sow doubt among the audience in the authenticity of everything other shows and the outside world promote with straight faces, presenting *The Gong Show* as the only true thing left because it is honest enough to admit that everything is false. These behind-the-scenes tell-all details in *Confessions* suggest that forgeries abound in Barris's universe to assassinate any sense of truth. When the so-called authentic is discovered to be fraudulent, questionable, or lacking in authority, one abandons authenticity in exchange for a cascade of fraud. The truth, then, becomes whatever works, and television becomes one spectacle after another.

Regardless, his show does manage to ratify Charles Van Doren's metaphor that television is a flame that people flock to like moths. *The Gong Show* obscures not only the validity of displays of talent but also the necessity for television to feature or select winners. Seeing people lose is the appeal of watching *The Gong Show*. Winners and losers cease to matter even to the contestants because *The Gong Show* provides something more valuable than money: "exposure" (Barris 155). "Everybody was a star," Barris explains, "for the first forty-five seconds of their act" (161). Barris discovers that people will "flock" to the show because they are "happy to be given the chance to be seen" (155). Being recognized and inducted into the community of television is the real prize because it frees people from the isolation booth of the self, validates their identity and talent (or lack thereof). As Thomas Doherty writes, "no humiliation is too demeaning, no intimacy too private, that it will not be bartered in trade for the vital oxygen of the airwaves," for "the warm glow of the cathode rays" ("Sex, Half-Truths and Videotape" 13).

After forty-five seconds in that "brilliant fireflash" of the studio spotlight, the contestants who have not kept their act "moving" get rubbed out by the sound of the gong. Clooney's film makes the connection between the gong and assassination explicit in the scene where Barris conceives of *The Gong Show*. As string of horrible performers struggle through renditions of "If I Had a

Hammer," including a guitar-strumming geisha, the camera pushes in on Barris. Inspiration strikes. In the reverse angle, a stagehand slides the audition room wall aside, unveiling a Central American hacienda behind the singing geisha. Her performance is abruptly stopped when a bullet strikes her from behind. She drops to her knees, revealing Barris standing behind her with a shotgun. The film cuts back to Barris sitting at the audition table. A gong sounds off-screen. Barris stands, embraces the geisha, and the rest is television history. The scene demonstrates how television allows Barris to make his deadly fantasies real, to present whatever self he wants and then broadcast that malleability to the world. The gong is the scythe wielded by television's grim reaper. "If I Had a Hammer" may be about eradicating violence and danger, but Barris's hammer—his penis, his gun, his gong mallet—spreads no such calm or certainty. It smashes stability in favor of a world in which fragmentation and indeterminacy free people from having to find out who they are. Everyone gets to perform until their self becomes so boring or unbearable that they must be "silenced" by the television assassins for the good of the nation. As such, Barris merges his bifurcated life as hitman and game-show host, smuggling his secret identity into the spotlight. As acts drop dead all around him, he remains standing as the only star, a status he achieves at others' expense and humiliation.

Where one might expect *Confessions* to end as a cautionary tale about how "one might become pathologically conflicted and divided, disabled from autonomous thought and action" after "radically shift[ing] identity at will," at the end of his book, Barris turns such oblivion into salvation (Kellner, "Popular Culture" 153). When Penny shares a Walker Percy quote with him, Barris pulls out a piece of paper from his pocket and reads, "In the affairs of the heart, I think I would rather suffer the emotional lows, the slings and arrows of defeat, the self-pity, the loneliness and discontent that comes with not knowing what's next, to the boredom and lethargy of a happy, secure household, knowing quite well what the next sentence, hour, and day will bring" (223). He claims to have written it himself, but, as with everything else in the book, it is difficult to know for sure. The "happy, secure" life that comes from having a stable sense of self represents boredom to Barris. Not knowing or caring who one is becomes a release from the burden of crafting a stable self.

Barris's book endorses a fragmented, fluid existence in which "there is no coherent core, no deep interior behind the surface appearance of a social self" and one is eternally on the run from stability and coherence (Morreale 104). The moment one settles down is the moment the hitman sounds the final gong. His final game show idea presents this idea quite clearly: each week, the show presents a thief at large to the audience, and whoever spots them first and calls the police wins the grand prize. Barris adds that "if the fugitive wasn't caught during that week, we could bring him back for another episode, double the reward, and send him out again to another part of the country" (239). As with most of the shows Barris creates, this one too is a projection of his own life: Barris hopes to remain on the run, undetected, impossible to pin down, hiding the fact that no one is at home, and the show never ends.

Barris's presentation of the self becomes the apotheosis of the postmodern self, "where images are no longer anchored by representation" and the "simulation" of an "unauthorized autobiography" "produces the real" (Morreale 104). David LaRocca reads this presentation of self positively, arguing that *Confessions of a Dangerous Mind* acts as "an unending project" of a "patchwork" self that is "stitched and otherwise mended" from "bits of disparate fabrics" to show how "as a community of fabulists and fabricators ... we neither draw away layers of fabric to reveal the truth nor drape lies in obscuring cloth, but spend our time on the surface, cutting and stitching, dwelling on the multifarious arts of illusion—where the truth really lies" (95, 97). However, the ironic, even gleefully cynical tone of Barris's book and Clooney's film make such a reading difficult to embrace. Like the makeover shows that Joanne Morreale writes of, *Confessions* "makes visible the ways that identity is created through rehearsal and performance of already fabricated images"—game show host, television producer, hitman—and "naturalizes the idea that identity is fluid and mobile, a commodity sign that we circulate in an endless attempt to make meaning" (104). If "our transformational potential [is] confined to image consumption and production," then Barris's fluid, unconfined self smacks of parasitic privilege because an audience must exist for Barris to project his "fuck-hate relationship with the passive viewing masses" onto (Morreale 105; Hampton 26). These masses, in turn, get trapped playing Barris's game, piling derision on "those eager unfortunates" on the show "even as they awaited their own turn as contestants" (Hampton 26). In order to achieve this feat, "an inverse Other has to be constructed—a boorish Them comprised of the white-trashed drooling class and sterilized suburbanites (the great unwashed) and a free-floating *Gong Show* of spasmodic losers, deserving victims, and walking clichés" who together form "a common denominator so low everyone could feel superior to it" (Hampton 27, 26). Or, as this round has come to know them, Herbert, Melvin, Jamal, City, Gabrielle, and the many more unnamed who did not appear on this or any other program.

The final verse of "Mack the Knife," which Brecht added for the 1931 film adaptation by G. W. Pabst, captures the dynamic between television and its audience today: "There are some who are in darkness / And the others are in light / And you see the ones in brightness / Those in darkness drop from sight." Those who remain in the light of television's "community" survive in the mediated world, while those who fall outside its glow vanish. The isolation booth of television allows for one to be displayed even in private, whereas the isolation booth outside the screen is death. Although it may not appear to be appropriate at first glance, the game show functions as a good metaphor for the self in the postmodern media landscape because its presentation of knowledge and intelligence matches Jean-Francois Lyotard's description of the relationship between knowledge and selfhood in the postmodern era. According to Lyotard, "the transmission of knowledge is no longer designed to train an elite capable of guiding the nation towards its emancipation, but to supply the system with *players* capable of acceptably fulfilling their roles at the pragmatic posts required by institutions" (48; emphasis added). Thus, the postmodern self remains available only to those with the buying power to adopt the new self "required by institutions," which makes this dynamic and fluid postmodern self a tool of capital.

Round Two

LOVE CONNECTION

The Game Show's Erogenous Zones

ONE WOULD BE HARD-PRESSED TO THINK OF A TELEVISION program less concerned with intimacy or love than a television game show. Even dating shows, which pair people who want to get to know each other better or reveal truths partners hide from each other, fail to inspire any sense of intimacy in the viewer. The entertainment of dating shows does not come from all the genuine and heartfelt love on display but from couples embarrassing themselves on national television. If anything, these shows seem to trivialize intimacy between lovers by unmasking it as based on misunderstanding or willful ignorance, and the transparency these shows present illuminates an absence of knowledge, of understanding, of intimacy, of love.

Dating game shows came to prominence in 1965 with the premiere of *The Dating Game*, just a few years after the quiz-show scandals of *Twenty-One* and *The $64,000 Question* nearly crushed the format into oblivion. Although they are not singlehandedly responsible for the game show's resurrection, dating shows, along with programs such as *The Price Is Right* and *Supermarket Sweep*, were instrumental in the television industry's effort to rebrand the compromised "quiz shows" by jettisoning the big-money quizzes' rarified (and rigged) displays of factual knowledge. These changes succeeded in keeping the game show alive as a television format, but this move also sunk the esteem of the now-disgraced format even further to an "entertainment [form] with low cultural prestige" (Hoerschelmann 13). Dating game shows perform the same function as any other game show, broadcasting the values of the dominant culture and instructing viewers on how they can rapidly assimilate into that culture. Olaf Hoerschelmann notes that while they may not have been something the culture was particularly proud of, dating shows promoted patriarchal American culture by presenting a "celebration of mandatory heterosexuality" that "focuses on the creation and maintenance of stable relationships and traditional family structures" (14).

Although not every couple on a dating show winds up living happily ever after (or even going on a second date), the programs "still operate with a narrative blueprint that emphasizes the primacy of healthy heterosexual relationships" even when "the overdetermined context of the dating show format" appears to be challenging it (Hoerschelmann 14). Romance might not be a stable force for the contestants on the show, but each day the viewer sees the persistent hunt for romantic fulfillment showered with free products, thus validating heterosexual monogamy as the only lifestyle where one can succeed materialistically. In celebrating mass consumption and connecting it to heterosexual monogamy, dating game shows project a utopian vision of capitalistic heteronormativity (or heteronormative capitalism) that encourages their audience, comprised mostly of women, to marry and fill their nest with the latest consumer appliances and handy solutions for modern living. Choosing not to follow the show's lead would compare to a contestant choosing not to spin the wheel.

As narcotizing as such an image of heteronormative bliss may be, however, these shows, in their implicit affirmation of the "ritual of coupling," wind up casting doubt on the very ideology they appear to promote (Hoerschelmann 14). Interestingly, the arrival of dating game shows coincides with the moment divorce rates in America begin their steady rise. According to the Centers for Disease Control's National Center for Health Statistics, 1965 only saw about 2.5 divorces per 1,000 people, with 479,000 total divorces and annulments; by 1982, that number had more than doubled to 5.2 per 1,000 people, with over 1.2 million divorces and annulments (Olson). A similar trend occurs in dating game shows: the number of potential partners to choose from and the number of relationships the shows encourage contestants to pursue increase. On *The Dating Game*, a young woman chose one man from three. *Singled Out*, MTV's 1990s foray into dating games, gave contestants a fifty-person "dating pool" to select from. Reality shows such as *Blind Date*, *ElimiDate*, and *The 5th Wheel* use hidden cameras to show audiences a highly edited version of a date, with the latter two programs injecting drama into the dates in the form of partners getting dumped while the date was in progress (*ElimiDate*) or switching partners midway through or contending with the arrival of a new contestant (*The 5th Wheel*). With the wildly popular dating show *The Bachelor* (and its spinoffs such as *The Bachelorette*), viewers watch a contestant explore relationships with two dozen people until they have decided on one to marry. Marriage becomes a prize on heaps of other reality programs as well: contestants battle to win the heart of a celebrity musician (*Rock of Love, Flava of Love*), a millionaire (*Who Wants to Marry a Multi-Millionaire?*), or someone they think is a millionaire (*Joe Millionaire*). However, while these shows ostensibly dangle marriage in front of contestants and viewers alike, the drama of the show involves watching players "shop" for the best partner to suit their needs and aspirations. But the shopping does not stop once one has made a purchase. *Temptation Island*'s high-stakes game put already-formed couples on an exotic island surrounded by hot singles (and hot tubs) to determine whether they are happy in their relationship or need to keep exploring the many attractive options on hand. This escalation in programming complements the shift toward relationships in American culture, where people discover that they have more freedom and choices than they once had and explore all their options to ensure that their freedom is in no way inhibited.

In presenting romantic relationships as fielding an endless array of choices, dating game shows destabilize the culture's conception of monogamy and heteronormativity, revealing both are based on exclusion, denial, and secrecy. In being undermined, the "true love" of game-show lovers follows Baudrillard's assertion that "*the discourse of truth is quite simply impossible. It eludes itself. Everything eludes itself, everything scoffs at its own truth*" because "seduction renders everything elusive" (*Ecstasy* 62). The dating game show assumes that lovers do not reveal certain truths about themselves to each other, and the show will manipulate them into telling each other things they have worked to keep hidden. In order for them to tell the truth, the prize must outweigh the damage that telling the truth will inflict, and only the capitalist wonderland of the game show can deliver such a bounteous return on investment in brutal honesty. However, this kind of honesty is never rewarded with more intimacy: in revealing these truths for material gain on the show, the contestant reveals to their partner a secondary truth: they value the prize of consumer goods over the prize of their partner's love.

This aggressive quest for transparency resonates with Jean Baudrillard's connection between obscenity and ecstasy in *The Ecstasy of Communication*. For Baudrillard, "obscenity begins when there is no more spectacle, no more stage, no more theatre, no more illusion, when everything becomes immediately transparent, visible, exposed in the raw and inexorable light of information and communication." When this occurs, "*we no longer partake of the drama of alienation*" with the "imaginary protector" of our own "private universe[s]"; rather, we "*are in the ecstasy of communication*," which Baudrillard defines as obscene (26). While game shows hardly do away with spectacle, stage, theatre, and illusion, the works that use game shows intermedially as metaphors for love illustrate how "the all-too-visible, the more-visible-than-visible" dynamics of the game show now govern romantic interaction (27).

In these works, destabilizing heteronormativity does not result in liberation from repressive heteronormative ideologies but rather substitutes the control found in repression for the market's control over intimate human interactions by packaging intimacy as a commodity. Even if intimacy is what someone wants—an assumption most of these works make—these works depict it as being unavailable, with nothing but advertising in its place. As late capitalism does so often (and so alarmingly well), it monetizes the decrease in stability of romantic relationships and sells empty solutions to this problem that perpetuate that instability without providing people with the fulfillment or the love that they are encouraged to seek. The discourse of capital overwrites the discourse of love, and these works suggest that the game show serves as the ideal site to witness this shift from "*the drama of alienation*" to "*the ecstasy of communication.*" The reimaging of love as displayed in dating game shows privileges the market over the lovers, refashioning them as points of sale in the amorous marketplace, objects of consumption for someone else's pleasure and profit. In such an environment, intimacy takes a back seat to the market's demand for an excess of variety and options, replacing the hunger for love with the hunger to consume more, but with fewer commitments and even fewer limits. In broadcasting intimacy to any and all who tune in, these works suggest intimacy to be a commodity like any other, one that can be traded for consumer goods. With three bachelors to choose from today and three more tomorrow, why would any bachelor or bachelorette settle for just one? The works discussed in this chapter will increasingly follow such reasoning to its logical conclusion, reframing the game show as capitalist pornography.

These works endorse Baudrillard's claim that "the market is an ecstatic form of the circulation of goods, as prostitution and pornography are ecstatic forms of the circulation of sex" by collapsing them all into one state (*Ecstasy* 27). Increasingly, the intermedial texts that talk about love through the game show gravitate toward pornography in form and content as an analogue for the way the consumption ethic has come to dominate human relationships under heavily mediated late capitalism. The game show is to capitalism as *Supermarket Sweep* is to shopping as *The Dating Game* is to dating as pornography is to love: all conceive of life as a frenzied high-stakes gamble devoted to self-gratification rather than a slowly development of cooperative bonds and relationships based in vulnerability and trust. In examining the similarities between the discourses of the game show, love, and capital, these works present America with a full-frontal view of its heavily mediated capitalist landscape to reveal a world in which intimacy and love are unstable, undesirable, even impossible. What the market demands of love, the game show delivers: a broadcasting of romantic relationships in which one is always shopping for a newer, better, more attractive partner in a never-ending, never-closing erotic marketplace where total romantic satisfaction is simultaneously unattainable and ever-promised.

Every work fails to present or conceive of an example where a relationship survives within a media-saturated world: couples wind up either separated, on the show with multiple partners, or off the grid forever. Characters who choose intimacy and commit to one person over the endless options of the market disappear from the media world because a lasting commitment to one person in a world in which love and intimacy have been commodified constitutes a closing of markets, an undiversified product line in the romantic exchange. Such a resolution, however, presents problems for readers and viewers because, as readers and viewers of a media product, they cannot follow the characters in their rejection of the media world. The audience remains trapped on the wrong side of the screen, separated from the intimate and the real.

CATEGORY

WHAT IS THIRST?

Intimacy and knowledge are, well, intimately connected. The lover wants to know their love object completely and to be known completely by the loved object. This impulse, of course, fuels the pursuit of love: the lover wants to get to know their loved one better because they love them, and in turn they love them more as they get to know them better. The dilemma arises, of course, that other people are, ultimately, unknowable. Roland Barthes describes this paradox in *A Lover's Discourse*: "on the one hand, I believe I know the other better than anyone and triumphantly assert my knowledge to the other ("*I* know you—I'm the only one who really knows you!"); and on the other hand, I am often struck by the obvious fact that the other is impenetrable, intractable, not to be found" (134). Individuals continually want to know their beloved better and yet continually encounter moments in which this loved one appears unrecognizable, a stranger in their bed.

As absurd as it may seem to apply Barthes's seminal tract *A Lover's Discourse* to the trivial erotics of the game show, Barthes himself justifies such an endeavor. "No love is original," he explains, and "mass culture is [but] a machine for showing desire" (136). Culture reflects the world but also acts as a lens that focuses one's gaze on whatever it puts before them. Little in fact could represent the desire exhibited by the mass culture machine better than the dating game show, for it (and depictions of it in fiction and film) substitutes "the description of the lover's discourse [with] its simulation" (3). Love's discourse, like game show answers, "exists only in outbursts of language, which occur at the whim of the trivial" (3). A show such as *Love Connection* may replace a genuine discourse of love with an ersatz simulation of it, but that replacement, as Barthes shows, represents "a discursive site," and understanding the sway this simulation has over the way viewers and readers perceive romantic relationships today offers the only hope they have of reclaiming or redefining love and representations of it (3).

As Jean-François Lyotard explains, institutions have discourses that "privilege certain classes of statements" while declaring "there are things that should not be said"; love and the game show are but two such institutions whose rules regarding play overlap in useful ways (17). Like Barthes's lover, most game show contestants enact their discourse alone. The discourse of the game show also "is today *of an extreme solitude*. This discourse is spoken, perhaps, by thousands of subjects (who knows?) but warranted by no one; it is completely forsaken by the surrounding languages: ignored, disparaged, or derided by them, severed" to "the backwater of the 'unreal'" (Barthes 1). The lover's discourse is based on figures of speech that contain "unknown (unconscious?)" sentences which operate within "the signifying economy of the amorous subject" (5, 6). These figures resemble "a 'syntactical aria,' a 'mode of construction'" rather than a complete and autonomous statement, and "occur to the lover without any order" as "the amorous subject draws on the reservoir" of available things to say to fit the moment (6). A lover's discourse is a random "encyclopedia or affective culture" for Barthes, governed by circumstance rather than logic: these figures "stir, collide, subside, return, vanish" (7).

Likewise, game show contestants find themselves presented with a series of categories and questions requiring them to scour the "reservoir" of their memories for the formerly irrelevant utterance that will match the interests of the group asking them questions. Contestants buzz in, utter a figure, and, like the lover, anxiously await a response from the other that validates their figure as harmonious with the other's values. These answers, like the "*I-love-you*" of *A Lover's Discourse*, are "without nuance" and reject "explanations, adjustments, degrees, scruples" because a game show cannot indulge in such ambiguity (148). An answer, like a declaration of love, is either accepted or rejected; the lover either wins or loses, but seldom draws. In love, as in the game show, "the true dismissal is 'There is no answer,'" because such a response, in both cases, negates the existence of the entire discourse: a game show cannot function without answers, and a lover cannot exist without "the last resort of [the lover's] existence," language (149). Thus, the game show discourse mirrors the discourse of love, where the $64,000 Question is always "do you love me?"

Barthes delights in the ultimate unknowability of the love object. Lovers continually encounter surprise in their relationships because they believe they have all the answers to the category—"I'm the only one who really knows you!"—and then find themselves stumped by the next question, unable to "solve the riddle" of their partner (134). When faced with the fact that they "shall never know" the loved one, the lover must choose whether to keep playing the game with the intention to win or change strategies (and perhaps even the game itself) and accept "that the other is not to be known" (134, 135). In using the game show to explore what it means to love, artists reveal that, with the exception of *Jeopardy!*, the game show's approach to knowledge has gotten things exactly backwards: where lovers buzz in to supply "outbursts of language, which occur at the whim of the trivial," intimacy demands that lovers place their buzzers aside and ask questions (3). When the lover accepts "that the other is not to be known," then "all that is left for [the lover] to do is reverse [their] ignorance into truth" (135). Once the lover reaches that state, Barthes claims, "the game of reality and appearance is done away with" and the lover is "seized with that exaltation of loving *someone unknown*, someone who will remain so forever: a mystic impulse: *I know what I do not know*" (135).

Ron Shelton's 1992 film *White Men Can't Jump* illustrates how interconnected game-show knowledge is to the lover's discourse by using *Jeopardy!*, the American symbol of the highbrow quiz show, to imply that love is a quest for knowledge and understanding that cannot be solved with answers and actions. Rather, the measure of one's love can be found in how much the lover learns about their beloved and how much they learn about themselves in the process. Shelton cleanly divides the world into doers and watchers, subtly proclaiming that love in its pure form represents an attempt on the part of ignorant masculine doers to more closely resemble feminine knowers. The comedy concerns two connected storylines: Billy Hoyle (Woody Harrelson) and Sidney Deane (Wesley Snipes) use Billy's visible whiteness and invisible basketball prowess to hustle people in pickup games, while Billy's girlfriend Gloria (Rosie Perez) studies to compete on *Jeopardy!* and tries to minimize Billy's stupidity and penchant for self-sabotage. The men are preoccupied with what they can do rather than what they know. They perform physical labor out of the house, whereas the women do intellectual work in the home. Instead of developing knowledge of their own, the men exploit the lack of knowledge in others, "triumphantly assert[ing] [their] knowledge" upon their opponents. In the game-show lingo of *Double Dare*, they take the physical challenge, every time, placing all their

Obscured by facts: Gloria's introduction.

hopes in the fact that everyone they challenge is ignorant of Billy's skill. They gamble because they cannot produce. They have but one piece of information to offer, and they go all-in on it every time to milk it for all it is worth.

As much as this situation may classify Billy and Gloria as opposites, Shelton carefully demonstrates how they function as ringers in their chosen rackets by challenging and defying cultural stereotypes. Like Billy on the basketball court, few expect a Latina former nightclub dancer like Gloria to dominate a game show like *Jeopardy!*. While her success does not involve deception in the way that Billy's does, it does surprise the white males running the game show. Billy's fruitless quest to back up his masculine bravado with action seeks to prove people wrong for judging him based on his appearance as a dopey white man incapable of jumping. Similarly, Gloria pursues learning because the knowledge she gains will supply her with the means to escape a life of debt and dependence on Billy. Shelton implies these parallels in how he edits key sequences. Shelton's montage of Gloria's dominating performance on *Jeopardy!* resembles other sequences of Billy and Sidney sinking basket after basket in their games, complete with similar crowd reactions. Just as each basket brings them closer to financial gain, each of Gloria's answers puts more money on her screen. This technique subtly characterizes both endeavors, *Jeopardy!* and basketball, as high-stakes hustles that rely on the other participants being unaware of Billy's and Gloria's gifts.

When Gloria first appears, an almanac blocks her face, suggesting that what she knows acts as a barrier between her and Billy. To know her, one must first know what she knows and grapple with it. Gloria even describes herself as "overloaded with more useless goddamn information than any human being on this fucking planet." Perez delivers Gloria's statement as a mixture of a boast and a lament that is no different from the trash-talking that Billy and Sidney engage in on the court; however, the prowess she boasts of here forces her to admit that her intimate command of the facts isolates her from the one thing she desires most: to be intimately known by Billy. Rather than fill Billy with awe, Gloria's knowledge intimidates him, so he treats her like a mystery that refuses to reveal itself to him. Gloria advises Billy against reducing the world to black-and-white facts that can only be taken at face value. Instead, she claims a person must intuit, ask questions of the answers they are presented with. She frequently attempts to communicate with him through Zen koans such as, "Sometimes when you win, you really lose, and sometimes when you lose, you really win, and sometimes when you win or lose, you actually tie, and sometimes when you tie, you actually win or lose. Winning and losing is all one big organic globule from which one extracts what one needs." Such a process requires people to be in dialogue with each other, to resist the urge to fetch a glass of water for someone and instead understand what it means to thirst.

Gloria may be overflowing with knowledge, but she is still thirsty. Conversely, Billy views his masculinity as a wellspring of answers and solutions instead of, as on *Jeopardy!*, looking at Gloria as the answer and striving to formulate the right question. The film's most iconic scene demonstrates how Billy and Gloria's problems with intimacy stem from their opposed approaches to knowledge and action. After they make love, Gloria announces several times that she is thirsty, and Billy promptly brings her a glass of water. To Billy's amazement, Gloria complains that her saying she is thirsty does not mean she wants him to bring her water. She claims that such behavior represents "a way of controlling a woman." Instead, she "wants [him] to connect with [her] through sharing and understanding the concept of drymouthedness" by saying, "Gloria, I too know what it feels like to be thirsty. I too have had a dry mouth." Billy rejects Gloria's plea for shared intimacy as absurd and ineffectual, saying, "When I say I'm thirsty, it means if anybody in the room has a glass of water, I'd love to have a sip." His understanding is based entirely in action, single problems with single solutions, and he remains oblivious to the possibility that problems can function as something other than an obstacle to intimacy. The thirsty scene shows why *Jeopardy!*'s inverted question-as-answer format is the perfect game show for *White Men Can't Jump*: like City in *Long Division*, Billy looks for answers and solutions without realizing that he is playing a game in which he should be lingering on the small steps and asking questions—learning, not solving.

None of his attempts to solve problems through action succeed. In fact, quite the opposite: they place him deeper in debt. After he and Sidney take their hustle as far as it can go by winning prize money at a tournament, Billy winds

White Men Can't Jump's romantic final frame.

up betting Sidney his share of the winnings that he can dunk. Sidney knows such a feat is impossible, but Billy will not back down; he must demonstrate what he can do and prove others' so-called superior knowledge as ignorant in the process. Of course, Billy loses the money because, as the title declares, Billy is a still a white man who cannot jump, but he takes home the trophy from the tournament as a parting gift, a perfect symbol of his empty masculinity. Even though he does dunk in the final basketball game and thus prove that at least one white man can jump on one occasion, the only lasting thing he has learned is his self-destructive drive to solve his problems through taking dramatic action has rendered Gloria lost to him forever. Sad as such a turn of events may be in the abstract, the film does not dwell on the loss too much. Gloria disappears from the film's consciousness entirely, as though returning to *Jeopardy!* as a wealthy champion means she must vacate her spot in the hypermasculine world of *White Men Can't Jump*. Winning makes her disappear from this world of losers, and her decision represents her running off with the one partner that can never disappoint her: facts.

The final shot of the film confirms that Billy and Sidney's relationship is the only kind of intimacy that can survive in a masculine world that privileges action over knowledge. Billy and Sidney experience no growth because they essentially end up exactly where they began, standing on the court at sunset, silhouetted by the golden sun, aggressively thrusting a basketball at each other and talking trash about all the ways they will embarrass each other on the court. It is written and photographed as a love scene, underscoring the homoerotic subtext of their relationship. The basketball serves as something they can pass back and forth between each other without jeopardizing their fragile sense of masculinity. They are not discussing what it means to be thirsty; rather, they are bragging about how they will make the other know something they are currently ignorant of, forcibly imposing knowledge on their partner rather than soliciting information from them. The dysfunctional male approach to knowledge and intimacy survives intact, and *White Men Can't Jump* gets the romantic ending it has been pursuing the entire time, only not with the couple viewers expected.

Even though the film may not ultimately embrace Gloria's point-of-view fully, it still proves that love can only occur when the doers acknowledge that there is a limit to what they can do. They must recognize that they cannot know or control everything, that all the answers cannot be found, that certain outcomes cannot be willed by force, that there is such a thing as mystery. Men will not be able to *know* love if they cannot abandon what they think they know about women. They must stop seeking to provide the answer like Alex Trebek and instead ask the question like Gloria. In love, the doers must prove that they can do one thing: learn.

CATEGORY

MARRIAGE MAZE

Three films lean heavily the game show's celebration of monogamy and heteronormativity to critique, both consciously and not, the destabilizing effect the capitalist media landscape has on intimacy. *Table No. 21*, *Stay Tuned*, and *Shock Treatment* depict a world so saturated with television that television and its forms has consumed reality. The market cannot promote intimacy because it cannot imagine such privacy between people. Intimacy, like monogamy, discourages competition, cuts into precious advertising time, and threatens to shut down the markets. As a result, these films illustrate how in the Land of the Game Show, every action, no matter how private, must conform to the normative demands of programming and the market, both of which demand the open-ended possibility of endless variety while simultaneously imposing patriarchal gender roles that celebrate men as doers in command of infallible phallic power and women as sexualized products who must market themselves to men and prop up the man's fragile masculine dominance.

The game show broadcasts a facsimile of honesty and intimacy to the largest market share, promoting knowing a lover's dirty secrets as superior to intimacy. In a statement that could also be a Daily Double, Barthes describes truth as "the truth: what is *oblique*" (231); however, game shows do not allow for nuance in their answers; in such a true-or-false world, nuance becomes a means of shielding the truth, mangling the purely factual answer, and compromise represents the height of dishonesty. Each of these films uses the game show's black-and-white discourse to adopt an intransigent, even self-righteous position on honesty, confusing the intimacy of *A Lover's Discourse* with the transparency and obscenity of *The Ecstasy of Communication*, treating the latter as a more honest and more market-friendly depiction of human relationships.

Baudrillard maps this process out in his description of seduction. According to Baudrillard, "the entire strategy of seduction is to bring things to a state of pure appearance, to make them radiate and wear themselves out in the game of appearance," which causes "the secret to lose its meaning, and only the visible has any value for us" (*Ecstasy* 55). The 2013 Indian thriller *Table No. 21*, directed by Aditya Datt, illustrates Baudrillard's ideas, showing what happens to intimate relationships when a game brings meaning and appearance into a state of equilibrium. The film uses the game show's commitment to right-or-wrong answers to embrace a view of love that more closely resembles a scorched-earth policy: the couple must destroy their relationship with radical honesty in order to save it, and even then, the relationship cannot survive because the game has revealed their love to be based on deceit.

In the film, newlyweds Vivaan and Siya (Rajeev Khandelwal and Tina Desai) win a vacation to Fiji, only to find themselves roped into playing for 10 million Fijian dollars on a life-or-death game show run by Mr. Khan (Paresh Rawal). The game, which he broadcasts to over eight million viewers on a live gaming website, involves rules as simple as the game's stakes are high: answer eight yes-or-no questions truthfully and perform a task tied to each question. No gray areas: yes or no, win or lose, action or inaction. The first question asks Vivaan whether public displays of affection embarrass him. Once he answers yes and the lie detector verifies his response as honest, he must kiss Siya passionately in the middle of the busiest street in town. Not surprisingly, the questions and tasks do not remain innocuous for long, nor do the stakes. By the time question four rolls around, Vivaan must prove that he can overcome his fear of blood by filling a bottle with a quarter liter of his own blood before Siva suffocates in an airtight chamber. (Admittedly, it escalates rather quickly.) If either of them tries to quit the game, the FitBit on their wrists will explode. Vivaan endures his share of humiliations, but the punishing nature of these questions and tasks falls disproportionately on Siya, making the game a not-so-veiled attack on women as vain, duplicitous, and promiscuous. By the end of the game, Siya eats meat, gets her head shaved, reveals that she cheated on Vivaan, and dances in a strip club. When Vivaan and Siya complain that the game and its threat to their lives violates the law, Khan tells them, "Laws are shallow. What's important are principles. Those of the game and the demands of the audience."

Khan's statement elevates the rules and practices of the game show above other, loftier principles, alleging that television's rules and methods lead to a greater and more significant truth by making hidden secrets visible. Even though Khan reveals that his motivation for putting the couple through such an ordeal is deeply personal, *Table No. 21*'s attitude toward love and intimacy is thoroughly derisive, seeking to humiliate anyone ignorant enough to proclaim that they are in a loving, intimate relationship by exposing how ignorant they are to their partner's duplicity and secrecy (and vice versa). Love can only exist among the delusional, the misinformed, the incorrect. *The Newlywed Game* employs this logic in its own way: the humor of the show derives in part from seeing how little these couples know about each other. So-called "true love" constitutes the ultimate oxymoron in this worldview; love is blind to the ultimate truth because it subsists on secrets and lies. The game, however, with its superior principles and audience demands, "seeks to produce meaning" and make their relationship "signify" by "render[ing] it visible"; however, such a pursuit, like the stakes in the game show itself, quickly becomes obscene, and their relationship becomes "gorged with meaning" it cannot sustain (Baudrillard, *Ecstasy* 55).

It may seem like the show is out to get them by forcing them to reveal these uncomfortable truths, but Siva and Vivaan are willing participants in this game. Before agreeing to play, their secrecy had a higher exchange value than the truth; however, now that they stand to profit from being entirely open and honest, they will break their silence. They play and reveal secrets to win money, not their partner's love, which is evidently not enough for them, and they continue playing to save their own lives, never challenging the game and its rules until the time for such defiance has long since passed. Even though Vivaan and Siya escape the game, *Table No. 21* offers viewers little in the way of optimism to suggest that this couple stands on the precipice of a bold new level of intimacy in their relationship, nor does the film inspire much confidence that their relationship survives the final round.

Its tone may be decidedly lighter, but Peter Hyams's 1992 film *Stay Tuned* presents a similarly nasty view of television's ability to tear love apart. Like *Table No. 21*, Hyams places the blame squarely on women, equating excessive television viewing with passive femininity. The film depicts television's endless entertainment options as a threat to the nuclear family and traditional masculinity, asserting that the only way love can survive is by conducting its business off the air. Roy Knable (John Ritter) represents the stereotypical milquetoast husband, a failed plumbing supplies salesman whose most intimate relationship is with his television set, while his wife Helen (Pam Dawber) is a career-woman whose success would embarrass and emasculate Roy if he were to take his eyes off the television long enough to notice. Helen tells him that he was a doer when she married him, but now he has turned into nothing more than a watcher. Fed up with Roy's unwillingness to unglue his eyes from the set and save their marriage, Helen chucks his fencing trophy, a monument to both his past phallic glory, through the television. Enter Spike (Jeffrey Jones), a sinister salesman for HVTV who offers Roy the ultimate in home entertainment: 666 channels. Naturally, Roy makes this Faustian bargain with "the Mephistopheles of the cathode ray," selling his soul for the promise of unlimited entertainment, a passive watcher for all eternity. Little does Roy know what lurks in the fine print: he and Helen are not proud subscribers to a great new cable service but are indentured servants of Satan, unless they can survive twenty-four hours trapped inside the demented programming of HellVision TV.

Of course, the first HellVision program they enter is a game show entitled *You Can't Win*, where they must answer embarrassing questions that reveal hidden truths about their relationship. Even though Roy watches more television, Helen performs better in the game when she correctly answers the question, "What former lover has your spouse been seeing?" "The former lovers we've been seeing are each other," she says. Helen getting the answer right perpetuates the association of daytime game shows with feminine domesticity and confirms Roy's weaknesses as both lover and problem-solver. Helen's answer may keep them alive and in the game, but it also announces with crushing finality that their relationship is so damaged as to qualify as infidelity to their television-centered lives. As a reward for answering correctly, they get to spin the wheel to find out which door they will go through next. Of course, since the show is called *You Can't Win*, every spot on the wheel is Door Number 1, and the Knables plummet into a distorted version of 1990s television programming, such as *The Fresh Prince of Darkness* and *The Home Shoplifting Network*, and battle to save their marriage—and their souls. Even though Helen's intellect bails them out of several jams, Roy reclaims his phallic power when he defeats Spike in a climactic sword fight. After the Knables return to the real world, Roy becomes a doer and opens a fencing academy where, in addition to teaching fencing, he tells kids not to watch too much television.

Although *You Can't Win* is the only game show portrayed in *Stay Tuned*, the film depicts all of television as a game show that the viewer cannot win. The limitless options, a now-quaint 666 channels, offer viewers like Roy Knable a way to pursue constant passive pleasure and avoid confronting their inability to fulfill the demands of normative masculinity, a low-calorie version of intimacy that may be less filling but certainly tastes great. *Stay Tuned* pushes this claim further by positioning television consumption as a threat to patriarchy and heteronormativity, making television a game that cannot be won by straight men. Going off the grid, unplugging the set, becomes the only solution to preserve a nostalgic form of normative masculine power that cannot exist among so many alternatives. Television's threat to masculinity, best represented by the game show *You Can't Win*, is not neutralized until Roy regains control not of the impotent remote but of his sword. Such a solution is hardly desirable or achievable. First, the more vibrant and unmediated masculine world that *Stay Tuned* imagines does not exist, nor does the film attempt to imagine it outside of the western serial Roy and Helen appear in on HVTV. Second, adopting this film's solution requires a wholesale embrace of a sexist patriarchal worldview that conflates patriarchy and intimacy, which, ironically, is the same worldview presented by the heteronormative game shows and television programs that this film finds so emasculating. *Stay Tuned* is also trapped in a game of *You Can't Win*, though that may be for the best. Although it captures a certain frustration with the limits a hypermediated world places on one's ability to interact with others meaningfully, it succumbs to a reactionary imaginary that only further limits human relationships and does not offer a new discourse for lovers in the Land of the Game Show but only immerses them more deeply in the world they are hoping to escape.

Where *Table No. 21* and *Stay Tuned* naively assume there is a real world off the air to which their couples can (and should) return, *Shock Treatment*, Richard O'Brien and Jim Sharman's 1981 sequel to *The Rocky Horror Picture Show*, illustrates there is no such thing as "Off the Air" anymore. Denton, the monument to all-American mediocrity that *The Rocky Horror Picture Show* so gently parodied, has now become the DTV studio, and all activity, both civic and not, occurs on the air in front of a live studio audience, formerly known as citizens. Cecelia Tichi argues that "the electronic hearth and individualist television potentially rival one another," but *Shock Treatment* regards all of television as a conformist force in American life that obliterates the individual and, like *Stay Tuned*, posits that an escape from the televisual landscape is the only hope love and individuality have for survival (63). The first shot of the film makes this transformation abundantly clear: a shadowy figure sits before a bank of television monitors in a control room. The camera pulls back to reveal that the control room sits in the heart of the iconic "Denton: Home of Happiness" billboard, which has been exhumed from the cemetery it was in at the start of *The Rocky Horror Picture Show* into the DTV studio. Everyone's hearts, it seems, have been struck by Cupid's antenna-shaped arrow, and they now, along with all our feelings of love, belong to television, *are* television. Sharman and O'Brien push Tichi's notion of the television as "electronic hearth" to its logical extreme, an electronic *heart*. To make the metaphor abundantly clear, if Denton

The Heart of America.

is, in fact, the home of happiness, then television is at the heart of all happy feelings. And now that the entire town has been transformed into a television studio, the control room functions as the heart of the town quite literally, keeping it alive by pumping images into its bloodstream. No one escapes from the televisual world, and no one wants to: the studio audience even sleeps in their seats. Watching is more than a person's job; it is their civic duty and their most intimate and enduring relationship.

Like *Stay Tuned*, *Shock Treatment* depicts the entirety of television as a game show out to split couples apart so that it can have the lovers' total devotion all to itself, keeping everyone's heart in the control room. After a brief news program, the first show on DTV's broadcast day is *Marriage Maze*, a game show featuring couples who have "made a hash of their marriage." The first contestants from the studio audience are Brad and Janet Majors (Cliff De Young and Jessica Harper). Although *Marriage Maze* purports to be a game, it, like *You Can't Win* offers contestants no options. In fact, *Marriage Maze* does not even ask any real questions: the moment Brad and Janet sit down, the host, Bert Schnick (Barry Humphries) tells Janet that Brad is "an emotional cripple" who should be sent to *Dentonvale*, a television program that doubles as a mental institution. Janet has no opportunity to respond because the game is rigged to break up their marriage so that she can wed studio chief Farley Flavors (also played by De Young), effectively marrying her to television itself. Marriage seems to be a maze that one is meant to get out of so one can enter another maze with no exit: television.

Sharman and O'Brien extend *Rocky Horror*'s satire of a repressive American culture that deems those who cannot live a heteronormative life as not just game-show losers but catatonic basket cases in need of rehabilitation. Remaking all life in the film as a television show allows *Shock Treatment* to portray Brad's failings as a lover and a man as game-show failings as well, with game-show prizes (and his failure to win them) serving as confirmation that his marriage has failed. After learning that Brad will be sent to *Dentonvale* for treatment, he and Janet sing a song to all the appliances being given away on the television screen, asking them to explain why they as a couple are "always sooner or later / bitchin' in the kitchen or cryin' in the bedroom all night" (DeYoung and Harper). People, it seems, no longer possess the answers in Denton's game-show world: the prizes, the rewards for successful play that also double as signifiers of domestic bliss, contain all the answers, suggesting that if one can simply play well enough to win them, then all the answers to a successful relationship will be revealed. Like unrequited love, the prizes mock the one who desires but cannot have them, and rewards those who join in the spurned lover's humiliation, like Janet's parents, who receive an all-expenses-paid resort vacation when they come on the show to answer questions about Brad's mental instability. Janet equates the lover's discourse with the discourse of the game show best when she sings that Brad would realize she still loves him, "If only you knew how to win some prizes / If only you knew how to play" (Harper, In My Own Way). With these details, DTV conflates the lover's discourse and the game show discourse with the goal of reeducating Brad in heteronormativity so that he and Janet can secure their rightful place as successful game show lovers in the normative media landscape.

Simultaneous to showing television and game shows enforcing heavily coded behaviors on men, *Shock Treatment* also presents television envisioning femininity as a market-driven spectacle, suggesting that the goal of DTV is not to keep lovers together but to place them on separate paths of endless consumption. The film depicts two types of love in the mediated world: intimate love and broadcasted love, the love between two people and the love between the spectator and the star. Barthes's concept of "all the delights of the earth" defines the love of broadcasting well. In *A Lover's Discourse*, Barthes describes a lover's fulfillment as an accumulation that "do[es] not abide by the level of lack," producing instead "an *excess*, and it is in this excess that the fulfillment occurs ... *enough* means *not enough*" (54). The game show, and television by extension, continually depict the desire for bigger, for larger, for more, discouraging the spectator from settling. While Brad undergoes his reeducation in masculinity in *Dentonvale*, Flavors gives Janet a star makeover that turns her into a stunning leading lady who quickly becomes a megalomaniac capable of singing a song whose entire chorus is "Me Me Me." In becoming a television star, Janet pursues the love of the studio audience to replace the lost love of Brad. This quest echoes the advice one character gives to another in Alexandra Kleeman's novel *You Too Can Have a Body Like Mine*: "think of yourself as a franchise" because "more outlets just mean greater reach" (101). Janet becomes, as Barthes describes, "the utopia of a subject free from repression" in whom "only the will to fulfillment shines, indestructible" (55). The "will to fulfillment" creates an excess of visibility that resembles and is fulfilled by the excesses of television, a broadcasted promise of emotional interaction that can be endlessly pursued but never rejected, so long as the viewer continues playing. The hunger for intimacy becomes a drive to consume, and Janet temporarily rejects a one-to-one form of emotional interaction in favor of a broadcasting of romantic feeling that can never be fully satisfied (on either end) but can be endlessly sought and sold. Janet's escape from repression, though, resembles less the "don't dream it, be it" liberation of *The Rocky Horror Picture Show* and more the "ecstatic form of the circulation of goods" and bodies that Baudrillard describes in *The Ecstasy of Communication* (27). Janet equates sexual liberation with commodity exchange when she sings, "I'm looking for love / I'm looking for trade" (Harper and Young, Looking for Trade). The song rebrands love as trade, a commodity broadcast in primetime to everyone gathered around the electronic hearth.

There are many necessary ways to reimagine love and intimacy as something other than heteronormative monogamy, and *Shock Treatment* shows how television transforms that necessity into an equally repressive entity that subjects every relationship to the demands of the market. Sharman's film sees the Land of the Game Show as a neofascist dystopia that simultaneously humiliates those who fail to conform to heteronormative living and reconceives love and intimacy with one person as a market-based public transaction with many. This commercial image of love-as-commercial promises the viewer fulfillment but only provides a dissatisfying exchange. Real love becomes impossible because love requires one to stop looking for more, to stop shopping, to put their buzzer down.

CATEGORY

CARNAL KNOWLEDGE

If it seems surprising to think of a game show as an erotic space, what is even more surprising is how many works do just that. From heavily promoted novels from major presses to full-length pornographic films to self-published erotica ebooks, the game show has certainly gotten around. *White Men Can't Jump*'s assumption that deep and intimate knowledge of another is possible, infinite, and desirable naively quaint when juxtaposed with game-show erotica. The mediated world frequently engages the broadcast model to argue that happiness can only be reached by consuming to excess. In a world of endless variety and options, brand recognition becomes an end in itself, a reward rather than an invitation. The following works blend the aesthetics, format, and methods of pornography with those of the game show until the two are indistinguishable, and the game show becomes the space where "ecstatic form of the circulation of goods" couples with the "ecstatic forms of the circulation of sex."

Although several of these uses of the game show are intended as absurd, their absurdity reveals how little difference exists between pornography and game shows. Game-show erotica effortlessly lays the game-show template over the template of a sex scene. Each round becomes part of the seduction and sex rituals that build in intensity and resistance, delaying gratification before the characters finally succumb to their desires and climax in the final round. This resemblance is only the tip of the iceberg for their deeper similarities, nor is clothing the only thing that these erotic works strip away. They also strip away all difference between game shows and pornography to reveal that porn's vision of love is the same as the game show's vision of capitalism. Just as a game-show contestant can win a new car without having to earn the money to pay for it, a character in a pornographic scenario can "win" sex-on-demand without having to work for it. When one takes these works more seriously than they take themselves, one discovers that the game show's portrayal of intimacy in American culture represents the fulfillment of the capitalistic impulse and its triumph over every aspect of life. The game show presents the market's erotic universe in which excess is the norm, every craving is satisfied, and the odds are ever in the contestant's favor.

The works in this category show, some more consciously than others, the ways in which a heavily mediated world swaps intimate knowledge of a person for superficial, physical knowledge of a body. Such a worldview falsely confuses visual and sensory pleasure for emotional intimacy, suggesting one's knowledge of another is incomplete if they cannot recognize every inch of the loved one, that intimate knowledge is best represented by touch or sight. In other words, capitalistic culture replaces intimacy with spectacle, turning the search for intimate connection into a game of its own, a pornographic fantasia of endless options (and orifices) to explore. Tully Krater's 2013 short story "Game Show" and the 2002 film *Who Wants to be an Erotic Billionaire?* offer the most literal depiction of the game show as orgy. In "Game Show," Dave is a lucky contestant on a show that tests his knowledge of his sexual partners' bodies. Krater makes the token silent female assistant of many popular game shows (best symbolized by *Let's Make a Deal*'s Carrol Merrill) into the prize itself. The first game, "Name That Orifice," requires him to guess exactly how one of the female assistants is servicing him: "What could it be? The sensuous wet grip of vagina? The warm suction of mouth? The trickery of a lubed fist? The snug-at-the-opening but hollow-within of anus? So many choices!" (Krater). Quite a stumper. In the second round, "Who's That Gal," also known as "The Fuck-Off," Dave must guess which female assistant he is having sex with, but not before getting "two minutes to familiarize [himself] with each of [the show's], um, assistants" (Krater). At the end of this round, Dave can either take home the kitchen appliances he has won, or return tomorrow to play another round. For all the alterations Krater makes to the game-show format, she preserves the domestic trappings of daytime game shows, even though her contestants are decidedly undomestic men. This decision makes the choice between increasing domestic knowledge or increasing carnal knowledge the falsest of choices. "A toaster or more time with Lina and the others?" Dave thinks, "It was no contest" (Krater). The contestants here would hardly accept being feminized by kitchen appliances over having their masculinity validated by women. In making the female assistants on the show the ultimate prize, Krater depicts women as appliances who eagerly service and maintain masculine fantasies of virility. For all its apparent transgressions, "Game Show" pushes few envelopes when it comes to gender politics, promoting instead a world of instant and effortless intimacy that believes sexual gratification is directly proportional to the sample size.

Where "Game Show" seeks to please men at every turn, *Who Wants to be an Erotic Billionaire?* evidently prefers embarrassing them. Its all-female sex scenes appear to privilege female pleasure even if they do not do the same for female intelligence. Like its namesake *Who Wants to Be a Millionaire?*, contestants on this show answer multiple-choice trivia questions, and for each question they get right, Bambi, the female assistant (Vivica Taylor), will remove one item of clothing. Contestants who answer all ten questions correctly get to have sex with Bambi (and win one billion dollars, though that prize would exceed the film's budget by a substantial margin). For the female contestants, the questions are ridiculously easy: what is your favorite color? how many sides are in a triangle? and so on. The second female contestant gets to Bambi even faster because the host, Remis Phildin (Julian Wells), skips the first five questions and asks one of the remaining five twice. By the end of the game, two women tie in the final round and request that Remis join them and Bambi in an all-female four-way. Unlike many porn scenes involving male-female intercourse, these sex scenes do not end until everyone climaxes. But pleasuring women is just half of the film's agenda. When the male contestants get their turn, the film shows just how rigged against men the game is. The first man, a trashy ex-con, receives questions such as "who was Richard Nixon's Secretary of Agriculture during his second term?" and "how many verses are in the national anthem of Greece?" Remis Phildin has a great time stiffing him, taking away only one choice for his 50–50 and dialing the wrong number for his lifeline. The second male contestant, an overweight bearded incel, has to use a lifeline to answer the humiliating question "when's the last time you had a friend?" only to discover that his "friend" is a pizza place.

However, the film only deviates from the male-centered norms of pornography so much. A film such as *White Men Can't Jump* privileges female intelligence, both intellectual and emotional, over masculine prowess and bravado, exposing how hard-won and deserving Gloria's success is. *Erotic Billionaire*, on the other hand, presents women with the same kind of everything-for-nothing rewards usually reserved for men in pornography and erotica such as "Game Show." No choices need to be made because no knowledge is required to win. In this respect, the show resembles the rigged contest of *Long Division's Can You Use That Word in a Sentence* in that it patronizingly lowers the standards for one group in order to ensure their success. While the film's humorous opposition to some aspects of patriarchy may elicit a chuckle or two, depriving the women in *Erotic Billionaire* of any intellectual acumen reduces them to sexual objects who do not need to know or learn anything in order to receive or give pleasure. Of course, just because no men are being pleasured in the film does not necessarily mean that the film's all-female sex scenes do not seek to gratify their desires. One must also recognize that heterosexuals are the film's likely intended audience. In this respect, intimacy is not so much off the table as it is nonexistent because even though they all achieve orgasm, the sex between women in the film is geared toward satisfying someone else entirely. Just as the game show erodes one's understanding of the values of hard work, the desire for intimacy suffers the same fate in these pornographic game shows. In that way, these works unconsciously reveal how all the knowledge game shows intend to measure merely gauges one's desire to trade that knowledge for the oblivion of consumer satisfaction, which is not all that different from the mindless sexual pleasure on full display in *Who Wants to Be an Erotic Billionaire?*

In a game show, the only rules are those of the game itself; the contestant does whatever it takes to win within those rules or risks going home empty-handed. When intimacy is off the table and all that remains is total consumer satisfaction, all desire becomes limitless because the focus settles on personal satisfaction of those desires by any means necessary. Woody Allen's game-show sketch "What's My Perversion?," part of his 1972 film *Everything You Always Wanted to Know about Sex* (but were afraid to ask)*, features a panel of celebrity guests (including future *Millionaire* host Regis Philbin) attempting to guess the secret fetish of the contestant. The final segment, where contestants act out their wildest fantasies, involves a rabbi getting tied up and whipped by a woman while his wife kneels at his feet and eats pork. In addition to being quite distasteful, Allen's film exemplifies creators turning to the game show format to show how the frenzied pursuit of big money and fabulous prizes can justify crossing previously uncrossable lines, if not erasing them altogether. When it comes to big bucks, the social rules outside the world of the game show no longer apply. The game makes its own rules, its own world, and the players must conform to them if they want a shot at the big prizes. Turning one's back on the game, either through committing to someone or simply tuning out, means turning one's back on an endless array of instant gratification.

Enter the next contestant, "Limitless Game Show" by Anya Merchant (2014), part of an ebook subgenre called Taboo Erotica. The series features stories that transgress normative social boundaries such as BDSM or affairs with secretaries and babysitters. In this story, the taboo is incest. Tessa, a struggling actress, signs herself and her stepson Sean up for "Limitless: Breaking Boundaries and Exploring Forbidden Territory," a web-based show where mothers and sons compete against other mother-son teams to see who can take things the furthest. When Sean realizes that the game is sexual in nature, he wants to back out, but Tessa thinks that being on the show could improve her stagnant acting career somehow. "If it gets too uncomfortable we can just walk away," she promises (Merchant). She also promises to let him have the $25,000 cash prize if they win. While both of these details are persuasive to Sean, the beginning of the story presents his deeper motivation: he has the hots for his stepmom. By the end of the show, of course, Sean and Tessa have had sex with each other before a live studio audience, as have all the other contestants. Even though they do not win, they leave the studio eager to "practice [their] approach and try again" (Merchant).

Like in "Game Show," *Erotic Billionaire*, and "What's My Perversion?" the material prizes pale in significance beside fulfilling one's most outrageous sexual fantasies. As in "Marriage Maze," the temptation to reject intimacy in favor of self-centered fulfillment becomes too much for just about everyone, and the contestants often choose to go against their own emotional interests in favor of improving themselves materially. However, these selections of erotica present a twist: rather than force the contestants to do something they do not want to do or reveal something they wish to keep hidden, the façade of the game show and its prizes permits them to acknowledge and indulge in desires that have been heretofore repressed, once again promoting the idea that the game show uncovers the "real" truth. However, "Limitless Game Show" turns out to serve as a strong rebuttal to this idea in its wholehearted embrace of it: the truth is not always the big winner because not all forms of intimacy are created equal or need be admitted, faced, and indulged. "Limitless Game Show" reveals how these works, in their literal approach to deep, complex issues such as honesty, truth, and intimacy, wind up settling for a superficial understanding of ideas that are by their nature meant to go beyond the surface. Taken together, as silly and disturbing as they are, these works perform a vital function by drawing a stark equal sign between game shows and pornography. Game shows present viewers with fantasies about money and things, while pornography presents fantasies about sex. People watch porn to see people copulate with each other and watch game shows to see people copulate with things. While the games they play may be as different as can be imagined, at their root they portray the same desire for acquisition, consumption, and repetition, what Baudrillard calls "a pornography of circuits and networks" writhing in the ecstasy of communication (*Ecstasy* 27). Each proves a basic tenet of capitalism: buyers and sellers want as much as they can get for as little as possible, but game-show erotica demonstrates that no matter what waits behind Door Number 3, intimacy will not be it. The two should be incongruous, but these amateur works depict how effortlessly they can be combined even by lesser artists.

The analogy equating the impersonal superficiality of pornographic sex with that of game-show capitalism comes to fruition in Helen DeWitt's 2011 satire *Lightning Rods* and Alexandra Kleeman's 2015 novel *You Too Can Have a Body Like Mine*. These two novels apply the methods of the game show to corporate and consumerist America, respectively, and, in doing so, reveal the game-show model not only as pornographic capitalism but the very fulfillment of a capitalist ethos, an orgiastic celebration of abundance with no strings attached and no money down. The characters in Kleeman's novel are average Americans, so average, in fact, that they do not even have names: A, Kleeman's protagonist, has a boyfriend named C who she fears will come to prefer her best friend B, who looks more and more like her each day. A states at the beginning of *You Too Can Have a Body Like Mine* (hereafter *YTCHABLM*) that "we care most for our surfaces" because "they alone distinguish us from one another" (Kleeman 2). According to her (and a story such as "Game Show" would agree), the superficial represents the first, best hope at achieving individuality. Ironically, though, it is the surfaces where characters lose their individuality and become unrecognizable to each other, making intimacy extinct in the modern world.

The game show in *YTCHABLM* is called *That's My Partner!*, the show where "couples in long-term relationships" face "a series of challenges designed to test how well they [know] each other" (98). *That's My Partner!* replaces the intimacy that comes from recognizing someone for who they are with its most superficial of counterparts: picking them out of a crowd. The first round makes them identify their partner through photographs of less recognizable parts of their bodies (backs of heads, hands, etc.), the second round requires them to pick their partner out from a group of silhouetted dancers, and the final level places contestants in a dark room full of naked people, where they "have three minutes to grope everyone they could get their hands on" in the hope of dragging their partner out into the light (99). Contestants who correctly identify their partner win a cash prize; losers must "dissolve their relationship" and adopt a "bidirectional" restraining order (100). Kleeman's qualification that the goal of *That's My Partner!* is "more specifically, [to see] how well [couples are] able to recognize each other" serves as her characterization of what passes for intimacy in American culture, and while these challenges seem easy enough, they almost always end in failure because the endless possibilities and varieties of consumer life have created a strange sameness that leaves everyone indistinguishable from everyone else (98).

Kleeman argues that love and intimacy are impossible in "the ecstasy of communication," and Baudrillard predicts Kleeman's world of obscenity and excess when he describes the world of the "all-too-visible" as "that which no longer contains a secret and is entirely soluble in information and communication" (27). This "soluble" culture places everything on display in the marketplace, and Kleeman's novel shows how individuality serves as a secret that must be dissolved by the logic of mass-produced consumer culture. By reducing everything, even interpersonal relationships, to "their exchange value," individuality and intimacy, the "message" of personal interaction, "ha[ve] already ceased to exist," leaving "the medium," a person's body, to "[impose] itself in its pure circulation" throughout the market (Baudrillard, *Ecstasy* 27). In the novel, men strangely wander away from their homes in a trance and turn up weeks later sitting in shopping malls several towns over. (The newscasters call it Disappearing Dad Disorder.) In an attempt to rationalize these men abandoning their lives, A says these men "were just seeking a perfect life":

> They wanted the good things.... They didn't want the gift-curse of recognition by those they loved and who loved them back, one consequence of love's durability being that they would be recognized and loved aggressively even on days when they couldn't stand to recognize themselves in the mirror, even on days when merely remembering themselves made them sad and want to sleep. Love that made every day a day that they had to live in a handcrafted, artisanal fashion, rather than being outsourced to someone who could do it happily and efficiently for a third of the price. (Kleeman 66)

In the novel, love and intimacy are not among "the good things" that people want. They represent instead a "gift-curse" that recognizes one's individuality and demands that one accept this love in spite of their own feelings of self-worth. But the curse does not end there: by describing such a life as "handcrafted" and "artisanal," Kleeman casts intimacy as a kind of radical authenticity amidst an "outsourced" world of mass-produced, impersonal exchanges. Even though they are marketing terms, "handcrafted" and "artisanal" connote a handmade uniqueness lacking in mass-produced goods, an intimacy of touch between maker and buyer. Such meaningful living proves to be too arduous for most in the culture to bear, and *That's My Partner!* becomes the site where this dilemma is enacted and transformed. Ironically, the final round involves touching, as if to prove to contestants that everyone's bodies are basically the same and that their love is neither "handcrafted" nor "artisanal" but impersonal and generic. Losing on *That's My Partner!* might dissolve a long-term relationship but it also frees contestants from this "gift-curse" of "handcrafted" love and "artisanal" recognition and rewards them with the loss of identity that often attends a breakup. Thus, the show not only functions as a product of its own but an instrument of the market that tosses couples out of their "handcrafted, artisanal" lives and into a world of anonymous variety.

Living an "outsourced" life renders everyone in the novel strangers to themselves. The title of the game show itself celebrates a kind of recognition that the show proves extinct: no one can say "that's my partner" confidently any longer because the statement could equally apply to anyone. A describes looking at herself in the mirror as "like waking up with a stranger" and lives in daily fear that C will leave her for B, her nearly identical friend (2). All she wants from C is a basic validation of their relationship as an intimate one, for him to tell her that she "is exactly who [she is], and that [she] couldn't ever be mistaken for anyone else" (102). C, surprisingly, refuses, or claims that he will not say it because "anyone could tell [her] that," so if he were to say it, he would "disappear" and suddenly "be someone [she] didn't recognize" (102). In other words, affirming her identity as an individual would compromise his own fragile individuality; to define their relationship as intimate would make it indistinct. This paradox traps A and C in a double-bind where they must remain more than acquaintances but less than lovers, a months-long one-night-stand, contestants forever stuck in the first round of *The Dating Game*. C does little to assuage these fears, telling her after they watch a man curl up into a ball after losing on *That's My Partner!* that she should "start dulling [her] fear" and "think of [her]self as a franchise" because "more outlets just mean greater reach" (101). He essentially combines the broadcast model of love from *Shock Treatment* with the franchise model of fast-food restaurants and big-box stores.

In C's way of seeing the world, individuality means exclusivity, which means fewer opportunities to capitalize on one's product or promote one's brand. He goes on to tell her that "any two people, on average, share 99.9 percent of their DNA sequences" (101). As he says this, she starts to "pull her knees up to [her] chest" like the man who just lost on the episode of *That's My Partner!* they are watching and looks at C, thinking that "he looked like someone [she] was just meeting for the first time, and didn't like all that much" (101, 102). His comment about everyone's shared genetic code makes him unrecognizable to her, and she assumes the same posture as the person on television who fails to recognize his partner and is now cut off from them forever. Since she will not get what she wants from him, he tells her to "think of something else [she] could want, and then just go get that instead. It's called 'transference'" (102). In response, A flips channels and feels "a smothered hunger beating out from the unseen places inside [her] body," and she realizes that what C's description of "transference" encapsulates "an essentially contemporary problem, a problem of supply and demand" that she can solve "by finding something new to want and pursuing that wanting instead" (104, 105). Kleeman characterizes the desire to consume as a transferred desire for intimacy: "Wanting things was a substitute for wanting people," and it is "one of the best possible substitutes" because there are always more and newer things to want, an endless supply to satisfy the "aimless hunger" of one's demand (106, 25). One can always desire more in this scenario and thus one need not feel saddened by never feeling full; never being full is, ironically, the goal of a consumption economy in materialistic America.

In *YTCHABLM*, to borrow a phrase from Mary Pipher, characters are starving in the land of plenty (Pipher 174). The possibilities corporate America places before A, B, and C overwhelm them so much that they cannot feel anything other than "aimless hunger." Like Kandy Kat, the Wile E. Coyote-esque cartoon character chasing the novel's ubiquitous snack Kandy Kakes in commercials, the characters in the novel find themselves consumed by the desire to consume, sharks surfing through a sea of endless channels. However, unlike sharks, the characters in the novel cannot "back that hunger up with such efficient action" (43). Instead, they eat and watch television with the utmost passivity. Rather than focus on a single television program (unless it happens to be *Shark Week*), A and C use their television's "channel seek" function, which "automatically cycle[s] through all of [the] stations one by one" without staying on a channel for more than ten seconds (53). A describes channel seek as "like experiencing several dozen small attachments and losses that you could maybe prevent but definitely would not do anything about" (53). Kleeman uses Channel Seek to present the whole of television in one small feature, characterizing its entire universe as episodes of *The Dating Game*, a galaxy of fleeting attachments and short-term bonds, which, as in *Stay Tuned*, threatens monogamy.

Although such a description sounds like the depths of disconnection, A sees such absent gazing as representing the pinnacle of intimate connection. Late in the novel, she describes C's "calmest and most relaxed state" in which she thinks that "by tracing his line of sight and fixing [herself] on that same TV show," she "could feel like [she] shared his mind, that [their] minds were one" in an intimacy that is "immediate but at a distance, as though [their] love were as swift and expansive as television" (206–7). A recognizes and yearns to be intimate with C through his gaze, but rather than gaze longingly into each other's eyes, they gaze vacantly in the same direction at an advertisement, waiting for the channel to change to something new. In the world Kleeman conjures, a world eerily similar to contemporary America, people connect via the "immediate but at a distance" intimacy that television offers. By staring absently at the same thing, couples can "tell exactly what [the other] was thinking about" because it would be identical to what was in their head (206). There would be no room for misunderstanding, only the intimacy of recognizing each other in our shared appetite for the consumed image. This kind of intimacy mirrors the final round of *That's My Partner!*, with Channel Seek morphing into a groping session where couples search for something they recognize as familiar. Even though they are bound to lose, it winds up being the kind of attachment whose loss "you could maybe prevent but definitely would not do anything about" (53).

Kleeman's couples experience intimacy through consuming images of other people getting intimate. A finds pornography lacking in recognition and information: "you watched them fucking and all you learned was that they were fucking," as though porn is a game show that mindlessly and repeatedly poses the same question. "These bodies were universally compatible, each to each, so the minds would be, too. There was nothing any of these naked bodies could do to truly surprise each other" (158). Although A intends for this criticism to be limited to the world of porn actors, she has already feared the same about herself because "any man's genitalia, however large or weirdly shaped, would be guaranteed to fit inside [her] own." Therefore, their "pairing," or any romantic pairing for that matter, rather than being based on love and trust (or even attraction and lust) would be "coincidental or, at best, lucky" (33). What perhaps stands out as the most troubling aspect of A's observation is the belief that one's superficial exterior can be as "swift and expansive" as one's interior.

In spite of this dire description, porn couplings in *YTCHABLM* represent the only successful couplings because they are wholly anonymous and impersonal by design; they are essentially the model that all other relationships in Kleeman's novel fail to measure up to. Like "cashiers at the grocery store," porn performers "carry out their tasks with a sort of faraway etiquette" (91). This "perfect world" is one of total access and constant consumption that A interprets as an image of consumer happiness as though sex is but another item selected from the shelf and carefully placed in a cart beside the eggs and Pop-Tarts. "Because in [the pornstars'] world everything offered is taken up and no proposition is refused," A reasons, "no excess desire is left behind" (91). Porn then is the erotic version of economic equilibrium where supply and demand come together. The comparison to a grocery store cashier is especially apt because pornography represents a supermarket where the only transactions are sexual in nature and are all equally priced: free, the shopping spree of all consumer fantasies.

Porn consumption connects every thread of the novel back toward a hunger for intimacy when A "come[s] to understand that the only stable point of orientation [in porn] was the stomach" (70). A explains that "all the ins and ups and downs and deeps seemed to indicate a line cutting through the vagina, through the uterus, and right into the center of the body, which also happened to be the center of digestion. This center seemed to be where everything wanted things to go, deeper and deeper to the innermost point, where they could finally rest" (70–71). A viewer of porn watches two (or more) people attempting to satisfy a deep hunger at the center of their being, never reaching their target or finding satisfaction, only the empty desire for more, just like Kandy Kat chasing Kandy Kakes. A's attempts at intimacy involve talking like adult film performers, but the most erotic text message A can think to send C is *"I'm starving!"* because she cannot find any language to use that she can recognize herself uttering (71). She explains:

> I always got lost in the parts of speech: if I wanted something involving one particular part of his body, I had trouble not using the preposition 'with,' telling him to do something 'with' it, or else I would be telling him to 'put' it someplace. Both structures made the part eerily passive, something he could pick up and set down and use or not use, like a hammer or telephone. (70)

The challenge, it seems, is mutual because, according to A, "the same thing happened when [C] talked about things he would do to a particular part of [her] body: the body that emerged from his description seemed to have only three or four parts, linked hazily by what [she] would assume was more body. Talking about [her] body in any way took [her] apart (70)." The erotic talk that the couple learns from pornography reduces them to consumable objects, each part of their body an individually wrapped package on a supermarket shelf (or a question on a game show). They cannot even recognize themselves in their own imaginations, identity-less parts lacking a coherent whole.

Focusing excessively on body parts reduces a person to an anonymous assemblage of parts. Baudrillard offers a similar diagnosis in *The Ecstasy of Communication* when he states "we are looking for a reduction into partial objects and the fulfillment of desire in the technical sophistication of the body," which "has been reduced to a division of surfaces, a proliferation of multiple objects wherein its finitude, its desirable representation, its seduction are lost. It is a metastatic body, a fractal body which can no longer hope for resurrection" (41). Kleeman naming her characters A, B, and C takes Baudrillard's ideas one step further by making them sound like parts in an IKEA box that must fit together a certain way to construct the desirable product.

As if to battle the mindless anonymity of pornography, A "fantasize[s] sometimes about an inverse pornography in which all that mattered was what was going on within what appeared to be a successful fucking":

> Everything would look the same, flat and happy, but as a viewer I would know that one of them felt an uncomfortable friction that they were concerned would turn into a rash, the other was worried about their unbalanced relationship, not sure what to think about or focus on, wishing they were fucking someone more energetic and distracting even if it was all staged.... You would know all the things that the body, in its busy activity, kept hidden. (158)

Of course, what A describes as "inverse pornography" many in the studio audience would define as reality; however, the notion of people possessing an inner life does not occur to A because she views everyone's minds as being as "universally compatible" as their body is (158). Inner lives, it seems, could only belong to those already "inside" the television landscape, where everything is "more exciting . . . instead of the calming numb of watching" television (28). Those outside the television remain anonymous: nameless, faceless watchers whom one cannot tell apart. In fact, she claims to have "a better understanding of what went on inside of [a man in a news story's] psychology" than she does about C, who "remains obscure" despite the fact that she has "spent hours and hours for months" with him (33). Therefore, intimacy is impossible outside of television, but it is also impossible on television.

Like in *Stay Tuned* and *Shock Treatment*, the goal of television appears to be to erode whatever sense of intimacy remains in the mind of the viewer because doing so makes the viewer anxious and vulnerable to the suggestions of advertising. The game show, like the Kandy Kakes A craves, creates an "aimless hunger" in the viewer and then markets itself to that viewer as the thing that will make them full, only it cannot because, also like the Kandy Kakes, it contains almost no calories. This method sounds an awful lot like Late Capitalism 101: identify a need created by an area where the market has failed, then manufacture a product that promises to fill that need but does not. Applying such a logic to romantic relationships would likely create the world of *YTCHABLM*, full of nameless hungry people searching for the product or person who will fill their empty identity.

The most successful instance of intimacy in the novel occurs in a dream A has in which all her ex-boyfriends appear and engage in an orgy with her and C. During the orgy, she says that she feels "happy and rested" because she "recognize[s] all of their bodies right down to the placement of body hair and freckles." She says, "I know them like I know myself, better than I know myself" (90). Her dream essentially merges the final round of *That's My Partner!* and the end of *Who Wants to Be an Erotic Billionaire?*, the major difference being that no one has to say "That's My Partner!" because they are all equally each other's partner's, or, as A puts it, all "the people I know best now know one another in the same way that I know each of them" (90). In A's fantasy, everyone is equally intimate and equally estranged because if no one knows anyone better than anyone else, there is no such thing as intimacy, only equilibrium. However, such a state appears to be what A describes later as a "better world," a world in which "we all could come home to the wrong house, sit down with strangers to a dinner that wasn't ours, treat them like family because we didn't know any better" (271). In this "better" world, "There would be nowhere you could go, nowhere you could run to, where you wouldn't be among family and friends. You would run away from home, to home, inevitably" (271). This vision imagines every aspect of the world as imitating a chain restaurant or big-box store: one would always know where everything is because everything is the same everywhere. When everyone is identical to everyone else, then everyone can go anywhere they please without distinction, equally friend and stranger, a world of superficial familiarity and intimacy where one no longer has to worry about getting to know anyone because everyone is the same, every relationship and emotion is transferable, everyone can turn to anyone and proclaim "That's

My Partner!," brought to you by endless repetition. In this world, watching television would likely be unnecessary because the world would look just like it.

Such a goal proves to be the hidden agenda of the New Christian Church of the Conjoined Eater, the bizarre cult that acquires a controlling share of *That's My Partner!* and supplies it with contestants from among its interchangeable acolytes with the intent to break up the show's couples and steer them into the cult. A winds up working as one of the "decoy girls" on an episode of *That's My Partner!* only to discover that her fears about C and B getting together have come true and they are now contestants on the show. She attempts to reveal herself to him, stripping off her makeup and clothes, but C's face betrays no "signs of recognition, but showing instead that grossed-out-but-thrilled look he used to get when watching *Shark Week* on television or really weird porn" (261). In trying to describe their previous state of total intimacy and recognition, A describes herself as a piece of food consumed by C, the shark who has long since digested her and moved on to another identical Kandy Kake. Nothing in her description speaks to her personality or any singularly identifying features for that matter. Readers are left with only her features:

> C had once touched every part of my face with his hands, with his lips and tongue. He had tried to find out how much of it he could fit into his mouth, licking my nose and then clapping his whole mouth over it, grunting as he widened his hold on my face. We practiced breathing through each other, sealing our lips together and relaxing the nasal passages, taking turns inhaling, drawing air through the holes in the other person's body, breathing circularly. We put our lips close and spoke down the other's throat so that we could feel the words trembling in our tissue, as if we had said them ourselves. We licked each other's ears, necks teeth. He had tasted every part of me, even some of the parts inside, but it didn't mean anything now. (264)

A and C trying to devour each other like they were Kandy Kakes leaves them both hungry and anonymous to each other because they have continually been viewing each other and their relationship as a product to be consumed. Barthes defines love as a "narrative ... a *program* which must be completed"; however, in *YTCHABLM*, completion vanishes in favor of a kind of endless repetition and duplication that the market prefers (93). Love is not possible, only hunger for it looming out of reach and scores of market-based solutions calling out from the shelves and the television screen.

Helen DeWitt's *Lightning Rods* concludes on the triumphant declaration that "in America, anything is possible" (273). DeWitt's satire, however, reveals how the game-show format and its successful infiltration of every aspect of the imagination, up to and including the erotic, invites people to dream of dehumanizing schemes that serve capital at the expense of intimacy and dignity. DeWitt's hero is Joe, a salesman in search of something to sell, something that "would one day lead directly to a multi-million dollar industry that would improve the lives of millions of Americans" (10–11). His brainstorming, however, frequently turns into masturbatory fantasies, which is how he lands on his million-dollar idea:

> He started wondering what it was about sex. Because if you think about it the pornography industry is a multi-billion dollar industry. Some people use it as an adjunct to a fulfilling sexual relationship, sure, but what about the rest? If you could figure out a way to deliver the real thing you'd really be onto something. A way to deliver the real thing where people did not have to worry about running into the criminal element, or getting arrested, or just getting recognized. (16)

Joe's idea starts out as a means of avoiding sexual harassment but quickly arrives at its true goal: male sexual release without the requisite amount of intimacy up front. In a worldview that elevates gratifying one's personal sexual urges over the mutual pleasure of an intimate sexual relationship, getting off becomes "the real thing," and intercourse becomes a more complex form of masturbation. Michael J. Arlen equates television viewing itself with masturbatory impulses when he describes it as "an act that we perform by ourselves and for ourselves" (Tichi 71). Rather than functioning as the "communal intimacy of the hearth," watching television represents a "private and autoerotic" act surrounded by "guilt and suspicion" (Tichi 71). As Cecelia Tichi explains, "engagement in the TV environment is per se autoerotic" where "all other areas of thought and feeling are precluded" (76). DeWitt's hero simply applies this view to all types of sexual activity, thus rendering all forms of sexual intimacy as autoerotic as watching television and the world a spectacle put on for one's viewing pleasure.

The narrator ends his list of worries with "just getting recognized," and while that may not carry the gravest legal consequences among the other items in the list, it is the most difficult to avoid in a consensual sexual relationship. Telling one person apart from another seems to be the most basic step toward building intimacy. Even in "Game Show" and *YTCHABLM*, recognition is the goal to the sexual game. Despite the fact that the contestants in that game are having casual, almost anonymous sex with several people, the goal is to be able to tell one person's body from the other. Recognition is the entire point. This fear of getting found out helps to characterize sex as an affair so private and shameful that the ideal number of participants would be one. In this context, "just getting recognized" carries with it all the shame of getting caught masturbating. "Humans do nothing without shame" according to Joe, and he regards sex as the most shame-filled human activity of all: "Well, just look at how much time people waste because they *can't* get it without shame! Look how much time people waste in conversations, asking people about their interests. Look how much time people waste fantasizing. And just look at the risks people take!" (24). Based on Joe's description, he sees what feels like the start of an intimate relationship as a shameful waste of time; what most see as a path toward long and meaningful love, Joe sees as the first step on a walk of shame that ends in a sexual harassment lawsuit.

Rather than spend money and resources educating employees about harassment and prosecuting those who harass, Joe monetizes and normalizes harassment with Lightning Rods: female employees who increase productivity and revenue while reducing stress and sexual harassment complaints in the workplace by having anonymous sex with male co-workers. The women, chosen at random, report to a room in which they undress from the waist down and stick their lower half through a hole in the wall and wait for a male co-worker (also summoned at random) to come in and have intercourse with her. These lightning rods "give people a way to get it out of their system" so that "they would be a whole lot more productive" and could "concentrate their energies on achieving their goals" and the goals of their company, who would not have to worry about the risk of sexual harassment lawsuits (24).

With Lightning Rods, Joe turns sexual assault in the workplace into a game show, with contestants chosen from the studio audience of cubicles and anonymous guilt-free sex as the prize. How does Joe arrive at such a bizarre idea? Like all million-dollar ideas, it came to him in a dream, a dream "about a game show with three contestants with their upper bodies sticking through a hole in the wall" and contestants asking them questions to guess which of the women was getting "penally challenged from behind" (11). From this vision, Joe conjures a sexual world full of satisfaction and free of the shame that he sees coming from intimacy. After all, how can anyone be ashamed by sex (or prosecuted for it) when the "penally challenged" woman does not even acknowledge—or even notice—that anything significant is happening? DeWitt demonstrates how the game show has found a way to deliver "the real thing"—massive wealth and material possessions—to people in reality without any effort or shame but rather jubilation. Further, *Lightning Rods* suggests that "the real thing" can be exported anywhere via the game show model because "the real thing" can be anything someone desires: a new car, a Caribbean cruise, or a roll in the hay. Meaning and intimacy can be removed from any activity, leaving only "the real thing" in its purest form, uncorrupted by emotion or knowledge.

This "real thing," of course, is a masturbatory fantasy transported to the real world. In "Fantasy and the Origins of Sexuality," Jean Laplance and Jean-Bertrand Pontalis show how autoeroticism comes from "the moment when sexuality, disengaged from any natural object, moves into the field of fantasy and by that very fact becomes sexuality" (334). The fantasy, they explain, "is not the object of desire, but its setting" (335). *Lightning Rods* illustrates how such autoerotic fantasies can move out of the realm of fantasy and enter the material world through a focus on setting. Much like the game-show set creates conditions that allow fantasies of wealth and success to enter the real world, Joe's autoerotic fantasy of women being unconsciously penetrated becomes flesh in the Lightning Rod system, practically merging the "object of desire," intimacy-free sex, with its "setting," an anonymous space in which such taboo behavior is permitted. Further, his scheme of having the women present only their lower half to the men in the office makes every effort to ensure that the men having intercourse with the lightning rods are as "disengaged from any natural object" as possible. The game show enables the leap for a masturbatory fantasy to be entertained in three-dimensional reality rather than in the two-dimensional space of one's mind or television set. Strangely, the game show proves to be a more logical jumping-off point than pornography for lightning rods because the game show already magically transposes consumerist fantasies into the real world by making contestants' dreams of becoming instantly rich come true by creating a real-life setting in which such fantasies can come true.

What becomes clear over the course of the novel is that Joe's invention actually sells ignorance. The only way to achieve intimacy-free sex is by ensuring that no one knows anything, to treat an intimate encounter almost as though it is not real. This ignorance, however, has unforeseen consequences: one kind of anonymous relationship casts a shadow of uncertainty over all human interaction. After all, "what do you say to someone if there is a one in five chance that you have had a close encounter of a ventro-dorsal nature through the wall of a disabled toilet?" (DeWitt 244). Complex lives and backstories are a liability to the lightning rod system because they lead to recognition, which leads to intimacy. In "getting it out of their system," the men in the novel spurn more intimate relationships, which reduces the women in the workplace to silent, anonymous objects, legs and vaginas without torsos, "a division of surfaces, a proliferation of multiple objects wherein its finitude, its desirable representation, its seduction are lost," the exact opposite of the women in Joe's fantasies (Baudrillard, *Ecstasy* 41). The system designed to protect people from sexual harassment instead normalizes objectification and abuse. Joe's game-show dream predicts this bug in his program when his quiz-show fantasy grows in complexity so much that he begins creating backstories for the contestants until they "would turn out to be ordinary people . . . only involved in a situation most ordinary people would not put themselves into" (DeWitt 16). Ironically, the more he imagines about these contestants as people rather than pieces of the game, the richer his fantasy becomes, yet the product he creates as a result of these fantasies actively dehumanizes everyone involved.

Thus, rather than "keep the atmosphere of the office from being poisoned" by sexual harassment, it has now been poisoned by an intimacy vacuum because now that men have limited all their sexual activity with women to an entirely depersonalizing affair, they suddenly lack the social skills for smooth sailing in a co-ed workplace, let alone intimacy (DeWitt 244). However, as so many of the works discussed in this round suggest, one does not need an invention like Lightning Rods to arrive at such a lack of intimacy. America is already well on our way, thanks to support from its sponsor, the game show.

CATEGORY

PARTING GIFTS

The finale of *Shock Treatment* presents Brad and Janet's expulsion from the studio as a victory over the image culture that DTV represents. As they are escorted out of the studio by the cops and the DTV hosts check into Denton-vale for treatment, Brad and Janet sing, "We're gonna do it / we just gotta keep going" (Cliff De Young). However, since the film does not show viewers a world outside the DTV studio, there is no indication that a non-televisual world exists for them to escape to, making their rebellion and the happy ending it represents the coldest of comforts. While most of these works admirably advocate an escape from the mediated world, they struggle as media objects themselves to imagine a way to represent the life they advocate. Whether they gleefully march off into the blinding light of day like Brad and Janet or discover their "truest and most recognizable self" after they are "sorted out" as ghosts like A in *YTCHABLM*, no work presents a picture of what true intimacy looks like in the modern world (Kleeman 266, 238).

Like Kleeman and DeWitt, Barthes identifies recognition as the key to intimacy by dismantling the biggest cliché about love there is. "Love is blind: the proverb is false," he writes (229). Rather than feed off blindness, the largest obstacle toward recognition, Barthes claims that "love opens his eyes wide, love produces clear-sightedness" (229). According to Barthes, this idea is the truth about intimacy: it is not about the final answer but rather the "lure" toward an answer that gives rise to love (230). Since the absolute truth about the loved one is forever out of reach, "it is not the truth which is true, but the relation to the lure which becomes true. To be in the truth, it is enough to persist: a 'lure' endlessly affirmed, against everything, becomes the truth" (230). The lure, then, reverses "ignorance into truth," and brings the lover to that "mystic impulse" in which "the other is not to be known [and] will remain so forever" (135). On a certain level, this "lure" of not ever being able to know another person and recognize them is tragic and makes love and intimacy seem impossible and loneliness all but guaranteed. Lovers, it would seem, are left with nothing but "aimless hunger"; however, on the other hand, the fact that there is always more to know, that the love object can continually reappear as a stranger, is a reason to continue a relationship. Within the lover's discourse, the lover is always seeking to recognize the loved one more, to know them on a more intimate level. The "lure" is not a decoy or an empty promise but rather the fullest promise imaginable: there are still more ways to recognize the loved one because there is always more to know.

Baudrillard too sees a way in which the embrace of the lure can lead to a greater and more authentic sense of intimacy in an image-based culture through "regain[ing] space for the secret" because, as Baudrillard asks in *The Ecstasy of Communication*, "what could be more seductive than the secret?" (55). Withholding information can lead to intimacy by inviting seduction. More importantly, however, "the secret challenges the order of production" and "the order of truth and knowledge" that initiated the ecstasy of communication (56). Baudrillard advocating for the secret reads as though he is calling for the abolition of the game show and its influence over human relationships: "there is nothing seductive about truth. Only the secret is seductive: the secret which circulates as the rule of the game, as an initiatory form, as a symbolic pact, which no code can resolve, no clue interpret" (56). As Gloria explains to Billy in *White Men Can't Jump*, intimacy does not come from solutions and answers but from questions, and Baudrillard agrees that "in seduction we rediscover the practice of this sharing and the intense pleasure which accompanies it" (56). Rather than looking to the game show or its sponsor, the market, to quench our thirst or satiate our "aimless hunger" through products, people can turn to each other to experience the "intense pleasure" of discussing what it means to be thirsty, sharing a secret between each other that disruptors like *Lightning Rods'* Joe cannot discover and monetize because "we will never cancel the secret" (Baudrillard, *Ecstasy* 56). By leaning on the game show and its true-or-false worldview, these works show how lovers "wear [them]selves out in materializing things, in rendering them visible" believing that doing so will generate greater intimacy by putting everything on display out in the open market (56).

This production-oriented mindset mistakes intimacy for a fixed state of being, a final answer, rather than what Barthes and Baudrillard see it as: a continual process, an endless becoming, a question that never finishes being posed: "Who are you and why do I love you so?"

Round Three

FAMILY FEUD

The Game-Show Families of Salinger, Wallace, and Anderson

DIANE F. ALTERS CALLS TELEVISION "THE MOST FAMILIAL of all media," and in *Prime-Time Families: Television Culture in Postwar America*, Ella Taylor agrees that television always speaks "the language of family in both its themes and forms": episodes frequently espouse traditional family values in predictably formulaic storylines that resolve themselves weekly in tidy half-hour chunks, as familiar and comfortable as the traditional family seen on television (Alters 55; Taylor 65). Television's appearance in many Americans' homes overlaps with the time period when the nuclear family enjoyed its largest influence on postwar American life. These concurrent events resulted in massive numbers of people viewing tremendous amounts of programming that depicted the nuclear family as the ultimate expression of American happiness and prosperity. In presenting a particular vision of the American family in a space where American families frequently gathered, television and the nuclear family effectively served as commercials for each other, broadcasting a redefined American Dream as a utopia available to anyone with a television set and a family in their living room (Taylor 40).

However, the "pervasive and resistant" "familial ideology" of the so-called "traditional nuclear family" often associated with the postwar baby boom and early television culture is not as "traditional" as this ideology claims (Carter 187). In actuality, the nuclear family is an "aberrant form of family life" historically, with the 1940s and 1950s acting less as a culmination of family values and domestic harmony than "a last-gasp orgy of modern nuclear family domesticity" before social and economic changes made the nuclear family both more difficult and less desirable to attain (Stacey 10). As Judith Stacey has shown, families have become more "diverse, fluid, and unresolved," much like everything else in postmodern society. The notion of "a single culturally dominant family pattern to which the majority of Americans conform and most of the rest aspire" ignores the "multiplicity of family and household arrangements" that "reconstitute frequently in response to changing personal and occupational circumstances" (17). Nevertheless, this "last gasp" quickly became established as the norm even though it more closely resembles a "fairy tale" that is "utterly unrepresentative of family life for most Americans" (Palmer 165).

Even as culture becomes more aware and accepting of other types of living arrangements, the traditional nuclear family's status as the "norm" persists thanks in large part to its ubiquitous presence on television, where viewers young and old were "inundated" by programs such as *Father Knows Best* that exalted the heteronormative nuclear family as the ideal marriage of tradition and modernity (Stacey 10; Taylor 27). Olaf Hoerschelmann argues cable game shows perpetuated this ideology well into the 1980s and 1990s, touting "the centrality of the family" to healthy, normal American life (119). Even without explicitly espousing a pro-family agenda, shows such as *Family Feud*, *Shop 'Til You Drop*, *Family Challenge*, and *Family Double Dare* promote the traditional nuclear family simply by refusing to feature contestants with any other family living arrangement (120). Presenting husband-wife or heterosexual family teams validates "the moral authority of the discourse of family" and normalizes "the primacy of family values" in American culture (121). On game shows ranging from *Family Feud* to *Extreme Makeover: Home Edition*, families receive large prizes for reifying the myth of the nuclear family. Often the prizes are intended to help that family become more traditional. After all, the goal on *Family Feud* is for a family to match the most people surveyed, rewarding the family that conforms with "average Americans" and punishing less popular answers as wrong, "abnormal," or deviant (115). The format of a game that showers dollars on families for being just like everyone else implies that living as part of a traditional family holds the path to all-American averageness and wealth.

In her book *Succeeding Postmodernism: Language and Humanism in Contemporary Literature*, Mary K. Holland examines how writers such as David Foster Wallace and Mark Danielewski seek to rescue family and language from "the destructiveness of unconscious mediation" brought on by television's incursion into the American home (92, 58). Writing about Wallace's novel *Infinite Jest*, Holland posits the novel's power derives from dramatizing not merely "the destruction of the family by our culture of narcissism" but how the effects of "family destruction reverberate far beyond the family unit" (83). Television infiltrates the home by becoming its electronic hearth; its presence in the home places families "at the mercy of the nihilism of forces of mediation and simulation" and makes the home no longer a symbol of escape from hypermediated culture but an extension of it (92, 96). Television usurps the family's authority in the home to the extent that "whatever [television] transmits disappears in the shadow of the authoritative fact of its transmission" (58). While Holland's book focuses on postmodern literary works such as *Infinite Jest* and Danielewski's novel *House of Leaves*, her analysis has broader applications to other contemporary works of literature and film that dramatize the effect of media on the postmodern family. J. D. Salinger, David Foster Wallace, and Paul Thomas Anderson extend Holland's arguments by creating intermedial texts involving families on game shows to demonstrate the degree to which televisual bonds have infected and superseded interpersonal, familial ones. The game show may pass itself off "as an esoteric intellectual game" in the popular imagination, but in these works it functions much in the same way as Holland sees the home in *House of Leaves*: "as a battleground," "an embodiment of those threats that bring the dangers of the crisis of signification to bear upon the vulnerable members of the family" (102, 99). What should be the most stable, dependable relationship in an increasingly disconnected and virtual broadcast world becomes the most fraught relationship of all in Salinger's 1961 novella *Zooey*, Wallace's 1989 story "Little Expressionless Animals," and Anderson's 1999 film *Magnolia*. These texts merge the impersonal realm of the game show with the intimate realm of the family to show that the true casualties of a media-saturated culture are the bonds that connect people to each other. To represent these damaged bonds, the authors create works about children left by their parents to fend for themselves in the televisual wild.

In emphasizing the need for connection as fervently as they critique the menaces of television, Salinger, Wallace, and Anderson make their audiences "face the problem of the contemporary family as central and fundamental . . . something that we cannot afford to ignore" (Holland 83). To illustrate the intersection between television and "the problem of the contemporary family," Salinger, Wallace, and Anderson go beyond using the game show as a narrative device and create familial relationships among the game show producers and contestants in the stories, transforming all conflicts over the game show into family conflicts and vice-versa. *Zooey* is where readers learn that all seven of Salinger's Glass children—Seymour, Buddy, Boo Boo, Walter, Waker, Zooey, and Franny—appeared as a "dynastic arrangement" of contestants on the radio quiz show *It's a Wise Child* from 1927 to 1943 (*Zooey* 53). The family tree in Wallace's "Little Expressionless Animals" more or less turns in on itself as the Goddard and Smith families intersect on both sides of the *Jeopardy!* set, which itself is part of Merv Griffin's extended family of shows and hosts, including Alex Trebek, Pat Sajak, Bert Convy, and paterfamilias Griffin himself. Finally, the families of Earl Partridge and Jimmy Gator, producer and host, respectively, of *What Do Kids Know?* form the hub from which all of *Magnolia*'s intersecting stories radiate.

Heading each of these families is a father figure whose "narcissistic parental cruelty" is enabled by television (Holland 69). Les Glass, patriarch of Salinger's Glass family, cannot interact with his children apart from watching them on television, and the influence of eldest, wisest child Seymour hovers over his siblings long after his death. In "Little Expressionless Animals," Merv Griffin stage-manages the relationships and fortunes of his employees and contestants, many of them abandoned, neglected daughters. Anderson features two fathers whose identities are thoroughly integrated with television game shows and who are also succumbing to cancer.

Cancer becomes a guiding metaphor for television in these works as a force within the body of the home that slowly consumes its host. These authors perceive the global village of television as a familial network of lonely people searching for warmth and connection that the electronic hearth cannot provide. Thus, the connection and dysfunction of the families that populate these texts stand in for the same need to connect between people in the world, whether they are related to each other or not. By making familial conflicts part of the inner-workings of the quiz show, the distinction between the family and the "global village" of broadcast media dissolves, allowing audiences to see how artificial the distinction is in contemporary society.

While the connection among these three works may appear to be "only a matter of chance" like the groupings of texts that comprise the other rounds in this book, their relationship goes beyond that of the coincidental or anecdotal. Salinger, particularly his Glass Family Saga, is an acknowledged, if underexplored, influence on the family dramas of David Foster Wallace, and Paul Thomas Anderson acknowledged in a 2015 interview with Marc Maron that he is not only a fan of Wallace's but that he was also briefly his student at Emerson College in the early 1990s. Further, Anderson's early work features the cinematic equivalent of Wallace's self-aware linguistic pyrotechnics and big-hearted empathy for freaks, addicts, and hideous men. More than being merely similar as a result of sharing a setting and subject matter, these authors comprise a continuum of artists who focus on how one can remain connected and human in an increasingly mediated, dehumanized world. Each work responds to its predecessor, and each exploits the disingenuous format of the game show to make earnest assertions about everyone's similarities as wounded humans. While a game show set may be the last place one would expect to find such artists preoccupied with authenticity, these works follow Holland's reading of *House of Leaves* and achieve "reconciliation and personal growth" through engaging with the "mediation and simulation that defines" the televisual era (98). Through the game show, they attack television's authenticity and demonstrate how mass media products can, under earnest circumstances, lead toward genuine connection between performers and their audience. Where one might expect them to find nothing in game shows but insincere grins and cheesy puns, they instead affirm their commitment to radical authenticity by finding moments of compassion and transcendence in the emptiest of places.

These authors, entranced by broadcast media's power, remain skeptical of its motives. Their repeated demonstrations of the power of television to connect people to each other makes clear that television is not the disease their works are helping to cure but rather a force that reveals "our larger cultural problems" of being cut off from each other in a world whose rapidly expanding media landscape continually makes the empty promise of bringing people together (Holland 83). These works come to adopt an ambivalence about mass media that regards it as a catalyst for connection, but not as connection itself, each critiquing its failure to function as a cure for loneliness. The works create a hierarchy of knowledge, using a quiz-show genius to expose the gulf between true wisdom and what mass media regards as "wise." By challenging the authority of both the father and mass media, the works show the potential for a new order or community. Exposing the limits of broadcasting's ability to connect people allows each author to further his project of "redeeming" fiction and cinema, respectively, as superior tools for empathy and connection (Holland 92). Broadcast media fails at its own promise in these works because it can only hint at satisfying the viewer's need for community, and the characters cannot free themselves from its grasp until they challenge broadcasting's authority. This intermedial conflict creates a stark distinction between broadcast space and literary/cinematic space, with the most honest moments of connection happening outside of the broadcast sphere and its representative capabilities.

Holland unpacks the intermedial strategies in Danielewski's novel *House of Leaves* to argue that the intermedial approach, or what she calls remediation, provides authors with a path to "redefine human agency, emotion, and connection" (102). The works in this round show through their intermediality how, as Holland writes of *House of Leaves*, a full understanding of the culture cannot be represented through "single acts of mediation" such as a television program. Rather, it is "the very self-consciousness of the multiple layers of mediation [that] allow[s] meaning and earnestness to emerge unspoiled by the taint of invisible manipulation" (109). This "multiple remediation," as Holland calls it, fosters connections between people and initiates a process of "recuperation" for the notion of family (109). In creating a network of texts that cultivate strong relationships between audience and text, the authors "create an escape route" from hypermediated culture that does not require a retreat from the modern world but rather a newer, more sincere kind of immersion in it through forming intimate networks to counteract the carcinogenic influence of traditional media (119). While these works may not necessarily "denaturalize[e] the cultural dynamics of familial ideology," they do call for "a new *ethical pluralism*" and "creat[e] spaces from which to challenge the ideological purchase of contemporary media representations of 'the family'" by depicting the cancerous effect television's game-show logic has on the ability to imagine new relationships (Carter 197, 187, 197).

Somewhat counterintuitively, the intricacies of the narratives encourage their audiences to connect, to make sense of the plot of the stories by connecting the dots of the dense familial relationships. The stories repeatedly call attention to windows, doors, barriers, and screens to show the ways in which mass media permeates every aspect of modern life, forming borders between lonely, disconnected people. However, within this fractured world, the family dynamics create a "semantic geometry" of plot and character that emphasizes points of intersection, alleging that everything is, in fact, connected, even in the alienated modern world they present (Salinger 49). These seemingly disconnected lines converge in the world of the game show as characters engage in familial conflicts that represent in miniature a larger conflict with mediated culture and the relationships it produces. The overwhelming intricacies of the plots and family relationships of each story stand in for the endless amounts of apparently meaningless and unrelated data that keeps people separated from each other in a confusing and uncertain "networked infotainment society." As masters of trivia, the genius quiz-kids of these stories manage to blur these boundaries created by mass media, and in bridging these gaps, they challenge the authority of mass media and the parental figures who thrust them into the world of the game show to establish new networks of relationships that repair the bonds severed by televisual networks. The process of connecting the narrative dots ends with the audience seeing how the solution to modern alienation lies in being connected to others and dissolving the borders that isolates individuals from each other, starting with the artificial but damaging boundaries created by the mass media, boundaries that the authors show to be mere representations of the rifts within families. Further, this work the audience does invites them to adopt Alison Alexander's and Judith Stacey's views of the contemporary family "as a system" or "part of a network" of "meaning and relationships" capable of battling the cancer represented by hypermediation (Alexander 280; Stacey 6). Through the magic of broadcasting and its merger of the sacred and the profane—family and television, art and commerce, religious epiphany and pointless trivia—the works destroy boundaries from within to present the holiness of the connection between other people.

* * *

CATEGORY

CHILDREN OF A LESSER GOD

In *Radio Days*, Joe's family runs into one of the "whiz kids" from a popular radio show during a visit to the zoo. They approach the boy (Marc Colner) and his well dressed family hoping to bask in the glow of his precocity, only to encounter an insufferably snobbish, verbose jerk who can barely deign to make conversation without lodging veiled insults at their lack of sophistication. Joe's family regards the whiz kid with a mixture of awe and contempt as though he were one of the animals in the zoo. As he walks away, Joe's father (Michael Tucker) smacks Joe, shouting, "Why can't you be a genius?"

This scene may not qualify as Allen's homage to the short stories of J. D. Salinger (Allen is usually more overt in his allusions), but the similar time periods and the erudite, contemptuous air of the whiz kid approximates what encountering a member of Salinger's Glass Family would most likely be like. Gifted and neurotic, the Glasses, like most of Salinger's protagonists, frequently disdain the world for failing to meet their high standards. Their backstory of appearing on *It's a Wise Child* may appear to be trivial; however, Salinger's novella *Zooey* demonstrates how this factoid becomes an incredibly meaningful piece of data when it comes to understanding both their conflicted family dynamic and Salinger's religious parables.

First and foremost, the Glasses, like the whiz kid in *Radio Days*, are radio personalities, and *Zooey* initially appears to place all the blame for the Glass family's problems on broadcast media. Radio and television do, after all, define their lives. They spent their childhoods "answer[ing] over the air a prodigious number of alternately deadly bookish and deadly cute questions . . . with a freshness, an aplomb, that was considered unique in commercial radio" (53). The Glass children identify themselves through the show so thoroughly that Zooey even names their flaws after it. He tells Franny "we've got 'Wise Child' complexes. We've never really got off the goddam air. Not one of us. We don't talk, we hold forth. We don't converse, we expound" (140). Zooey spends most of this novella "hold[ing] forth" and "expound[ing]," first to his mother while he takes a bath, then to Franny, and much of the scholarship devoted to the novella questions how much it turns not only its protagonist but also its author into "The Prince of Bores" (140). Regardless of whether the character or its author notices the irony of Zooey's statements, its sentiment strikes at the core of the family's dysfunction. Wise children, or more accurately, precocious children, are the plague on the Glass House. Even though Zooey names the family's condition after the radio game show, he claims their problem is not a media problem but a family problem. He tells Franny "you're way off when you start railing at *things* and people instead of at yourself." Television is not to blame, "It's *us*," he says. "We're freaks, that's all. Those two bastards got us nice and early and made us into freaks with freakish standards, that's all. We're the Tattooed Lady, and we're never going to have a minute's peace, the rest of our lives, till everybody else is tattooed too" (139). "Those two bastards" are Seymour and Buddy, the "dead ghost" and the "half-dead ghost" who took it on themselves to host "home seminars" and "metaphysical sittings" educating their youngest siblings on Eastern religions and philosophy with the goal of turning them into "wise" children (103, 66). The tutelage of Seymour and Buddy, the first wise children, binds the Glass siblings together in a legacy of dysfunction and trauma. Salinger's decision to diagnose the family with the "Wise Child" complex presents the game show and the Glass family's "dynastic arrangement" on it as a public representation of a private family drama. The Glasses have been torn apart by their own precocious genius, and, in some ways, by one particular precocious genius: Seymour.

As in every other story in the Glass Family Saga, all lines of insight and conflict point back to the eldest child, Seymour, whose suicide, captured in "A Perfect Day for Bananafish," both shatters and defines the connection among his surviving siblings: his death deprives them of his enlightened insights and intensifies his influence over them. Buddy, Zooey, and Franny preoccupy themselves with preserving Seymour's legacy as a guru too good for this world even as doing so limits their own pursuits of self-expression and enlightenment. This conflict comes to a head in the stories that comprise *Franny and Zooey*. These stories nominally concern the weekend when Zooey pulls college-aged Franny from the precipice of a nervous breakdown; however, they also involve the first—and strongest—moment in which the broken family confronts and critiques the wounds left by Salinger's ultimate wise child. Although the resolution may wind up cementing Seymour's posthumous authority over the family, the story's critique of him, despite Salinger's obvious adoration of him, lingers nevertheless and demonstrates to readers the possibilities for connection when one abandons the self and uses the tools of mass media to restore others.

Zooey begins at the pinnacle of the Glasses' disconnection from each other. Arthur Schwartz identifies disconnection as the signature problem of the Glasses throughout Salinger's stories, caused by their inability to communicate with each other directly (95). For the voluminous amounts of talking in the novella, little of it occurs via face-to-face communication, and even though Zooey seldom has a moment to himself, he remains isolated from everyone via a series of barriers he employs to separate himself from his family. He spends nearly half the novella in the bathtub behind a shower curtain mercilessly mocking his mother, and his second, more significant conversation with Franny occurs over the telephone despite being in the same apartment as she. Similarly, Les Glass, Zooey's father, "lives entirely in the past," listening to the radio expecting to hear his children, especially the deceased Seymour and Walter, on *It's a Wise Child* (83). His only engagement with the present comes in the form of watching Zooey on television. These details suggest Les cannot recognize or interact with his children outside of their mediated personas. Because the Glasses have difficulty engaging with the real world, their only familial interaction comes through mediated forms like letters, phones, televisions, and radios (Schwartz 95). Broadcast media beams the Glasses into the homes of thousands, but it keeps them separated in their home.

Salinger implies that *It's a Wise Child* and all public displays of knowledge represent the opposite of true wisdom. Franny broadens Zooey's critique of game shows to dismiss knowledge in general as "piling up treasure on earth": "Sometimes I think that *knowl*edge—when it's knowledge for knowledge's sake, anyway—is the worst of all. The least excusable, certainly." "Knowledge *should* lead to *wisdom*," she says. "If it *doesn't*, it's just a disgusting waste of time!" (146). Implicit in Franny's critique are Seymour and Buddy, who, above everyone else, are responsible for filling Zooey and her with the false wisdom that has disconnected them from the world and made them into freak geniuses who elicit only contempt and pity from the audience. For Salinger, true wisdom lies not in the accumulation of random bits of trivia but in the connection between people. Salinger achieves this connection, oddly enough, not through Seymour's brand of rigorous religious instruction but through acting for a mass audience.

The road to enlightenment in *Zooey* is acting, or, more specifically, an approach to acting in which the performer connects with a mass audience through the selflessness of their performance. A veneration of acting is a rather surprising discovery in Salinger's authenticity-obsessed *oeuvre*, but here Salinger posits acting need not represent the height of phoniness as it does in *The Catcher in the Rye*; it can instead signify the pinnacle of selflessness, provided that the performer focuses their performance fully on the audience's needs. In Zooey's speech to Franny at the end of the story, he encourages her to act because, he claims, "the only religious thing you can do is *act*" (198). Zooey determines that Franny's "Wise Child" complex moves her to feel nothing but contempt for everyone around her and pushes her toward her breakdown, but Franny's disgust with the inauthenticity of others is, according to Zooey, "none of [her] business" (199). She should perform nonetheless. Myles Weber reads this urging toward performance as one of the cornerstones of Salinger's work. Where it would seem like a true artist must turn away from mass media in order to preserve their artistic integrity, as Salinger seems to have done in real life, Weber shows how Salinger uses Zooey's Parable of the Fat Lady to assert that "the artist owes it to the public to create and share that creation with a mass audience" (132).

The Parable of the Fat Lady is certainly the most famous section of the novella. In it, Zooey tells Franny about the time he refused to shine his shoes before one of his early appearances on *It's a Wise Child* because he was convinced that "the studio audience were all morons, the announcer was a moron, the sponsors were morons, and [he] just damn well wasn't going to shine [his] shoes for them." Seymour responded by telling him to "shine them for the Fat Lady" (200). This imaginary Fat Lady becomes a real person in Zooey's mind, and he shines his shoes for her during his entire run on *It's a Wise Child*. "I don't care where an actor acts," Zooey tells Franny, "*There isn't anyone out there who isn't Seymour's Fat Lady*" (201).

Acting and religious insight hinge on the performer's relationship to the audience in the parable: if the performer holds the audience in contempt and dismisses them based on what they respond to or fail to respond to properly, then the actor is headed straight for a breakdown like Franny's. However, Zooey suggests, if the actor goes out and dedicates their performance to an audience member who represents abjection, then they will arrive at the mystical epiphany that the Fat Lady is not only everyone but "Christ Himself" (202). The selfless performer both overcomes their contempt for others and makes a genuine connection with each audience member as a result. Distilling the vast audience of a radio broadcast into one person not only intensifies the sense of intimate, personal, one-to-one connection, but it also illustrates the central message of the Parable of the Fat Lady and Salinger's body of work: it dissolves all mediated distinctions and boundaries between people, collapsing everything into an ecstatic unity that brings everyone closer to God.

Readers can see the positive effects Salinger's parable promises within Franny and Zooey's conversation itself. Franny becomes Zooey's Fat Lady, the person Zooey performs for despite his many objections, and the story implies that Franny's peace at the end of this intimate performance equates to the ecstatic contentment that Seymour's Fat Lady will experience. Zooey spends much of the novella refusing to help Franny; his attempts at reaching her via face-to-face communication fail as he grows increasingly impatient and abusive. When he finally does reach out to her meaningfully, he does so through several layers of impersonation and mediation: he calls her on Seymour's telephone line and pretends to be Buddy checking up on her. This transcendence of the story's climax would not be possible without performance: Zooey's final breakthrough on the telephone to Franny comes as a result of his impersonation of Buddy. Performance and impersonation are central to the Glass family not only because they are entertainers (and the children of vaudevillians), but, as Salinger reveals in "Raise High the Roof Beam, Carpenters," all of the children "appeared on the show under pseudonyms" (7). Their selves disappear from the start of their careers in showbusiness, permitting them to focus more attention on their audience, who comes to be personified by Seymour's Fat Lady. Buddy defends Seymour against a charge of exhibitionism in "Raise High the Room Beam, Carpenters," claiming that Seymour "went down to that broadcast every Wednesday night as though he were going to his own funeral" (59). The comparison here between performance and death is crucial. Seymour's performance is a type of funeral because the performer's self must die in order for them to truly connect with the Fat Lady. Salinger's brand of performance becomes an act of martyrdom rather than exhibitionism, where the performer dissolves one boundary, the self, in order to escape solipsism and connect with their audience.

Zooey reaches Franny by allowing himself to disappear. Their connection becomes intimate because Zooey and his needs disappear and he becomes entirely focused on helping Franny, which he seems unable to do without the distancing device of the telephone. Furthermore, Franny takes the call from their parents' bedroom, which potentially shows how Zooey may also be working toward a transcendence of his own. Salinger's decision to make the imaginary audience member the Fat Lady may be as simple as trying to create an image of abjection, but she may also be an avatar for a specific Fat Lady, Bessie Glass, whom Zooey repeatedly calls "Fatty" in their conversation. By taking on roles and forgetting themselves through all the conversations and performance, both Zooey and Franny appear to overcome the burden of both their quiz-show legacy and the overbearing influence of their brothers and achieve something close to religious insight that has the potential to dissolve the biggest boundary of all, the boundaries between the members of the Glass Family.

Rather than demonize broadcast media as an entity that generates trauma, Salinger goes so far as to suggest that mass media can provide people with a way out of trauma. The Parable of the Fat Lady demonstrates Salinger's main project, according to Ihab Hassan: "The movement of love or holiness in everyday life"; and in this story Salinger shows how this movement can be accelerated through broadcasting (19). The selfless actor becomes a "professional ecstatic" who shows "that the sacred and the profane are always interfused," and their voice is "merely the voice of steadfast love struggling with the locutions of art—the sacred and the profane intermingling—and making itself audible in new ways" (19–20). This description resembles Seymour's characterization of the end result of religious study: according to Buddy, Seymour asserted that "all legitimate religious study *must* lead to unlearning the differences, the illusory differences, between boys and girls, animals and stones, day and night, heat and cold" (Salinger, *Zooey* 67–68). Seymour's philosophy is that all religious pursuits seek to tear down barriers and boundaries, to connect and unify everything as One. The detail that his revelation takes place on "a crosstown bus" only furthers the notion of bridging gaps between separate things (67). Such unity is essentially the message of the Parable of the Fat Lady: despite the fact that the Glass children may not want to go on the radio and perform, they must overcome their own selfishness and do it for the Fat Lady, and when they do, they discover everyone is connected, leaving no division between Self and Other. This blurring of boundaries brings heaven and earth together and is facilitated here by something as crass and inauthentic as *It's a Wise Child*. Salinger posits that if something as vacuous and inauthentic as a radio quiz show can foster true connection, then connection is possible anywhere: it is not the medium that keeps people apart; it is rather themselves.

Ihab Hassan views the ending of the novella as a triumph, a true defiance of Seymour in which "Zooey *succeeds* in clarifying Franny's spiritual dilemma in the absence of both Buddy and Seymour. He succeeds in calling her back to things of this world, the profession of acting, just as Buddy, in his inchoate manner, had tried to advise Zooey in his own acting career." Thanks to Zooey, Hasan claims Franny, "the youngest of the Glass children has at last achieved a measure of independence from the guru of the house" (12). While Zooey may achieve this independence without Seymour and Buddy, he does everything he can to make them present for Franny: he calls her from Seymour and Buddy's room in the Glass apartment on Seymour's phone line which is kept operational by Buddy, whom Zooey impersonates in order to keep Franny talking. Hassan views these layers of impersonation as "a parody of the older brothers, and therefore both an appeal to their authority and a way of undermining it" (13). Although it is accurate that Zooey does not succeed in getting through to Franny on this phone call until she unmasks him, the Parable, the ultimate insight that leads Franny away from a nervous breakdown and toward her epiphany is not Zooey's story but Seymour's. In fact, Seymour had already told Franny a version of the parable when he told her "to be funny for the Fat Lady" before she appeared on *It's a Wise Child* (Salinger, *Zooey* 201). However, Zooey, not Seymour, adds a crucial addendum to the Parable of the Fat Lady: "*There isn't anyone out there who isn't Seymour's Fat Lady. . . . don't you know who that Fat Lady really is? . . .* Ah, buddy. Ah, buddy. It's Christ Himself. Christ Himself, buddy" (201–2). One should not underestimate the importance of Zooey's addition because it escalates the story from one about other-directedness and compassion to one about religious transcendence, and Franny's epiphany does not occur until after Zooey makes this revelation.

However, even Zooey's addition has the fingerprints of his brothers all over it. He does not exactly deny Seymour's authority as attempt to take his place as the spiritual adviser to the family, which does not involve any renouncing of Seymour's teachings but rather continues them. Zooey's implied insistence to Buddy that the episode with Franny constitutes "mysticism, or religious mystification" only further supports this view (Salinger 48). Further, the repetition of "buddy" can hardly be seen as accidental: it places his other brother, who just so happens to be narrating this "prose home movie" after interviewing each character in "somewhat harrowingly private sittings," firmly at the scene of this revelation (47, 49). As if that were not enough, Zooey reveals that he heard this story from Seymour when he "subbed for Walt" on *It's a Wise Child* (another layer of impersonation), associating all but two of the seven Glass siblings with the scene (200). Each of these details undermines any claims to Zooey's newfound authority and independence from his older brothers. At the very moment that Zooey appears to be breaking away from the damaging influence of his older brothers and passing along new and insightful wisdom to his suffering sister, he passes along acting advice he received from Buddy and by embellishing a story he heard from Seymour in a way that subtly acknowledges the influence (and authorial presence) of Buddy. So while it does seem like Zooey wins the battle against the influence of his older brothers and tormenters through impersonating them, the war is less decisively in his and Franny's favor because all insights, epiphanies, and revelations bear Seymour's signature. Seymour's authority reigns supreme in the Glass House. Even when he is not present to preach to and instruct his siblings, his message lives on in them, even when they are trying to defy him.

Qualified as this victory may be, Salinger's suggestion that such connection and transcendence in broadcasting seems possible, at least for the genius performer, remains. Seymour's and Zooey's Fat Lady parable make these performances acts of charity that can lead the performer to enlightenment and a sense of being connected to everyone, thus creating a true state of total knowledge and awareness that the quiz show is but a pale facsimile of. As Franny drifts off to sleep after the phone call from Zooey-as-Buddy-as-Seymour, she becomes entranced by the "Om" of the dial tone and drifts off to sleep as a truly wise child. Her enlightenment only results from Zooey's challenge to the authority of his intellectual parents and the game show they both appeared on, an authority that Salinger shows to be one in the same.

CATEGORY

THE GREAT CONVEXITY

It seems as though there are no boundaries between show and family, television and reality in David Foster Wallace's story "Little Expressionless Animals." If anything, Wallace's story suffers from overconnection: half the work of one's first few readings of the story involves delineating the various family trees that dot the story's landscape. There is the Smith Family, consisting of *Jeopardy!* contestants Julie and Lunt; the Goddard Family, comprised of Faye, the researcher, Dee, her mother and the show's producer, and Janet, the director of the show and Faye's ex-stepfather's wife; and then there is the Merv Griffin family, which most prominently features the patriarch himself and the family of hosts Alex Trebek and Pat Sajak.

Paul Giles views Wallace's project in "Little Expressionless Animals" as offering "human perspectives to subvert a culture of corporate images in which the legends of TV advertising have become naturalized" (331). By placing a family at the heart of the game-show culture, Wallace demonstrates the extent to which this "naturalization" has taken over contemporary culture: television aesthetics and rhythms become the natural state of being, nurturing people in its cathode-ray glow. The game show itself is now the family drama because there is no world outside the screen. What was once "a haven from culture" becomes ground zero for promoting that culture; the parent, the figure once charged with protecting a child from the threats of the outside world, now invites the threat into the home (Holland 96). While Wallace's critiques of television are by now so well known as to be synonymous with his name and image, looking more closely at "Little Expressionless Animals" in dialogue with Salinger's *Zooey* and Anderson's *Magnolia* reveals that his attack in "Little Expressionless Animals" may have a larger target than the television industry. Holland aptly describes how Wallace's fiction, particularly *Infinite Jest*, "forces us to face the problem of the contemporary family as central and fundamental" to "our larger cultural problems" (83). By creating a story in which televisual drama and family drama blur together, Wallace merges his critique of television with his diagnosis of "the broken contemporary family" (Holland 83). In "Little Expressionless Animals,"

America's broader societal problems are familial in nature, and culture's most tightly knit connection, the family, may be getting dissolved by one of the its least intimate creations, the game show, which in this story serves as the hearth that the families gather around only to have their bonds blurred beyond comprehension, erased before they can be fully formed.

Holland notes that Wallace's critique of television-as-babysitter borrows from Christopher Lasch, whose work *A Culture of Narcissism* decries television's ascendancy to a position in which it has "replace[d] traditional paternal authorities, creating disaffected mothers and fathers as a consequence" (66). As with many narratives critical of television, the first two scenes of the story depict spectation as a condition brought on by abuse and neglect. The first displays how Julie and Lunt Smith's gift for trivia has roots in trauma: their mother abandons them beside a cow pasture with little more than a copy of *LaPlace's Data Guide*. They absorb enormous amounts of data in *LaPlace's Data Guide* to compensate for the knowledge their mother deprives them of a family, of why they were abandoned, of how to live in the world. Wallace connects media and trauma to the Goddard family in the second scene. Dee Goddard remains inert, expressionless, and silent in a movie theater while a man sitting behind her fondles her red hair because she does not want Faye to be disturbed by what is happening. By reducing abused characters to mute, disconnected spectators in this opening, Wallace shows how characters use spectation to retreat inside themselves in an effort to escape from trauma. This coping mechanism comes to define their interaction as they become expressionless spectators unable to interact with the real world.

Marshall Boswell has adroitly demonstrated how "Little Expressionless Animals" concerns itself with "the fluidity of boundaries": nearly every scene in the story features characters viewing something through some kind of transparent barrier, be it a window, a screen, or a doorway (70). Almost no one views an event directly or sequentially; reality is so thoroughly filtered and mediated that the world of the story does not need cameras or televisions in order to feel framed for our viewing pleasure. David Hering sees every setting in the story as "characterized by glass," and Carlton Smith and Deborah Paes de Barros remark that "Julie's house is merely an uninhabited high-tech TV show set," all emphasizing how even the off-camera world of the story feels like a mediated space one watches rather than interacts with (Hering 93; Smith and Barros 6). The television show and its production appear to be the most fluid sites of all because Wallace blurs the lines between what is on- or off-camera, inside or outside the set (both the *Jeopardy!* set and the television set itself). Boswell notes how these blurred boundaries extend far beyond the confines of the story's events to "complicate the traditional boundary between phenomenal reality and the mediated world of television or language" (Boswell 71). Wallace's choice of *Jeopardy!* as his quiz show opens these porous borders even more because its very format inverts convention: the show's "questions" are actually answers, to which the contestant "answers" with a question (Boswell 71). The one space seemingly free of boundaries is the nude beach where Julie and Faye talk about love and waves. Released from the borders of clothing, Julie and Faye can interact freely in open, unmediated space; however, Faye and Julie spend their time on the sand looking at and talking about the ocean, essentially on the border between land and sea, which does not make this space as different from the framed media landscape as it would first seem. Clare Hayes-Brady reads this scene as illustrative of "another kind of solipsism" in which love constitutes a kind of reflection that emphasizes the space between the lovers instead of their connection to each other (183). This world where even the beach becomes a potential space of inverted reflections showcases "the worst excesses of narcissism and entrapment," leaving readers uncertain whether such a thing as outside exists anymore (Hering 79).

The only true boundary that seems to exist is the boundary between people who are part of the Merv Griffin Family and the people who are not. There are no characters in the story who do not wind up involved in the production of a Merv Griffin show. Of all the families that intersect in the story, the only parent with authority and control is Merv Griffin, whose power is so absolute that he not only makes the rules of the world but can throw them "out the window" whenever he pleases, no matter how such an action may affect his "children" (Wallace, "LEA" 25). Merv Griffin's manic dream of Julie's appearance on the show, of "the mystery of total data" creating "a sort of antic, ontic self-perpetuation" of "fact sustaining feeling," seeks to preserve the world of the game show, and Julie's "oneness with the board's data," indefinitely (28). Griffin, unlike Salinger or Wallace, fails to see the influence of the quiz-show genius outside of the show because his vision does not go beyond the dimensions of the set. All of Griffin's employees suffer the same delusion. Dee Goddard smugly tells Muffy du Mont that she works behind the scenes in the television industry to ensure that she will never be "inside the set"; however, the *Jeopardy!* world itself is so insular that no one in Dee's life, or the life of anyone else on the staff, is not involved in the show. They are so completely "inside" the set that there is seemingly no need to actually watch television. The only person who seems to watch television is Dee, who talks back to the set, answering all the questions the commercials ask her as though the people on television are in the room, or, more frighteningly, as though Dee herself is inside the set in a state of "oneness" with television. Wallace underscores just how inside the set Dee and the other members of the *Jeopardy* staff are by having Julie and Faye watch Dee converse with the television on a monitor inside Julie's office. The way that the Merv Griffin family avoids ever getting outside the set is by bringing everyone they encounter onto the show. Thus, according to Boswell, for all the fluidity of boundaries, one boundary seems impermeable: the boundary between "the real" and "the game" (72). For Boswell, "'fluidity' occurs *only* within the story, which is irrevocably cut off from the real world. . . . the story paradoxically proposes that fluidity in order to prove the impossibility of *actually* breaking through" (72). Hari Kunzru agrees with Boswell, viewing the story as being about "the difficulty, the near impossibility . . . of interpersonal connection" (98). Without the ability to break out of the television landscape, or the story itself, the world of "Little Expressionless Animals" becomes a closed loop, the televisual equivalent of incest. No one gets outside the screen.

Kunzru's reading, with its emphasis on "near impossibility," is slightly more optimistic than Boswell's conclusion of absolute impossibility or Hayes-Brady's reading of Julie's love of Faye as being solipsistic. However, these readings do not linger over the moments in the story where Wallace gestures toward a solution and shows readers where they can succeed even though his characters fail. David Hering reads "Little Expressionless Animals" as an early attempt by Wallace to formulate "an 'ethics of watching'" in which spectation becomes, much like in *Zooey*, "a communicative, dialogic gesture" between performer and audience, "text and reader" (87). Readers, unlike the characters (or television viewers), have the privileged position of seeing both sides of the window: readers look through the control room onto the *Jeopardy!* set, from Julie's apartment out onto the city of Los Angeles, and from the world of the story out into their own. On one level, this positioning means that readers continually view each moment of the story through a screen of mediation; however, taken another way, Wallace puts the readers in the control room and gives them the ability to see the manipulation and limitations of a heavily mediated world and to resist succumbing to its influence. The windows, screens, and lenses in Wallace's story stand in for the invisible walls and masks people put between each other in the real world, and by identifying them as such, readers can "avoid the delusion of imagining the screen as mirror or as reality" (Hering 96). To paraphrase Zooey Glass, in Wallace's story, the problem again is not the game show: it is us. While Holland has noted that Wallace's fiction "does not imagine for its characters a way to eschew" the "self-reflexive loop" of a society dominated by mediation and "empty irony," Wallace gets closer to imagining it in this reading of "Little Expressionless Animals" than he does in many of his later, more mature works (57).

Julie is one of the characters in Wallace's work who comes close to breaking out of the prison of corporate mediation. Ironically, she does so through almost complete immersion in it, and although she is not successful, Wallace does provide the reader with a formula for escaping "the narcissistic loop" of life in contemporary society. Wallace describes Julie's first appearance on *Jeopardy!* as a transcendent moment: "Something happens to Julie Smith when the red lights light. Just a something. . . . Every concavity in that person now looks to have come convex. The camera lingers on her. It seems to ogle. . . . Her expression, brightly serene, radiates a sort of oneness with the board's data" (17). Trebek describes Julie's "oneness with the board's data" as "an intellectual caress" (21). "She's like some lens," Merv Griffin claims, "a filter for that great unorganized force that some in the industry have spent their whole lives trying to relocate and focus" (24). Griffin defines Julie's force as a performer as a force with

> the capacity of facts to transcend their internal factual limitations and become, in and of themselves, meaning, feelings. . . . This girl informs trivia with import. She makes it human, something with the power to emote, evoke, induce, cathart. . . . She is, or can become, the game show incarnate. She is a mystery. (24–25)

As humorous as Griffin's speech may be, Wallace does more than merely poke fun at his nemesis, television. Quiz shows, one would assume, are the opposite of mysteries because the goal of the show is to find answers; however, the inverted form of *Jeopardy!*, viewers give questions, makes the show not unlike fiction's famous goal of provoking questions rather than providing solutions. Of course, *Jeopardy!* does not actually achieve this; it can only produce a trivial facsimile of the questions of fiction, but in using *Jeopardy!* in his story, Wallace can call attention to both the possibilities inherent in *Jeopardy!*'s inversion of the game-show format while also elevating fiction as the more meaningful arbiter of mystery.

Julie not only becomes the quiz show in becoming "convex," she appears to become television itself, "like some lens." (All camera lenses and television screens at the time of the story are convex in shape.) Compared to the fake charm of Alex Trebek, Julie's ability to go convex makes her a unique performer in the television landscape, one capable of reaching outside herself and providing viewers with "an intellectual caress" akin to Zooey's other-directed shoe-shining. In his description of her appearances on the show, Wallace attributes Julie's success on *Jeopardy!* more to her convexity than he does to her impressive body of knowledge. Once again, the effect a broadcast has on the audience depends on the heart of the performer.

Hering does not share this optimistic view of Julie's appearance and considers her as trapped by the camera's gaze, "unable to look *into* or *through* that glass" of the lens "but only *at* it" (94). This reading, however, views all television performers as equal in skill and effect, limited by the "technological materiality of the medium" and does not give enough consideration to the convexity characters such as Zooey and Julie enact when on screen (96). Further, Wallace contrasts Julie to the other characters in the story by with an anecdote about a TV addict seeing themselves on a screen. The TV addict staring at themselves is the ultimate closed loop, a true narcissistic mirror where a person stares at themselves staring into a lens, thus looking right back at themselves. No connection can occur this way; it is pure concavity brought on by the erosion of boundaries between televisual space and reality. When the TV addict sees themselves on TV, they are on both sides of the screen, whereas Julie remains only on the set, showing that the connection over broadcast only works in one direction, from performer to audience.

Julie's performance shatters the form of the show in many subtle ways as well. Her "oneness with the board's data" allows her to subdue the conventions and personnel who make game shows into ersatz simulations of human emotion. Julie's ability to run the board, answering all questions herself "before [Trebek] can even end-punctuate his clues," undermines Trebek and the other contestants' necessity to the proceedings (17). Her performance on the show is so dominant that the canned chit-chat of the game show host never takes place during Julie's run. She goes one step further by correcting Trebek when he tells another contestant that her answer is wrong. The producers seem to acknowledge her authority as well, frequently cutting to her even "while Trebek is still reading a clue" (17). Trebek, the consummate quiz-show host "who has never before had an audience get away from him," loses not only the audience but the camera's gaze as well (18). The eyes of the metaphorical rabbits in the field of clover from his dream are not looking at him, and, without the camera on him, he cannot look at them either. Julie's ultimate coup comes when she gives Trebek the finger on television, rejecting him and his authority thoroughly, allowing Julie and the audience to connect without anyone mediating their interaction. From this point on, Julie is virtually unstoppable: it takes an act of sabotage to end her 700-episode reign over the show. By becoming convex and outwardly focused on the show, Julie challenges its control over her and the audience and dissolves its sham-intimacy, opening the door for the kind of actual intimacy and connection that she and Faye experience to occur.

Julie's subversion of the authority of the quiz show carries over to her life off-camera as well through her relationship with Faye Goddard. Paul Giles describes Faye and Julie as "characters who are adrift in a sea of commercialism" attempting "to retain an idea of human otherness as a means of resisting incorporation into imperial forms of homogeneity" (331). As genius contestant and researcher respectively, they corner the market on facts, information, and authority in the story, and much of their off-set conversation concerns how much information they should share about their lives and their relationship with the media. They choose to share little, preserving a boundary between private life and broadcast life that allows them to remain connected to each other. Wallace, through Julie, actually seems to claim that knowledge stands in the way of humans connecting to each other. Julie claims that "little ignorances ... line the path to any real connection between persons," implying that knowledge is anti-geometric because it does not create lines but rather terminal points (4). Later in the story, Julie offers an even more damning depiction of human relationships when she describes what she sees as the three stages of love: in stage one, lovers "exchange anecdotes and inclinations. Then each tells the other what she believes. Then each observes the relation between what the other says she believes and what she in fact *does*" (9–10). Placed on a continuum of knowledge, these three stages of love progress from trivia ("anecdotes and inclinations") to ideals ("what she believes") to contradictions ("the difference between what the other says and what she in fact *does*"). With trivia at the first stage of love, Wallace seems to equate trivia with "the little ignorances" necessary to connect people, which seems to bode well for the *Jeopardy!*-style trivia; however, when one looks at where the stages of love end, one sees that this progression does not end with total connection but rather in disconnection. Like the waves that build and break at the end of the story, it seems that love and connection between people in Wallace's story are not possible, only approachable via ignorance or deception. But this impossibility is only how things appear, even to Julie, for she claims that "the whole point of love is to try to get your fingers through the holes in the lover's mask," meaning that love is by definition a difficult and necessary struggle between image and reality (32). In "observing the relation between what [the lover] says and what she in fact *does*," the lovers are perhaps not so much disconnecting from each other in the third stage of love (i.e., falling out of love) but rather encountering the existence of "the lover's mask." The third stage reveals that some of the information in the first two stages of love may in fact be part of the mask, which means that stage three represents not the final stage of love but rather a moment where love can either, much like a wave, break or continue to build into a new stage, depending on whether the lovers choose to continue after encountering the borders of the lover's mask.

Marshall Boswell rightly regards the story itself as an ocean: waves of language that approach "its signifier but 'breaks up' before it can make contact" (76–77). "Oceans are only oceans when they move," Julie says, because "oceans are just their waves. And every wave in the ocean is finally going to meet what it moves toward, and break" (Wallace, "LEA" 42). Boswell views this statement as an expression of the impossibility of connecting with anyone else; however, this wave does connect: it "meet[s] what it moves toward" *before* it breaks. This moment does, of course, destroy the wave, but it also represents the wave achieving its purpose: contact. Julie places this occurrence in the context of human expression, which she views as what "keeps people human, interesting, loveable" (Hayes-Brady 182). Expression, emoting, revealing something to someone else is "a wave, breaking on a rock, giving up its shape in a gesture that *expresses* that shape" (Wallace, "LEA" 42). This phenomenon is what happens to Julie when she goes on-air: it represents a face going convex, expressing the shape of what is building up inside a person, the opposite of a mask, which is designed to conceal the surface and the interior. This movement from the inside to the outside constitutes the attempts of people to connect with each other, to step out of one's own mask and get through to another person, without resigning itself to "the inability to reach through the glass to the other side" (Hering 94). In *Zooey*, this movement is possible on another type of wave: the airwaves, and although Wallace does not appear to share Salinger's optimism about broadcasting, he does acknowledge that such connection is possible provided that those on-camera are able to become convex. This quality places Alex Trebek in direct opposition to Julie because he is concave, concerned only with whether people are looking at him, even in his dreams. Furthermore, becoming convex may be essential, for as the world grows increasingly more mediated, people will need to know how to navigate a landscape in which there are few unmediated sites of interaction. In this respect, the final sentence of the story, "Julie and the audience look at each other" represents the moment before Julie's wave breaks (she is about to be defeated by Lunt); however, omitting a description of her defeat from the story and ending the story on such a suspended note transforms this moment into Wallace himself looking out as well, "daring his reader to unmask" (Kunzru 99). Wallace defers the story's resolution, ending the story the moment before the wave meets what it is headed toward, before "at" potentially becomes "into."

Kunzru characterizes this dare to the audience as a dare to avoid becoming like the expressionless animals of the story because to be expressionless is "to wear a mask" (Kunzru 98). Wallace includes several vignettes depicting the docile, compliant audience commercial television desires in order to turn the reader away from such obedience to television's crass materialistic influence and toward expression-fueled connection. Alex Trebek's megalomanical dream of being stared at by "a million bunny rabbits" constitutes one not-so-subtle description of a game-show host being watched by a wide television audience (Wallace, "LEA" 36). Similarly, when Julie makes up phony explanations for Faye's lesbianism, she describes a fictitious relationship in which Faye's boyfriend becomes so obsessed with Faye's body that he makes her lift weights nude while he watches from outside, through a window, with his friends. "You can see them through your own reflection in the black glass," Julie says, "the faces are rigid with fascination. The faces remind you of the carved faces of pumpkins" (35). In both anecdotes, expressionless faces become inhuman, the faces of animals and vegetables. The image of the carved pumpkin also gives the reader an image of a mask, the same kind of mask perhaps that Julie says it is a lover's job to get their fingers through. These stories and dreams serve as Wallace's warning about the dangers of the blank spectation that television encourages, for these stories all amount to a description of audiences. It is quite tempting to read this in concert with Wallace's well known takedowns of television; however, there appears to be something else at work in "Little Expressionless Animals" than Wallace's typical critique of television. For all its focus on the inner-workings of television production, there are no audience members as characters in the story; all the characters either appear on the show or work behind the scenes. The only audience member here is the reader, whose reliance on spectation, Wallace warns, will turn their faces into expressionless masks reminiscent of a rabbit, carved pumpkin, or cow, leaving them so trapped within themselves that they will be unable to connect with anything outside themselves, just like the story's ultimate expressionless animal: Lunt Smith.

Julie's traumatized brother Lunt is "a damaged person," a "mannequin of a kid" who lives in "a private hospital in the desert" because he "has trouble living in the world" (20, 27, 20, 25). Lunt's appearance on the show represents not so much another boundary becoming fluid as it does a connection being severed. (Julie appears on *Jeopardy!* in the first place to raise money to pay for Lunt's psychiatric care.) Lunt's slumped, barely audible stage presence is the opposite of Julie's intense convexity: Lunt is the eternally closed loop, so concave that he cannot even lift his head to look at anyone, let alone through them. Merv Griffin's move to depose Julie as *Jeopardy!* queen by having Lunt compete against her effectively turns her "convex" televisual presence in on itself and replaces it with "imperial forms of homogeneity" represented by Lunt's appearance on the show and by Merv Griffin Entertainment itself (Giles 331). The show, and Julie, implode in "a regressive move into infantile solipsism" (Hering 96). She no longer "radiates a sort of oneness with the board's data," and her withdrawal into herself strips trivia of its import. Any attempts at connection with those outside the set evaporate. Lunt's deposing of her into a cynical ratings stunt, a moment where the impersonal formula of the quiz show reasserts itself. Although *Jeopardy!* will certainly continue as a successful quiz show, Wallace implies that the show will never again achieve the transcendent kind of success that it has during Julie's 700-episode run. While it may seem like pulling everyone onto the world of the show would make everyone one and thus more connected than ever, all movement across boundaries ceases. For Wallace and Salinger, the meaning, the holy sense of oneness, comes from movement because the goal of broadcasting is not to please the performer, the self, but rather to reach out and connect with the audience. Absorbing everyone into the world of the show represents turning a window into a mirror; everything becomes incorporated into the self: the Fat Lady, the other, the lover and their mask, cease to exist. This area is where the true transcendence of *Zooey* and the failure of "Little Expressionless Animals" lies: the former features a moment in which mediation helps to rescue someone from the depths of self-absorption, whereas the latter shows how "the vast cynicism of corporate decision-making" conspires to trivialize the very means of connection it offers (Kunzru 99). In ending the story this way, Wallace shows that he views broadcast television's potential to connect people as imperfect, all potential with no achievement, a rising wave that breaks before reaching where it wants to go.

While much of the data on Lunt appears at first to characterize him as an autistic, traumatized "other," a concave figure to his convex sister, Wallace's various descriptions of him do not render him all that unique. Even though Lunt lives in an institution, this institution "specialize[s] in sort of . . . *yanking* people outside themselves. Into the world" (20). On one level or another, everyone in the story has "trouble living in the world": Dee Goddard speaks to her television set, Alex Trebek is narcissistic and delusional, and even though she is higher-functioning, Julie shares all of Lunt's trauma. These facts, after all, help explain why they work in television: the Merv Griffin family becomes a world onto itself that seeks to absorb everything it comes into contact with, keeping them out of the real world. Putting Lunt on *Jeopardy!* hardly yanks him outside himself and into the world. However, simply because Lunt's doctor fails in preparing Lunt for life in the real world does not mean that there is not a force present in "Little Expressionless Animals" that is not successful in the same endeavor. The goal of Wallace's fiction, from *The Broom of the System* to "This Is Water" and *The Pale King*, is very much about "yanking people outside themselves into the world." This movement outward is what happens to Julie when she becomes convex: she momentarily projects outside herself and "radiates" across the airwaves to connect with a television audience. This "yanking" creates movement; it makes a "very big puddle" of broadcasting into an ocean of connection (41–42). Without movement, without expression, people would simply be mannequins, expressionless animals like Lunt. Through the movement of fiction, Wallace hopes to yank the reader out of their own isolation within a "fake, regimented, spiritually exhausted" game-show world, turning a puddle into an ocean (Kunzru 98). In this regard, Wallace becomes the doctor, and the reader is Lunt, his patient.

Wallace employs this characterization to privilege fiction's ability to create meaning over television's. While the story's structure, with its fragmented, non-linear narrative and commercial interruptions, may appear to mimic channel-surfing, it more accurately represents the reader's (or the human being's) process of connecting discrete, fragmented bits of text in order to make sense of a seemingly disordered mass of information. The act of reading and interpreting the trivial data becomes an act of connecting, of making meaning by discovering where all the discrete points of data intersect, and Wallace designs the story to make the reader undertake this work of imposing order and meaning on the story (Severs 157). As incestuous as everyone is on the show, only the reader comprehends the full extent of the story's events and the relationship everyone has to each other. Like Julie, the reader "will always know every fact [the characters] know plus one" (Wallace, "LEA" 39). For example, readers know the "woman with hair like fire" is Dee Goddard, and readers can sort out which of Julie's hypothetical explanations for Faye's homosexuality are true stories from her own life and which are not. In forcing readers to track the myriad points of connection and intersection among characters, media, and reality, Wallace highlights the failures of television to bring people together, but more importantly, he "reaffirms the text as a site of human interaction between author and reader" in the belief that his fiction can produce the convexity that television only fakes (Boswell 73).

However, suggesting that Wallace's story preserves the world outside the text from the heavily mediated world of "Little Expressionless Animals" by rejecting the possibility of the latter breaking through to the former seems to be wishful thinking. Sadly, the world of "Little Expressionless Animals" is not all that alien from the reader's own world. Wallace's story has its own kind of twisted realism to it, so for Boswell to suggest that the reader's world and the world of the story are different, separate, misconstrues both the story's relationship to the world and its potential to guide us through it. Wallace's story looks out from the world of mediation to the real world without being able to break through because the real world is just as compromised by mediation, and while this failure is significant to the story, the movement matters most, the gesture toward the outside that aims to cross boundaries and get one's fingers inside the lover's mask, where "something like living occurs" (Boswell 74). Although the fluid boundaries of "Little Expressionless Animals" may not succeed in dissolving any of the boundaries created or framed by television, Wallace's repeated mentions of screens, windows, open doors, and other permeable borders invite the reader to see the possibility of escaping from the televisual loop. The story's untidy resolution leaves its wave, and hopefully the reader's wave as well, convex, unbroken, still rising and moving toward the shores of connection.

• •

CATEGORY

WISE UP FOR THE FAT LADY

The challenge to the reader to become convex, to emote and be vulnerable within a heavily mediated landscape remains implicit in Wallace's story. In Paul Thomas Anderson's film *Magnolia*, however, this challenge becomes the jumping-off point of the story, wherein Anderson dares his media-savvy, skeptical audience to let down their guard and, through his 188-minute epic, be yanked out of themselves and into the messy contemporary world. The film "enacts a kind of return of affect" Holland sees in *House of Leaves* (99). Like Danielewski, Anderson attempts to "recuperate[e] the earnestness and emotional connection that have been lost in an age of constructed realities" (99). This challenge to connect materializes not only in the conflict between parents and children but also in an intermedial conflict among "film, television, and digitality" (Lane 96). The gaps between the parents (who are all hosts, producers, and actors) and their children who are performers and contestants equate to the boundaries between media, especially cinema and television, and together point to larger crises in American culture such as those involving masculinity, addiction, family, and community. *Magnolia* immerses viewers in these contemporary problems in pursuit of an authentic way to connect in a world dominated by the inauthentic connections of mass media. Anderson uses "the sprawling uncertainty" of hypermediated networks to form new bonds between people isolated by media culture and create space both for sincerity and a new conception of family (Holland 99).

Geoffrey O'Brien finds the abundance of makeshift families throughout Anderson's career as expressive of "a peculiarly American disconnectedness" that compels his characters to form "protective families or parodies of families" to alleviate the "deep loneliness" that is their daily experience as Americans (292). The emotional content of each scene and Anderson's *mise-en-scène* emphasize this loneliness in *Magnolia*. Characters seldom share the frame with each other when they express their overwhelming loneliness and heartache, but the structure of the narrative and the film's approach to music and editing foreground connection, simultaneity, and intersection at every moment, forging a kind of familial relationship the characters are not aware of. The montage and soundtrack of the film repeatedly tie these lonely characters together to reveal that they are part of a larger tapestry and are, therefore, a community (Jeffrey). The film's style and structure can be viewed as polyvalent, with characters (and the viewer) continually inside and outside of the film's story and structure; the full scope of the film's mosaic functions in a similar way to how Holland reads *Infinite Jest* because it can only be accessed through "paying attention to *individual* voices at individual moments" (61). Anderson's structure permits the viewer to connect with the film in a way that both reinforces the power of cinema while also creating a distance that encourages the viewer to transport this sense of connection into the real world. Anderson may frequently remind viewers that *Magnolia* is, in fact, a story, but he always follows such reminders with an assertion that "these strange things happen all the time."

Unlike the game shows in *Zooey* and "Little Expressionless Animals," *What Do Kids Know?*, the game show in *Magnolia*, makes generational conflict a part of the show by pitting a panel of precocious children against a team of genius adults, thus unifying the plot, characters, and themes of the film within the game show itself. The game show stands in for the dominance of television. On it, people are as disconnected from each other as possible, despite their sharing the same stage: their interactions are disingenuous and canned on-camera and rude during the commercial breaks. Because it is a live broadcast, no one is allowed a moment to do anything that is not in service of the show, not even go to the bathroom. Everything must follow the script down to the second, and no one can go off-script because going off-script ruins the flow of television. In a game show, anything off-script is, in truth, a wrong answer; however, *Magnolia* is almost solely made up of moments where characters go off-script to show how real answers and knowledge come from moments of disruption and intersection that disturb the smooth flow of television.

Like "Little Expressionless Animals," *Magnolia* focuses on two families, the Partridges and the Gators, who are part of a larger, more figurative family. Earl Partridge's family encompasses the stories of Earl (Jason Robards), his son Frank T. J. Mackey (Tom Cruise), Earl's nurse Phil Parma (Philip Seymour Hoffman), and Earl's wife Linda Partridge (Julianne Moore). Jimmy Gator (Philip Baker Hall) hosts *What Do Kids Know?*, and his family drama contains the storylines of his daughter Claudia (Melora Walters), his wife Rose (Melinda Dillon), police officer Jim Kurring (John C. Reilly), and quiz show contestants Stanley Spector (Jeremy Blackman) and Quiz Kid Donnie Smith (William H. Macy). Both family dramas fall under the umbrella of Earl Partridge's production company and are thus part of his television family, much as the Smiths and the Goddards become children of Merv Griffin in "Little Expressionless

Animals." The quiz-show families of the film are decaying from the top down, with both father figures dying of cancer, and their position as patriarchs of families and television programs allows Anderson to suggest that television itself has succumbed to its own cancerous growth. The true cancer eating them from within is a visual simulation of human relationships represented by the game show that has metastasized and cut them off from their families, leaving damaged and resentful children in its wake. While the rain of frogs at the film's climax introduces an overtly apocalyptic element to *Magnolia*'s narrative, this event merely prepares the viewer for the more significant apocalypse in the film: the death of the fathers and the television ethic that they represent. The film ends on a measured note of healing and redemption, where the children come together to create a new community free from the sins of their fathers. In this way *Magnolia* uses the tools of cinema to look past the shortcomings and empty promises of television to stress intersection and simultaneity as the necessities for keeping people connected in the twenty-first century.

At first glance, viewers may have trouble deciphering exactly how all of *Magnolia*'s characters and storylines link up, leading many to dismiss the film as a mess, "a swirling, barely controlled fantasia of juxtaposed emotional predicaments" designed more to give actors the chance to indulge themselves in scenery-chewing dramatics than to tell a coherent story (Jones 38). Some go even further to characterize *Magnolia* less as a film and more as a soap opera, a work of television rather than a work of cinema (Dillman 146). The film appears both intricately designed and entirely haphazard in its architecture, but for the film's apparent sprawling aimlessness, its structure is incredibly unified (Toles 23). The film's structure is so tightly connected that one image links the stories. When the quiz show abruptly ends, credits roll on the television screen inside Earl Partridge's house. The last credit declares that *What Do Kids Know?* Is in fact, "A Big Earl Partridge Production," which collapses the diverse storylines in *Magnolia* into the story of Earl Partridge's extended family. As chaotic and messy as the events of the film appear to be on one level, *Magnolia*'s "own style and structure *feel* as though nothing is left to chance, appearing to have an organic and pre-conceived architecture," with all its disparate strands merging in specific locations: an intersection in the San Fernando Valley and a quiz show featuring children (Lane 15). The film "solicits spectators who are active and film- and media-literate" and "rewards those who pay attention" by embedding visual and aural clues into the film's design (Lane 42). The most well-known of these would be the multiple appearances of the number 82 in the film that foreshadow the rain of frogs, which is mentioned in Exodus 8:2; however, the Big Earl Partridge logo and the intersection of Magnolia and Laurel Canyon Blvds. would also serve as strong examples of crucial visual cues. These details

The Big Earl Partridge Productions logo.

call for and reward repeat viewings and invite the audience to participate in discovering, decoding, even constructing the design of the film (Holland 122).

While this tension between chance and order is most apparent at the level of plot, it spills over into other parts of the film as well. Directors of Anderson's generation, heavily influenced by directors from the French New Wave and the New Hollywood, frequently apply "pre-conceived" styles to their films as a means of announcing their presence and mastery of the medium. With *Magnolia*, however, Anderson appears both to "attempt to control reviewer and audience response" as well as reject "a unified or authoritative point of view" by "creat[ing] deep pockets of space for characters to exercise their own voice," resulting in multiple voices and culminating in the film "encourag[ing] viewers to construct their own meaning by singling out what *Magnolia* means to them" (Lane 9, 8). The film's open, participatory design symbolizes a reconceiving of family not as a concave space of patriarchal (or directorial) control that silences other voices but as a convex, child-centered space based in listening and cooperation. The size and scope of the film's plot initiates this search as viewers seek to figure out what the film means, and Christina Lane argues that this search for "a grand design ... insinuates more than a search for meaning": it "constructs an ethical position" for living in the world (29, 3). This search for meaning connects to the preamble and the title image of the film because both allege that if viewers are able to accept that stories like the ones in the preamble are not only possible but frequent, then the linear grid of the streets of Los Angeles will open up to them like a circular flower, revealing not a series of disconnected dots but rather a community in which every piece connects to the center.

Television dominates the world of *Magnolia* so much that its main goals seem to be to perpetuate itself and its influence over everyday life. The film uses this omnipresence to critique it, "treat[ing] television as both content and form" (Lane 70). Joanne Clarke Dillman and Lane both describe how the style of the film mimics the "flow" of television, particularly the soap opera, to such a degree that "all of the characters of *Magnolia* are bound to and mediated by television" (Dillman 147). The contestants not only appear on the show but also intend to use their appearance to get them onto other television shows: Stanley's teammates (Natalie Marston and Bobby Brewer) brag about auditioning for "MOWs" and encourage Stanley to use his notoriety to gain entry into the lucrative world of "endorsements and shit." Stanley's father (Michael Bowen) also views Stanley's success as a chance for him to further his own stalled acting career. Meanwhile, Quiz Kid Donnie Smith has been living off his appearance on the quiz show as a child for so long that being "Quiz Kid Donnie Smith" seems to be his entire career, and his fame gets him a job selling televisions. Frank T. J. Mackey's "Seduce and Destroy" program exists mostly as a seminar, but he appears first in an infomercial that plays on several characters' televisions during the credit sequence. Jim Kurring's only companion appears to be television, which he watches while he eats breakfast, and he narrates his own imaginary episode of the television program *Cops* to himself in his squad car. Claudia Gator appears to actively shun her game-show-host father, but she still watches his show when she gets high. Even minor characters such as Gwenovier (April Grace) and Solomon Solomon (Alfred Molina) earn their living through television. (Gwenovier is a television journalist and Solomon sells televisions.) Television constitutes such a pervasive presence in the film that scenes that do not involve television production or feature a television playing in the background still call attention to television through its absence. Like the world of "Little Expressionless Animals," there is no world outside the set in *Magnolia*, and because the world of television in the film is a world run by fathers who abuse and abandon their children; this fact also means that there is no space in the film unaffected by trauma. This motif, as Dillman shows, makes the film into "a highly reflexive media text that interrogates its own system," and declares television "morally bankrupt," "an empty distraction" that turns knowledge into a parody of itself (149, 148, 149). The film's merger of televisual life and family life demonstrates how everyone in contemporary America is in effect a child of television.

Dillman separates *Magnolia* into four parts: "preamble, credit sequence, main story, and coda" (143–44). The preamble and the credit sequence constitute a dual prologue for the film and highlight its main themes: loneliness and chance connections. It may appear at first that connections and loneliness would represent opposing concepts; however, the narrative of Anderson's film effectively shows how loneliness is what connects people to each other: Anderson's "characters ache . . . to connect" because they are lonely, and they base these connections on their shared loneliness (Jeffrey). In the preamble, the audience hears three stories of strange coincidences surrounding the deaths of a pharmacist, a blackjack dealer, and a teenager. These vignettes invite "spectators to open their eyes to a new—or at least renewed—way of seeing" by preparing the audience for the wide array of unexpected coincidences and strange-but-true phenomena that will occur throughout the main story (Lane 14). As unbelievable as the stories are, and as unbelievable as the many elements of the main story will be, the preamble asks that a jaded movie audience suspend its disbelief and remain open to the possibility of such events occurring regularly. It offers trivia—the organized, empirical explanation behind the strange events—as a means of creating belief in events that do not get explained. Knowing this seemingly trivial information prepares the viewer to get the film's more significant questions correct later.

The credit sequence, on the other hand, is integral to the main story, and not simply because it introduces the main characters and their storylines; it also presents the organizing principle of the film: the tension between community and loneliness. Anderson achieves this tension in the credit sequence in two ways, both cinematic. The first comes from the soundtrack via Aimee Mann's cover of Three Dog Night's "One." The song's refrain "one is the loneliest number" clearly announces one theme of the film; however, its use in the film simultaneously announces the other. Its appearance underneath seemingly disconnected scenes introducing each of the major characters shows the audience that these stories are not separate stories viewers are channel surfing through but are connected in a way that viewers cannot yet see (Lane 65). The credit sequence promises that all of these stories will intersect, and viewers familiar with cinematic storytelling expect the film to make good on that promise. After all, these stories would not appear in a montage if they were not in some way related. The film even makes this promise before introducing any of the main characters when the title of the film appears over two images: a time lapse of a magnolia blossoming and a series of closeups of maps of the streets of Los Angeles. Frame-by-frame scrutiny of the shot also reveals that scenes from the main narrative fade in and out in the background. This juxtaposition captures all of *Magnolia*'s themes. The endless grids of streets and freeways suggest the distance that exists between everyone in a major city, as well as the unlikelihood of any two people crossing paths in such a large space, and the blooming flower assures that everything connects to and radiates outward from a central hub. Things are spread out, yet are together as one, and while one may be "the loneliest number," it is also the number of community. Like the song "One," however, the map of Los Angeles only appears to show a lack of connection, but it actually foreshadows the climax of the film where frogs fall from the sky at the intersection of Magnolia Blvd. and Laurel Canyon Blvd., stressing

Circles and lines: the film's title card.

that this film is more concerned with points of intersection rather than the spaces between things. Lane looks at these tensions between connection and disconnection to conclude that "*Magnolia* resists binary oppositions and instead incorporates circular shapes and cyclical patterns" into its narrative, with this title card showing that the "round shape and ever-expanding movement" of the flower serves "as a metaphor for community" and "signals the film's governing principles of circularity" rather than linearity (13, 95).

Magnolia's circle expands outward from Earl Partridge. By uniting all of the characters and their stories under Big Earl Partridge, Anderson equates game shows and television with fathers, or, more broadly, masculinity, in order to challenge and deconstruct a bankrupt, obsolete mode of male behavior. According to Lane, the fact that every male character besides Jim Kurring works in television or for someone involved in television shows the men (and perhaps masculinity as well) are "trapped within a world of mechanization and objectification motored by consumer culture" in which they "play out patriarchal modes of identity" that are inadequate at best (32). The men in the film avoid connecting with those close to them, especially their children, preferring the transient and distant connections provided by broadcasting and predatory dating. Anderson's choice to have television represent toxic masculinity is refreshing since television, especially the daytime television of soap operas and game shows that *Magnolia* traffics in, has generally been characterized as feminine. Anderson shows how this image of masculinity is "a direct function of the media industry" surrounding the men, and it appears to be so fragile that any kind of meaningful connection with another person constitutes a threat to it (Lane 32). The film carries this behavior to its grotesque extreme through Frank T. J. Mackey. Mackey is essentially a game-show host: despite the fact that he is a living and breathing person, he is nothing but image, and his seminars essentially immerse (or indoctrinate) attendees into the world of television, broadcasting its predatorial superficiality to the real world. "Seduce and Destroy" teaches men how to eschew committed relationships in favor of temporary and abusive relationships that preserve the fragile image of their masculinity. Based on the chapter titles Frank mentions, the "Seduce and Destroy" program is less about wooing women than it is about managing one's appearance by faking emotions. Lecture titles like "How To Fake Like You Are Nice And Caring" and "Form A Tragedy" speak to creating scenarios in which a man can appear like he wants to connect with someone when all he really seeks is self-gratification. Once the man gets laid, he abandons the woman and leaves her betrayed and abused, much like the women in "Little Expressionless Animals" and the kids in *Magnolia*. Like a game show, the techniques in the "Search and Destroy" program feature a contrived setup, and, after a few rounds of carefully orchestrated play, the show ends with a clear winner who goes home with fabulous prizes and a clear loser who will receive some lovely parting gifts if she is lucky. In this case, everything becomes a game, only now without a show. Now it is just life.

Like the families in *Zooey* and "Little Expressionless Animals," the children in *Magnolia* are products of trauma and neglect, with the parents continually abandoning their children and the real world in favor of the world of the image. If the fathers are being consumed from within by cancer, the sons suffer from identity crises. Frank T. J. Mackey evades his identity as Jack Partridge by creating a completely new persona; Stanley's father's obsession with Stanley's performance and financial dependence on his winnings from the show reflects his own failed manhood; and Quiz Kid Donnie Smith is "a man without an identity," still defining himself as a kid and failing to find a stable adult identity in the world (Sperb 143). Stanley rejects the identity his father and television attempt to impose on him, which requires him to abandon his life as he knows it. These wise children do not get the luxury of a "wise-child complex" because no one cares about them beyond their utility as spectacle and their potential to accumulate free money. The very title of the quiz show captures the parents' attitude toward children well: *What Do Kids Know?* Simultaneously praises and dismisses the children's intellect, claiming to marvel at the amount of trivia the young people have absorbed while also regarding it as "worthless knowledge." Jason Sperb reads the show's title as "an ironic reference to the abuse and neglect that several children throughout the film suffer at the hands of their respective parents" (113).

Ironically, of course, the kids know quite a bit more than the adults. Diane Sippl characterizes the kids in *Magnolia* as "truthseers and soothsayers," and Lane describes them as witnesses who give the film "a larger narrative economy that values childhood (especially boyhood) over almost any other circumstance"

(Sippl 7; Lane 92). It is through the treatment of the children that Anderson mounts his critique of televisual culture, and he appeals to their knowledge and sense of wonder to point the way towards a new community free from the domination of the televised image. Although only two major characters, Stanley and Dixon (Emmanuel L. Johnson), are actual children, the film's definition of child extends to characters like Claudia and Frank, who are children of the quiz-show fathers of the film, and Donnie Smith, who is always identified, even in the closing credits, as "Quiz *Kid* Donnie Smith." Each of these characters' parents abuse them, and each holds special or secret knowledge that is the key to learning the truth about the events of the film. The young boy in the preamble (Cory Buck) knows why Sydney Barringer (Chris O'Hara) loaded his parents' shotgun. Stanley not only knows all the answers to the questions on the show, but his knowledge that raining frogs is actually "something that happens" allows him to respond to the event entirely differently from every other character. Dixon knows who killed the man in Marcie's closet and is able to convey that knowledge through a creative rhyme. Claudia knows that her father molested her, whereas Jimmy claims to be unable to recall it. Frank keeps his true identity as Jack Partridge a secret from everyone and protects his mother by keeping her alive in his false autobiography. Finally, Donnie Smith knows what it is like to survive being struck by lightning, another freak occurrence, and bears the knowledge that his parents stole all his winnings from his appearance on *What Do Kids Know?*, leaving him with only the title "Quiz Kid Donnie Smith" but none of the material benefits or independence that would come with it. Despite the enormous amounts of knowledge, both trivial and otherwise, that the kids possess, they are continually patronized, condescended to, dismissed outright, or, worse, abused and taken advantage of. Jim refuses to listen to Dixon's rap because he objects to both hip-hop and to Dixon's use of profanity. The only time anyone pays any attention to Stanley is when he fails to perform by wetting his pants and refusing to answer questions on the quiz show. The adult children respond to their childhood trauma by hiding from their past: Claudia hides via drug addiction and her isolated existence (all of her windows are covered), Frank hides behind his new identity and persona, and Donnie hides behind his celebrity. Each of them represents the future for Stanley and Dixon if nothing is done to break the abusive cycle created by the quiz-show fathers.

As in *Zooey* and "Little Expressionless Animals," the child contestants possess the power to challenge and reform their culture's media landscape, making them not only "truthseers and soothsayers," but forces of resistance and reconciliation in the film who free the community from television's grasp. Although Dixon attempts to cooperate with the police by giving Jim the clues to solve the case, he refuses to do so on Jim's terms, and encoding his special knowledge in a riddle ensures that no one will know the truth until they meet him on his own terms. The real force of resistance in the film, however, is Stanley, whose knowledge and curiosity are so comprehensive that no one knows how to relate to him other than to make him perform. Like a puppet, no one acknowledges that Stanley has any needs or desires of his own, even the need to use the bathroom. The producers not caring for Stanley's basic needs matches the neglect that all the children in the film face at the hands of their parents, yet another example of Anderson equating television and abusive parenting. In order to preserve the image needed to sustain television, these children must become "spectacle and commodity" and forfeit all human needs (Dillman 149). Fittingly, Stanley's last name, Spector, shares its roots with "spectacle" and "specter," reinforcing his status in the eyes of adults as an immaterial image without preferences. Stanley rebels against television, his father, and all parents who put the needs of their children second to the needs of their image-oriented culture by declining to participate: he stops buzzing in. While this behavior may not be against the rules of the show per se, it does defy the purposes of the game. Without Stanley's participation, the show comes to a halt because neither of his teammates wants to play the final round in his place. Stanley lets many attacks against him slide throughout the film, but when Jimmy jokes to the audience that Stanley is exemplifying "the indecision of a child" by refusing to play the final round, he responds with

> This isn't funny. This isn't cute. See the way we're looked at? Because I'm not a toy. I'm not a doll. The way we're looked at because you think we're cute? Because, what? I'm made to feel like a freak if I answer questions? Or I'm smart? Or I have to go to the bathroom? What is that, Jimmy? What is that? I'm asking you that.

Jimmy's only response is, "I'm not sure, Stanley." Stanley, in full violation of game show convention, asks Jimmy a question, and Jimmy must admit that he, the host of the show, cannot answer the one question he is asked. This simple bend in the rules causes the entire façade to crumble. This exchange causes the show to self-destruct and end early, which presents a major problem for the television station that now has air time to fill and little to fill it with. Dillman claims that "Stanley's moment of rebellion plainly exposes the game show and, by extension, television, for what it really is: an empty distraction" whose "knowledge is obscure and ephemeral, a meaningless diversion of no real value" to anyone, performer or audience (148). While there are moments in "Little Expressionless Animals" in which the game show verges on collapse,

Magnolia's breakdown is far greater because the show does not get to its final round, which means that no one can determine a winner, and without a winner, a quiz show becomes completely meaningless. Stanley's tirade against Jimmy becomes a dress rehearsal for the more significant standoff that he has later in the film with his father, and in both cases, Stanley reduces these men's power, revealing to be empty vessels of authority as transparent as television.

Stanley's monologue comes at the end of a seventy-seven minute sequence during which the score (and the actors) builds in intensity toward this major cathartic moment, the premature termination of the quiz show. Without this abrupt end to the quiz show, the viewer would not see the credits for the show and the Big Earl Partridge Production logo, the crucial clue to the film's structure. Thus, Stanley's rebellion against meaningless trivia grants the audience access to the knowledge needed to connect all the stories, and because the information only appears on a screen, *Magnolia* reveals that the viewer is the only person equipped to make sense of the story and tie it all together, not just in terms of plot and family relationships but in terms of themes and meaning. The quiz show does in fact contain important knowledge, but that knowledge comes from outside the game during the part of the show that few watch, the credits. For Anderson, television only reveals the larger connections underneath the flow when someone challenges its conventions and power in a way that disrupts that flow. This disruption of television's flow signals to the viewer that anything in the film is possible, including a musical number and frogs falling from the sky.

Anderson's critique of television is not as comprehensive at it first appears, however, because there is one force in the film that is associated with television that does similar work of unmasking its image culture from within. Gwenovier's investigative journalism stands as far from a quiz show as a television program can get, and Anderson uses her character to show that television does have the ability to unmask the truth and convey meaningful information beyond mere "rub-a-dub"; it just frequently prefers not to. Frank enters the interview under the illusion that he controls it because "this media apparatus" represented by her camera "enables him to project a self" rather than be real (Lane 55). However, when Gwenovier's questions begin to deconstruct his persona, he finds himself in a very different relationship to her lens. Now he becomes trapped, out of control, feminized, a position he claims to be able to save men from. Gwenovier's best "gotcha" questions concern the only women in Frank's life with whom he had a caring relationship, especially his mother. Christina Lane believes that this interview represents a moment of "ironic realism" in that it reveals "identity is heavily mediated and technologically inscribed in this millennial age of mass media. Frank believes that these commercial tools only work toward his benefit, not realizing that they contribute to the incoherence and uncertainty of his identity" (Lane 55). In the same way that Stanley's challenge to Jimmy ends the game show, Gwenovier's probing questions about Frank's past cause him to terminate the interview. Rather than storm out of the room, however, Frank retreats into silence, claiming that he is "quietly judging" Gwenovier. Storming out would have made for good television; silence, on the other hand, does nothing for the interview, just as Stanley's refusal to play does little for the quiz show. However, Stanley's challenge to television's form gets to a greater truth; Frank's represents a last-ditch attempt to shield the truth. Frank's silence makes him a spectator staring into the lens as though it were a screen, closing the loop, becoming an expressionless animal in order to avoid the real.

Magnolia uses both ends of television's spectrum, the investigative journalism profile and the quiz show, to show that television cannot sustain the kind of genuine truth or challenge to its image that Gwenovier's and Stanley's questions represent. The incredibly elaborate, borderline-ridiculous trivia questions of *What Do Kids Know?* Engage in the same kind of surface gamesmanship that Frank Mackey does, and both share the same relationship to the truth in that both distract from the real. The presence of these shallow questions encourages the viewer to look for more significant questions about knowledge that the film poses. Knowing in *Magnolia* means "wising up" to everyone's shared frailty. The true pitfalls of television's focus on the image is that it makes people, especially men, into disconnected narcissists who "yearn for mastery" over the world (Congdon 410). By interrogating the patriarchs of the televisual medium and showing them to be dying from within, characters such as Gwenovier and Stanley strip them of their power.

After the breakdown of *What Do Kids Know?* And Gwenovier's interview, television all but disappears from the film as the characters confront the real source of their trauma: their fathers. The "Wise Up" musical sequence follows the breakdown of both television programs, as though the disappearance of televisual space opens the film up to a cinematic space that television cannot accommodate. Much like "One" in the credits sequence, "Wise Up" presents the audience with the tension between loneliness and connection, only now the film provides a solution of sorts: the loneliness and disconnection "is not going to stop until" the characters in the film "wise up" to the fact that television is not the cure to their problems but is rather a symptom of the disease (Mann). This appeal grows in meaning as each character sings it, and the choice to end the sequence on Stanley, the real wise child, surrounded by books in the library, affirms the song's statement as true wisdom. David Congdon shows how the final lyric to "Wise Up," "No, it's not going to stop / So just give up," does not proclaim the futility of trying to connect with others but rather the futility of

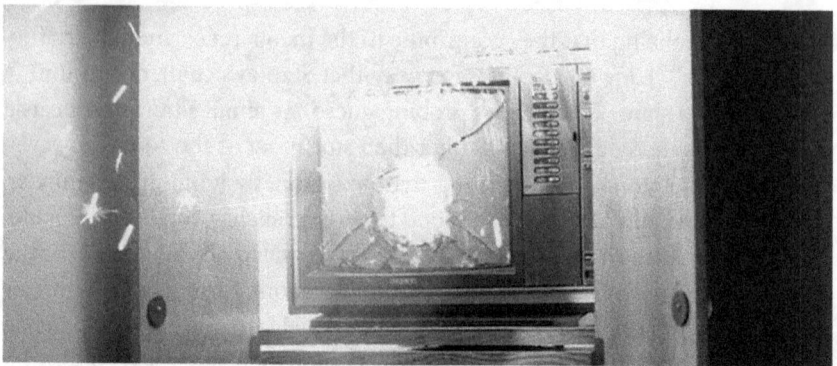

The death of television.

characters trying "to master their existence and control their destiny" because their "attempt to control their destinies through sheer self-determination has resulted in despair and self-destruction" (Mann; Congdon 410).

Accordingly, the male characters who are the least image-conscious and narcissistic (Phil, Jim, Stanley) succeed in facilitating the most change. In this context, a line from another song, Dixon's rap to Jim, becomes instructive. Before Dixon tells Jim who killed the man in Marcie's closet, he says, "Check that ego—come off it," and David Congdon reads this lyric as showing that "the characters have to 'check their ego' and give up on the notion" that they can control everything (410). "We only 'wise up,'" he writes, "when we 'give up' this fantasy and come to terms with the past. However such coming to terms requires a violent interruption from outside ourselves, since a self-realized coming to terms would only further confirm us in our delusions of autonomy" (411). Congdon's reading makes Dixon's rap and Mann's song resemble Seymour's Parable of the Fat Lady and the goal of Lunt's doctor in "Little Expressionless Animals": all call on people to move beyond the self and reach out to others. The rain of frogs that follows "Wise Up" yanks the characters out of themselves and into the new community, but the groundwork for this transformation comes first in the form of Stanley subverting the codes of the quiz show and causing it to self-destruct.

The rain of frogs reifies an idea implicit in *Magnolia* all along: real knowledge leads to belief because meaningful discoveries transcend factual information and become cause for wonder. There is a scientific explanation for the rain of frogs just as there is for the events in the preamble, but this explanation fails to demystify the reality of it being "something that happens." While most characters respond to frogs falling from the sky with fear and screaming, Stanley's discovery that "this is something that happens" transforms him, turning his formerly trivial knowledge into deep belief (Lane 104). The transformation at this moment is not limited to Stanley; his wonder transforms the film itself: the speed of the film slows down and fills the previously terrifying event with beauty and elegance. The rain of frogs becomes a moment of cleansing and a moment of apocalypse because it ends with the death of both quiz-show fathers, showing that the cleansing is not complete without the death of the patriarch. Jimmy's death scene can be read as even more significant than Earl's. Although he does not die on-screen, Anderson's shooting script indicates that Jimmy dies as the result of the house fire caused by the bullet that hits the television set. Therefore, television is killed twice in the film: once through the death of Jimmy and Earl, and again by Jimmy shooting the television set itself. No televisions appear in the film after this moment.

Congdon defines "apocalyptic" as "a cosmic divine invasion of the 'present evil age' which inaugurates a radically new age, a 'new creation,'" and *Magnolia*'s treatment of television, represented by the game show, as a pervasive, cancerous cycle of abuse in which "the sins of the father [are] visited on the children" certainly qualifies the film's story as apocalyptic (406). Although the coda of the film most clearly concerns itself with "inaugurating a radically new age" in which children break the cycle of abuse and seek out new communal networks, the film as a whole attempts to forge a new community based on active intersection, not passive spectation. Congdon writes that this new community can only come about if "something 'from above' or 'from the outside'" rescues the characters from their "self-enclosed crisis" (411). In other words, only something that crosses a border or dissolves a boundary. Within the film, the intersection of the characters and their storylines through both time and space creates this transformation. Once television disappears from their lives, they "wise up" to a more authentic and connected way of viewing the world. But this perspective does not only apply to the world within the film. The more significant boundaries *Magnolia* blurs are the ones outside the world of the film, those between the film and reality, between the audience and the director, between television and film, between cynicism and naivete. Each of these tensions gives *Magnolia* its power and encourages a back-and-forth dialogue between the audience and the film that mimics the kind of ongoing engagement the film encourages viewers to have in the real world with other people. Therefore, the film "occur[s] both outside (in the characters, in context) and inside (within us)" (Lane 27).

Anderson uses coincidence and simultaneity to make the audiences' reception of the film into "a question of faith—a refusal to believe only in chance" and believe in a structure that may be beyond one's immediate perception but is not beyond the capabilities of cinema (Lane 15). Congdon explains faith's role as being necessary to apocalyptic events if the event is going transform a community: "the transcendent significance of [an apocalyptic] event is visible only to the one who has the bifocal vision of faith, the one who can see the true state of things" (412). This figure would appear to be Stanley in *Magnolia*; however, for all that Stanley appears to know, there are significant portions of the story that he does not have access to. Like in "Little Expressionless Animals," it is the audience that possesses the most knowledge, who has been able to assemble all the separated bits of data into a connected whole. Christina Lane argues that, in asking the audience to believe the story, Anderson asks audience to have faith in cinema itself (104). This insight also captures the importance of Franny's epiphany at the end of *Zooey* coming over the telephone rather than in person. These three works imply that more meaningful discoveries and revelations take place when a performer is able to cross over (or become convex) and move from inside the world of media and reach outside into the world of the real. No particular character moves outward in *Magnolia*, nor does Anderson necessarily; rather, the film itself becomes convex. No matter how "bifocal" any one character may be in each of these works, the audience truly has the ability to "see the true state of things." The viewer can see what is on television and off, inside the screen and out in the world, and they are the ones whom each work calls on to believe in the power that the mass media can have to connect lonely people when a performer is able to "check his ego," become convex, or "shine [his] shoes for the Fat Lady" (Congdon 413). The final image of the film, in which Claudia Gator looks into the camera and smiles, recalls the final sentence of "Little Expressionless Animals": Claudia "and the audience look at each other." Where David Hering reads the last sentence of Wallace's story as indicative of "the kind of entrapment imposed" on people by mediation, *Magnolia*'s dialogic overtures enact the kind of "ethics of watching" that Wallace calls for and attempts in his work, making the ending a release from the cancerous entrapment of television (94).

Although television may seem to dominate the world of *Magnolia*, it cannot compete with the dominance of cinema in the film itself. Anderson continually distinguishes between the space of the television, both on-set and on-screen, and the world of the film, showing that cinema is convex because it has the power to navigate both televisual space and cinematic space, whereas television can only explore itself. He covers Stanley's arrival at the television studio in an extended Steadicam shot that traverses several floors of the building, declaring that his camera (and therefore cinema) commands complete knowledge and dominance over television. Anderson's camera, montage, and sound design capture the reality off the television screen, whereas television can only broadcast the image or appearance of things. Anderson demonstrates this several times throughout the film, starting with the dissolve from an image of Frank

Claudia and the audience look at each other.

Mackey on television to inside the infomercial itself. Seeing Mackey on television underscores his status as an image, and viewing the cheesy, overdone, stilted environment of the infomercial goes even further to critique his idealized world as a contrived, hollow world, an impossible (and undesirable) fantasy that only works when everyone agrees to pretend that it does. Additionally, after Jimmy Gator arrives at a doctor's office to receive test results, Anderson cuts to an *Entertainment Tonight* profile of him that presents him as a legendary game show host. Anderson immediately tarnishes this laudatory television image of Gator by cutting from the puff profile to Gator having sex with a showgirl in his office just as the profile proclaims Gator to be "a dedicated family man." Even though Frank's resistance to Gwenovier's interview may render her footage useless for television purposes, Anderson's camera has more access and continues to roll even after the interview concludes to capture Frank's off-camera attack on Gwenovier. These details privilege cinema over television as a truth-telling medium and an outlet for genuine connection and sincere emotional expression in the same way that Salinger favors radio over television and Wallace privileges fiction over television. All three artists view the language of their art form as a language game that constructs a social bond similar to how Wallace interprets Wittgenstein's definition of language as "a function of relationships between persons" that is "dependent on human community," and engaging in that discourse is "redeeming, remedying" for all involved (McCaffrey 44, 33). Finally, without cinema's ability to move fluidly through all visual boundaries, the larger structure and meaning of *Magnolia* would not be possible. In inhabiting both the inside and the outside of the television set, *Magnolia* provides the viewer with the information they need, and Anderson's film makes an argument for cinema as the more reliable conveyer of meaning than television.

Magnolia uses the unlikeliness of its connected events—its movieness—as a reason for its plausibility, appealing to the audience's jaded knowingness as citizens of a media-saturated culture in order to invite viewers to believe in the story. Nowhere does Anderson's complicated navigation of his audience's media-saturated knowingness manifest itself more than the scene in which Phil Parma successfully convinces a "Seduce and Destroy" telemarketer to put him in touch with Frank Mackey. This plea is as much Anderson's plea to the audience as it is Phil's to the telemarketer:

> I know this sounds silly, and I know that I might sound ridiculous, like this is the scene of the movie where the guy is trying to get a hold of the long-lost son, you know, but this is that scene. This is that scene. And I think they have those scenes in movies because they're true. You know, because they really happen. And you gotta believe me: this is really happening. I mean, I can give you my number and you can go check with whoever you gotta check with, and call me back, but do not leave me hanging on this, all right? Please—I'm just—please. See, see this is the scene of the movie where you help me out.

To many, this monologue may seem like an overly clever way to sell an implausible plot twist, an interpretation that has a good deal of credibility; however, viewed another way, the speech represents the film's honest invitation to believe. Lane views this monologue as representative of the film's unique approach to irony: rather than using artifice to expose the hypocrises of reality, *Magnolia* suggests "real life seems to be filled with movie-ish contrivances and because of this, conversely, we should perhaps believe in [the film's] synchronicity" (104). In other words, rather than using irony as a tool to encourage skepticism and superiority, Anderson employs it to encourage connection, belief, and humility. Instead of emphasizing the unreality of the film, this scene instead argues for the unreality of everyday life as a means of getting viewers to see their world differently and, hopefully, embrace the connections that they have not seen before and become less lonely as a result, suggesting that jaded irony bears responsibility for loneliness and isolation. The knowledge that "this is that scene" in a movie becomes the equivalent of the trivia questions on *What Do Kids Know?*: it is "ephemeral" and of "no real value," whereas the belief that "this is something that happens" opens events of the world up to beauty and wonder and has the power, Anderson suggests, to create a new community apart from television. The film ends with Claudia, the daughter of and prey to the cynical game show host, ending up with the most sincere character in the film, Jim, revealing the redemptive possibility of the film's end, in which the next generation will repair the sins of the parents and form real connections in real space rather than present false connection across the airwaves. The last image of the film extends this possibility to the audience as well because the film ends with Claudia looking into the camera and smiling, inviting the audience to share in her redemption not as spectators but as one of the redeemed.

In his "transparently, almost embarrassing sincere" film, Anderson enacts cinema's version of what Wallace calls for in fiction in his essay "*E Unibus Pluram*: Television and U. S. Fiction" (Udovitch):

> The next real literary "rebels" in this country might well emerge as some weird bunch of anti-rebels ... who dare somehow to back away from ironic watching, who have the childish gall actually to endorse and instantiate single-entendre principles. Who treat of plain old untrendy human troubles and emotions in U.S. life with reverence and conviction. Who eschew self-consciousness and hip fatigue.... Real rebels, as far as I can see, risk disapproval.... The new rebels might be artists willing to risk the yawn, the rolled eyes, the cool smile, the nudged ribs, the parody of gifted ironists, the "Oh how banal." To risk accusations of sentimentality, melodrama. Of overcredulity. Of softness. (81)

Together, these works expose the artifice of game shows—and mass media in general—in order to expose a hidden truth. If viewers are perhaps able to be both cynical about television's motives but naïve enough to believe that it can offer insight and connection, then they can view television as both an enemy and a tool that can prevent them from being manipulated by it and rather use it to connect with other people. The trivia that the film fills viewers' heads with proves itself to be true, "something that happens," "is really happening" and filled with real import until viewers can only believe in it, and in believing be healed by its wonder.

- -

CATEGORY

SO NOW THEN

Holland argues that "the symbol of family *images*" in *House of Leaves* "reminds us that the power to redefine both the self and the familial bond" lies in mediation, or, more specifically, "remediation" (103–4). But the question remains, how? Unlike many works of fiction that concern themselves only with identifying problems, these three appear to offer relatively concrete solutions, and the end of *Magnolia* echoes a sentiment that Wallace expresses in an interview with

Larry McCaffrey. After the death of the fathers and the television universe, the children are left alone to develop new bonds in a world where the old rules have been shown to be carcinogens. The coda represents the moment in which the children realize that their "parents," as Wallace says, "aren't ever coming back [and that now] *we're* going to have to be the parents" (McCaffrey 52). Holland defines "being the parent" in *Infinite Jest* as "reaching outside oneself and taking responsibility for oneself and others as they negotiate the seductive cycles of narcissism in which everyone takes a wild ride" (84). Holland claims that for Wallace there is no other option because being the responsible party represents "the only [option] that seems to offer a method for making and maintaining human relationships in an intensely infantile and solipsistic world" (84).

Zooey's conversation with Franny represents the Glass children taking care of each other without any help from their actual parents, Bessie and Les, or their intellectual parents, Seymour and Buddy. While Zooey appeals and/or succumbs to the authority of Seymour and Buddy, Franny's epiphany comes as a result of Zooey "reaching outside" himself, pulling himself out of his own narcissistic focus on television acting so that he can become convex enough to rescue her from a solipsistic breakdown by encouraging Franny to step outside herself as well, asking her to live her life "for the Fat Lady." Although a cynical gimmick on the part of Merv Griffin ends Julie's dominance on *Jeopardy!*, her performance does break the rules of the show and allows her to go far beyond the five-episode limit for a contestant. More significantly, however, her dethroning by Lunt breaks the loop formed between them. While readers do not know what will become of either of them, their separation does seem to yank Julie out of the closed loop of Merv Griffin's television universe and into the world. The story ends not with her looking down like Lunt, who only becomes further trapped within himself and the world of television, but rather looking out at the audience. As the earlier parts of the story make clear, when she looks at the audience, she becomes convex, making the end of the story a hopeful moment full of potential that will carry over to the reader, who is left to connect the different scenes, characters, and ideas of the story. The coda of *Magnolia* consists only of scenes in which the children clean up the mess left in the wake of the death of the quiz-show fathers and the rain of frogs. These children, much like Zooey at the end of his novella, step in to care for each other and form networks that did not exist at the start of the film. Frank returns to play parent by visiting Linda, his stepmother, in the hospital, caring for her the way he cared for his mother; Jim counsels both Donnie and Claudia; Claudia opens herself up to Jim; and, most importantly, Stanley establishes a new relationship with his father. Anderson photographs the scene to resemble a parent scolding his child, only with Stanley standing in the adult position over his father, who lies in bed like a petulant child who refuses to wake up. "You have to be nicer to me, Dad," Stanley says. His father, still clinging to his empty authority, says, "Go to bed," but Stanley refuses and instead repeats his request: he will not be ignored, and his conditions, like Dixon's identification of the murderer, are nonnegotiable. As George Toles notes, the position of Stanley's father on his bed echoes that of Earl Partridge's, suggesting that this new day will have echoes of the previous day, except with different, more productive results (12).

The final song "Save Me" may sound on its face like a cry for help, just as "Wise Up" initially sounds like a song expressing defeat; however, the characters' salvations do not come at the hands of an all-powerful parent or some kind of dependent relationship. Rather, *Magnolia* shows how people must save each other by "reaching outside" themselves to help others. The film, like Mann's songs, is "wise enough to know that there is strength in vulnerability," and the film shows how this strength cannot be acknowledged, let alone employed, until the illusory dominance of the game-show fathers and their image culture is unmasked and defeated (Lane 86). Anderson achieves this in a visual medium, and as Holland and these works argue, a successful return to earnestness and affect as forms of human interaction can only emerge from the hypermediated culture that laid waste to them in the first place (123). Although these artists show that television cannot deliver all of the connection it promises, their intermedial approach does show that other media can use the game show as a device to create works that deliver on television's unfulfilled promise to connect, creating spaces that "make present not only the self and empathy between selves but also belief, truth, and the real" (Holland 123).

Round Four

FEAR FACTOR

Game Shows, State Power, and Death

REALITY TELEVISION TRANSFORMED THE LANDSCAPE OF game shows. The traditional game show certainly went into decline after *Who Wants to Be a Millionaire?* and *Deal or No Deal* faded in the early twenty-first century; however, when one considers that a large portion of reality television is made up of game shows, game shows are as, if not more, popular in the twenty-first century than they were in their 1950s heyday. Reality programs in the vein of *An American Family*, *The Real World*, and *Celebrity Rehab* may not operate like game shows, but the most successful and influential reality programs of the twenty-first century do. Su Holmes argues that competition-based reality shows—also termed "gamedocs"—borrow many of their formal elements from game shows: these reality shows often feature celebrity hosts—Joe Rogan, Heidi Klum, Donald Trump, RuPaul—who preside over a game that is "structured by rules, and pivot[s] on the competitive philosophy of a winner-takes-all gamesmanship" (25). Shows such as *Survivor*, *Fear Factor*, *The Amazing Race*, *Big Brother*, and *The Apprentice* derive a great deal of their entertainment power from "the spectacle of 'ordinary' people under extreme (television) pressure," which has been an integral part of game shows since their inception (25). While reality shows incorporate material from other television genres, especially soap opera and documentary, without the structure of the game show, many of these programs would not likely thrive.

The ubiquity of reality-based competition programs, or "gamedocs," in the post-9/11 television landscape prompts one to ask what ideologies are on display in the most popular game shows of the twenty-first century. As Su Holmes and Olaf Hoerschelmann show, there is little frivolity at the root of any game show. "Game structures are never innocent of power"; rather, game shows express (and are expressions of) "very specific ideological formations" (Holmes 116; Hoerschelmann 152). Likewise, John Fiske states in *Understanding Popular Culture* that culture "is centrally involved in the distribution and possible redistribution of various forms of social power," and can be as effective as military action (1). "Sociopolitical systems depend upon cultural systems," Fiske writes in *Television Culture*, because "the meanings people make of their social relations and the pleasures that they seek ... stabilize or destabilize that social system" (243). Reality game shows such as *Survivor*, *The Apprentice*, *Big Brother*, *Fear Factor*, and *The Amazing Race* all involve some form of humiliation, pain, and aggression for the contestants, be it physical, mental, emotional, or all of the above. Hoerschelmann claims that "the recent spate of torture quiz shows express the corporate need for a docile workforce psychologically equipped for the shifting demands of corporate culture" because these shows "require their contestants to do whatever is necessary to mold them to changing corporate demands in the interest of their personal enrichment" (152). While Hoerschelmann's analysis here has much to recommend it, it is nevertheless odd that he stops his statement at the level of corporate culture and does not extend it to the state. The same shifting demands that drive the corporate sphere to yearn for a compliant workforce would also provoke the state to use media to cultivate an obedient populace. A person willing to eat worms on live television would not only be an ideal employee but an ideal subject of any kind of institutional or autocratic power.

Jérôme Bourdon acknowledges this connection in his essay "Self-Despotism: Reality Television and the New Subject of Politics." For Bourdon, "the ideology of the 'real' at work through reality television is not specific to television" but an illustrative example of the triumph of late capitalism and its ability to define reality (67). Gerald Gaylard agrees that the "virtuality [of reality television] is not confined to technology but involves a wider set of cultural practices that tend to rework the 'real' in the service of commodification," which he calls "postmodern archaic." Both agree with Hoerschelmann in that reality contestants mirror the "service economy of capitalism" and its demands that "individuals must adapt to an unstable and uncertain market" exemplified by the game (Bourdon 74). For example, contestants on *Fear Factor* must submit themselves to whatever stomach-churning test the show places in front of them or they lose out on their chance at success, modeling the atmosphere of a hostile workplace where the dictum is, "Do it or you're fired." Bourdon emphasizes that "bodies must learn how to present themselves adequately in order to perform in the new capitalistic world," which transfers impositions formerly instituted by the governments to "the needs of global capitalism" (75, 76). Bourdon reads reality television as a new form of political submission: "submission of the candidates to the rules of the games" represents "submission to the new social norms at work in the new spirit of capitalism" (77). Contestants on competition shows never question the purpose or worth of each task, no matter how absurd or dangerous they are, because the unwritten rule of these shows is that one does not question the rules: one either plays by them or goes home empty-handed. This submission to reality television, however, reveals an ambivalence within the fabric of democracy, a "self-subjection that democratic citizens seem willing to impose on themselves" (Bourdon 79). Reality shows such as *Big Brother* proudly display, represent, and normalize "new mechanisms of surveillance," leading critics of the shows to call them examples of "electronic fascism" (Bourdon 70). (Even the show's name unironically concedes that Orwell's world has appeared not as tragedy but as farce.) Gerald Gaylard points to the "illusion of spontaneity" as the hallmark of reality programming and argues that this illusion "normalizes surveillance" as well as "culture and patterns of consumption . . . to reify the products of the imagination . . . to sell them."

Popular culture frequently taps into the longstanding fear that "viewers' voyeuristic desire for realistic sensationalism" and "networks' desire to make a huge profit" will inevitably lead to snuff television (Gaylard). The arrival of reality television certainly increased the number of books and films depicting death and torture-based game shows; however, works that imagine a game show that makes players compete for their own lives have been around almost as long as the game show itself. Philip K. Dick's 1955 novel *Solar Lottery* may be the first instance of it in fiction, closely followed by Robert Sheckley's story "The Prize of Peril," which formed the basis for the first film to use the conceit, the 1970 German TV movie *Das Millionenspiel*. With each new development in broadcasting or technology, another version of this story arrives, be it exploitation fare such as 1983's *Endgame* or 2007's *Live!* and *The Condemned*, indie releases such as Daniel Minahan's 2001 film *Series 7: The Contenders*, or major releases such as *The Running Man* and the massively popular series *The Hunger Games*. The popularity of this conceit demonstrates the public's fascination and concern with the extremes to which television can go. A closer look at several of these works, especially the most popular among them, reveals that these concerns also stand in for the culture's fears of state and corporate power, which many of these works collapse into one.

Writers and filmmakers gravitate toward entertainment media, particularly the game show, to present this sinister convergence of media and state. Works that deploy the game show as a metaphor for state power envision a hypercapitalist dystopia in which corporate media's interests merge with a totalitarian government's oppressive interests to create a game show that turns the state's power to kill into a narcotizing spectacle where audiences consume their own helplessness and death as the ultimate in entertainment. Such a division between the corporate sphere and the domain of the state is not as distinct in a neoliberal world as one might think. Reality programs may be funded and broadcast by private, multinational conglomerates; however, these conglomerates exist and flourish precisely because they are supported and stimulated by the state in the form of tax breaks, increased control and influence over basic social services, lenient anti-trust laws, etc. In his book *Capitalist Realism*, Mark Fisher demonstrates how "neoliberalism surreptitiously relie[s] on the state even while [it] ideologically excoriate[s] it" by cutting the state "to its core military and police functions" (2). These works depict a pure rendition of Fisher's capitalist realist world, where the state exists solely as an instrument of deadly force that exercises its power through the media. Rather than taking a back seat to the media, as many might suggest, the state instead has entered into a mutual partnership with the corporate world for total dominance of market and political power.

In "The Media and the State," Colin Sparks adumbrates the symbiotic relationship that media has with the institution it supposedly keeps in check. After discussing the more clear-cut ways that the interests of government and media converge—the state acts as not only a source for news but also a censor, subject, manager, and masseur of it—Sparks claims that because the state is "an instrument of coercion" and the media "instruments of persuasion," they "influence each other as if they were the two arches of a bridge" (89). Because "the people who call the shots in the state and the media are indistinguishable" and have mutual relationships with people in "the boardrooms of industry and finance, both public and private," both together constitute "the ruling class" (89). Together, Sparks writes, "these people take all the important decisions about what is going to happen, how it is going to be reported and what will be done with anyone who objects" (89). Ultimately, Sparks consolidates both the state and the media as "weapons" used by those in power to maintain that power (89). Such a two-front strategy of control on the part of those in power renders the populace (or the audience) trapped in a struggle wherein they "conspire to change the world" while the state and the media "conspire to keep us in our places" (87). Sparks uses the ways that the state interacts with the news media to reach this conclusion; however, in looking at the books and films discussed in this round, one can see how intermedial works reveal how prevalent and pervasive this symbiosis of control is.

The relationship between gameplay and politics becomes more integral to the plots of these works because the protagonists physically enter a game space to compete for their lives, and their doing so frequently inverts John

Fiske's concept of play from *Television Culture*. For Fiske, play is empowering because "it pushes rules to the limits and explores the consequences of breaking them" (238). The first rule to be inverted, and the one that grants power to every aspect of play, is that of choice: choosing to participate in the show, choosing to play the game, choosing a role to play, even choosing to sit out one round or leave entirely. Fiske writes that "play, for the subordinate, is an active, creative, resistive response to the conditions of their subordination" and is thus empowering, with "the power to be different" serving as the most active, creative, and resistive of all (238). Fiske also describes how game shows follow "the main structuring principle of play" because they present "the tension between social order and the 'freedom' of anarchy or chance" (236). The particular type of play on display in game shows serves the same purpose as a carnival because their play reverses the consumer-producer power dynamic. Normally, the consumer's tight budget and limited control of price-setting constrains them from exerting any power over the market, but according to Fiske, the game show's "release of the economic constraints which ensure [one's] subordination allows shopping skills to become agents of empowerment" (279). Fiske's view of game shows takes on an even more optimistic air when he argues that the joys stirred up on the show "always produce a threat that puts social control at risk" because the joys the shows stir up cannot be fully integrated into the status quo (279).

Su Holmes, conversely, argues that while these shows may permit mischief, this mischief only works to reaffirm the ideology it nominally challenges (80). The books and films discussed here side firmly with Holmes over Fiske, even when they seem to endorse Fiske's optimism. Works such as *The Hunger Games*, *The Gladiators*, and *The Running Man* have the appearance of the type of game show that Fiske describes, with one major exception: there is no choice. Within the world of the story, these games, like the states they represent, give the illusion of freedom while secretly controlling people's roles, movements, even their emotions. Players are forced into their roles and have no choice but to play the game as thrown at them, a game whose layout, gameflow, and even rules can change dramatically without a moment's notice or a player's awareness or consent, turning a model of participatory, merit-based democracy into a tool of oppression. The production of the show masks this reality by turning the lack of choice in the game into part of its entertainment for the audiences at home, discouraging the audience from identifying with the contestants and instead aligning themselves with the show or its ruling body, which has the power to reward or kill. The game shows in these films persuade their audiences to shift their allegiance by portraying the contestants as social undesirables (criminals, the poor) or disposable people (draftees).

Therefore, game spaces within these works do not qualify as "utopian space[s]" where the rule of law does not apply, but rather these shows are actually the strongest articulations of the laws that govern a culture (Holmes 80). Rather than affirm the relationship between people and institutions, this kind of space, according to Jean-François Lyotard, uses the attributes of language games, social bonds, and democratic norms to actively destroy those very things (46). These works stretch Lyotard's claim that "institutions impose limits on the games, and thus restricts the inventiveness of the players in making their moves" to the absolute limit: life and death (17). In *Just Gaming*, Lyotard states:

> The question of the social bond, when it is put in political terms, has always been raised in the form of a possible interruption of the social bond, which is simply called "death" in all of its forms: imprisonment, unemployment, repression, hunger, anything you want. . . . isn't such a language game always assisted by the sword? (Lyotard and Thebaud 99)

Within this situation, writers and filmmakers find an uncanny metaphor for state power in the media age. In purporting to provide unparalleled freedom, the state uses the tools of a free society—the media—to exert more control over the population without making major changes to the imagery that it projects. Thomas Doherty characterizes the films in this round as part of "the cinema of surveillance," films "challenging video hegemony even as they exploit video imagery" ("Video" 71). These films are political, according to Doherty, because "the center of state power is no longer the palace but the government broadcasting station" in which "democratic capitalism exploits television" as "a conduit for entertainment and commercial selling" ("Video" 73). The films discussed in this round depict "video-sustained dystopia" that "blur the difference between totalitarian and democratic television," perfectly illustrating Wendy Brown's conception in "American Nightmare: Neoliberalism, Neoconservatism, and De-Democratization" of "democratic subjects who are available to political tyranny or authoritarianism because they are absorbed in a province of choice and need-satisfaction that they mistake for freedom" (Doherty, "Video" 75, 73; Brown 705).

This world corresponds with Jean Baudrillard's "The Implosion of Meaning in the Media," in which "more and more information" produces "less and less meaning," which allows the state to consolidate its control (79). Where one might expect information to produce meaning via communication, instead information "exhausts itself in the staging of meaning" and "devours its own content," "devours communication and the social," making the implosion of meaning the real Hunger Games in media culture (80). The amount of realism in reality programs thrusts a "tainted" quality on "less realistic footage," which leads viewers to accept more of what they see as real than they should; conversely, the influx of reality programming into reality contaminates the real by lending it "an element of the bizarre and predictable about it" (Gaylard). This confusion over what is and is not real ultimately works to benefit those in power, the ones producing and controlling the images at the expense of those consuming them. With the ability to confuse or even obscure what constitutes reality, the state can now control reality.

Lyotard argues that "knowledge and power are simply two sides of the same coin" and that "the question of knowledge" in the information age becomes "a question of government," which is to say that the two are inextricably linked (8–9). Game shows serve the same function that Lyotard believes legislation serves: the rules of the game "formulate prescriptions that have the status of norms" for the larger society (31). Although the games in the films this round examines may seem to be solely about physical ability, knowledge serves a more vital function because in most cases, the state uses these games and the media to limit and control the amount of knowledge that both the players and the people have about the state's oppression. When the players gain knowledge about the state's abuses of its citizenry, their quest becomes twofold: stay alive and broadcast their knowledge about the state to the populace to incite a revolution. Seizing command of the control center of the games may seem to be a transfer of power from the state to the resistance, but these works ultimately express a pessimism when they reveal that, regardless of which group the revolution topples, a larger power remains undisturbed: the power of the image.

. . . .

CATEGORY

PAWNS IN THEIR GAMES

The Hunger Games that Suzanne Collins creates in her book series of the same name collapses so many different types of reality television programming—sportscast, reality show, newsmagazine, fashion competition, political campaign ad, even a dating show—that it is, in effect, the totality of television. It depicts the "total screen" of Jean Baudrillard's "Hypermarket and Hypercommodity," where products and objects in the world cease to function as messages conveying particular meanings but rather as "tests." Tests, Baudrillard argues, do not inform or communicate: they serve as "referendum, perpetual test, circular response, verification of the code" in which citizens respond to an interrogation by giving the answer that the test simultaneously demands and provides (75). In watching the Games, citizens verify the state's total power over them. Collins's world is "a total functional screen of activities," a "hypermarket" in which the screen is "the model of all future forms of controlled socialization" (76). In the Hunger Games arena, even the sky is a screen. This "total screen" world, then, becomes "a space of direct manipulation" where repression acts as "an extra sign in the universe of persuasion" foisted on viewers by the "'policing' television" (76). The Hunger Games, both within the game and in the studio audience that is the nation, is how the state tests obedience, how well one can conform to its whims and will, how good of a subject one can be to its power.

The wildly popular book and film series takes place in a not-too-distant dystopian American future. After a series of climate-change fueled ecological catastrophes, America descends into violence and chaos and is reborn as Panem, a "shining Capitol ringed by thirteen districts" that supply the Capitol with resources and, most importantly, entertainment in the form of The Hunger Games, an annual televised contest in which one male and one female aged 12–18 from each district (called tributes) fight to the death in a high-tech arena (*Hunger Games* 18). The winner receives instant and permanent celebrity, and their district receives free food for a year. The losers die violently on live television. The series follows Katniss Everdeen, a tribute from District 12 who becomes an unlikely victor and an even more unlikely revolutionary whose notoriety and anger become the fuel that ignites an uprising against the Capitol.

The Hunger Games broadcast expresses Panem's identity as a nation, which is not as foreign a notion as it may seem. Shows such as *Survivor* also articulate a sense of national identity because its series of tests set in primitive landscapes assures viewers that, regardless of what tragedy may befall their culture, "their culture could still flourish because their culture is natural," thus stoking one's sense of national identity even when the structures surrounding that identity—i.e., civilization—appear to be in ruins (Gaylard). This combination of the latest in technology with the most rustic of circumstances makes the game and its outcome seem "'natural' and therefore 'unquestionable'" (Gaylard). Gaylard describes how these qualities turn *Survivor* into a validation of capitalism:

> Capitalism must be the ultimate culture because it is not a culture as such but in fact unmediated nature, verisimilitudinous naturalism; the divide between nature and nurture collapses. So the totem of the tribe is not the desert island, the outback, or the savannah, but the game itself—competition with winner takes all as its crowning decapitation. The totem is capitalism, the law of the jungle, the constitutive principle of the tribe as such.

Thus, the competition model that *Survivor* endorses is the capitalist model transposed to a pre-capitalist society, and one that Suzanne Collins's book series *The Hunger Games* (and its four film adaptations) emulates and extends by merging the capitalist media engine with the power-hungry one of an autocratic regime, using a televised and ritualized game show to make both capitalism and totalitarianism appear to be the natural state of the world. The game worlds of *The Hunger Games* (2008) and its sequel *Catching Fire* (2009), with their forest and tropical island settings controlled by state-of-the-art technology, function as the "postmodern archaic" in their blend of primitive wilderness and high-tech virtuality where "the ancient myths of purification and justice via abasement and suffering are reinforced" (Gaylard). Further, its merger of capitalist entertainment with state power validates Gaylard's claim that "capitalism must contain the archaic in order both to conceal and to justify its savagery."

Like capital, the Capitol becomes immune to all critique because it has already absorbed its failures and used them to its advantage. Panem may be a failed state, but through the media, it renders its inability to provide for its people natural by turning it into endless, self-perpetuating spectacle. The media's desire for higher ratings becomes indistinguishable from a government's desire for increased control in that both continually up the ante to maintain dominance over their audience. The Capitol created the Games to punish the districts for a failed revolt and remind citizens "how totally [they] are at their mercy. How little chance [they] would stand of surviving another rebellion" (*Hunger Games* 18). Collins demonstrates throughout the books how the children "reaped" for the Games become a "human shield" that protects the Capitol from dissent (*Mockingjay* 345). This dynamic becomes most apparent in *Catching Fire*, when the Capitol fills the 75th Hunger Games, the Quarter Quell, with returning victors in the belief that this violent extravaganza will both captivate the citizens of Panem and "quell" the fomenting rebellion by killing off its leaders in the Games.

The Games themselves become more than a representation of the Capitol's power: they are the expression of it, its lead instrument. In fact, they may be all the Capitol is apart from the militarized police force because Collins makes no mention of the Games generating any revenue, nor does she mention or depict other television programs unrelated to the Games. Collins shows how this figurative power is tied to the literal power of electricity, which in District 12 only works for telecasts of The Games or "some important government message on television that it's mandatory to watch" (*Hunger Games* 80–81). When the victors grasp hands during a televised interview in *Catching Fire* and create the "first public show of unity among the districts since the Dark

Days," the Capitol cuts the power to the studio and cancels coverage of the Games temporarily to stop the uprising's power from spreading (258). Finally, The Hunger Games themselves are destroyed via an electrical malfunction in *Catching Fire*, extinguishing their literal and figurative power simultaneously.

The Games themselves may only be held annually, but the Capitol orchestrates events that keep the Games and "the horror fresh and immediate" in people's imaginations year-round, such as victory tours (*Catching Fire* 4). Like Olympic stadia, the Capitol preserves the arenas after each Hunger Games as historic sites, promoting them as tourist attractions where people from the Capitol can "rewatch the Games, tour the catacombs, visit the sites where the deaths took place . . . even take part in reenactments" (*Hunger Games* 144–45). This memorialization of the Games further depersonalizes the dying people on television and rebrands state executions as theme-park entertainment. As a whole, these events become "the Capitol's way of reminding people that the Hunger Games" and their power over the districts "never really go away," forcing "the colonized to celebrate their own defeat" and to "remember the iron grip of the Capitol's power" (*Hunger Games* 370; Fisher, "Precarious Dystopias" 30; *Catching Fire* 4). And so Collins presents a totalitarianism that transforms oppression into a celebration of absolute power, a pageant of force that the oppressed must enjoy, asking them to be not only desensitized to totalitarianism, but entertained by it.

The Hunger Games emphasize a tribute's individual performance and participation to conceal how every detail of the Games is in the control of the Gamemakers, who not only design each arena, but manipulate every aspect of the game while it is going on from a gleaming, high-tech control center that in the film resembles a combination of NASA mission control, a broadcasting studio control room, and the White House Situation Room. Even though they can, if they desire, kill all the tributes immediately in the form of fire, deadly creatures they fashion on-the-spot, or other imaginary means, they frequently "manipulate [the tributes] into confronting one another face-to-face" by changing the environment of the arena (*Hunger Games* 177). However, the Gamemakers do sometimes kill a tribute themselves "just to remind the players they can" (177). The Games, then, enact the power of the totalitarian state: both have the power to kill players at any moment but refrain from exercising such outward displays of hard power in favor of stage-managing the world to control its citizens' behavior, turning their aggression against each other rather than against their true oppressor.

Although calling them the Hunger Games makes it sound like the people of the districts are competing to be fed by the Capitol, Collins's language suggests that these people are the food harvested to sustain the Capitol's insatiable hunger for mindless entertainment and violence. She names the selection of tributes a "reaping," the preparation room for the Games "the Stockyard," and the cache of weapons and supplies that sits at the center of every Games space the "cornucopia" (*Hunger Games* 144). These words connote bounty, harvest, captivity, and slaughter, a Thanksgiving feast of carnage. For contrast, Collins uses gluttonous language for the Capitol, which is filled with "oddly dressed people with bizarre hair and painted faces who have never missed a meal" who gleefully "[vomit] for the pleasure of filling their bellies again and again" (*Hunger Games* 59; *Catching Fire* 80). The Hunger Games themselves epitomize this binge-and-purge culture: viewers stuff themselves with young lives at the reaping and then violently purge them in the Games, only to repeat the action again next year. Katniss even wonders to herself "what do they do all day, these people in the Capitol, besides decorating their bodies and waiting around for a new shipment of tributes to roll in and die for their entertainment?" (*Hunger Games* 65). The novels and the films depict luxury as oblivion to the suffering of others, with the Games acting as the ultimate distraction for the privileged, an all-you-can-eat buffet of sadistic entitlement. The films light and design the Capitol like a cross between a game show and a Super Bowl halftime show, a decadent, candy-colored world of excess à *la* late Rome or Las Vegas. Despite being styled as the embodiment of spectacle in vividly saturated neon and fluorescent colors—in stark contrast to the drab, desaturated, and flatly lit districts—the people of the Capitol are a perpetual audience. They view The Hunger Games but will never be called to participate in them. Their democratic participation comes in the form of vigorous consumption. Collins's Capitol and its Games are little more than America's game-show culture reimagined as a totalitarian state.

The first *Hunger Games* film (2012) pushes Collins's imagery even further. Director Gary Ross stages the reapings in a manner reminiscent of concentration camp intake scenes in Holocaust films such as *Schindler's List*, with militarized, jackbooted Capitol police (called Peacekeepers) herding frightened citizens into rigid lines by gender while Capitol officials set up small tables and paperwork for processing them. Many of the sequences depicting the Capitol and the Games lean on a blend of Nazi architecture and imagery, referencing structures of Albert Speer and the rally scenes of Leni Riefenstahl's *The Triumph of the Will* (1935). While Ross's decision leans heavily on Nazi iconography as visual shorthand for evil, his choice does further the "postmodern archaic" of the Games, considering that the Nazis also valorized "ancient myths of purification and justice via abasement and suffering" to justify their atrocities as natural. The three subsequent films preserve Ross's Nazified representation of the Capitol, ensuring that viewers always associate Panem's state-sponsored death with

The Hunger Games' Nazi aesthetics.

the Third Reich's brand of fascism and genocide. Collins makes a particularly biting connection between the state and public executions when Katniss sings an old folk balled called "The Hanging Tree" in *Mockingjay* (2010). The title and lyrics immediately remind viewers of Jim Crow-era lynchings, another instance of state-sanctioned violence carried out in front of an entertained audience and broadcast to the nation in the form of postcards and news reports. This moment further contextualizes the Games as a form of terror condoned and facilitated by the state that used the public nature of these crimes as a means of entertaining the dominant culture and terrorizing oppressed people, keeping them from gaining access to freedom and political power.

The districts serving the Capitol in *The Hunger Games* series represent Baudrillard's "negative satellites of the city" that "translate the end of the city ... as a determined, qualitative space, as an original synthesis of society" (Baudrillard, "Hypermarket" 78). Their only purpose is to supply the people in the Capitol with the resources they need to continue their extravagant lifestyle—coal, fishing, lumber, textiles, and, of course, tributes. They are subcontractors performing outsourced labor for a leisure class, with geography being the sole determinant of their relative value. Typically, reality shows divorce their contestants from their relationships and associations (region, culture, family, etc.) to emphasize the "internal politics of the game" (Holmes 116). Within *The Hunger Games*, however, no such separation exists because the rules of the game simulate the external politics of Panem, acting as a learning tool that reinforces the Capitol's ideology. Therefore, contestants are continually identified by their district, and their fate in the game often depends on the socio-economic situation of wherever they come from. In effect, the Games facilitate "the implosion of the social in the masses" because they enforce the disparities not only between the Capitol and the districts but among and within the districts themselves (Baudrillard, "Implosion" 81). Most of these districts experience abject, oppressive conditions.

The Hunger Games' Nazi aesthetics.

Districts closer to the Capitol tend to be wealthier and win the Games more often, earning them more food from the Capitol and more resentment from other districts. Within each district, poorer families put their child's name in the drawing more times in exchange for more food, which Katniss's friend Gale says represents "just another tool to cause misery" by "plant[ing] hatred between the starving workers of the Seam and those who can generally count on supper and thereby ensur[ing] [they] never trust one another" and therefore cannot rebel against their common enemy (*Hunger Games* 14). Solidarity becomes impossible because any reaping could turn an ally into one's victim or one's murderer.

To escape that subjugation, their district must win at the Games, which involves turning eleven other districts into victims. Thus a player in the Games faces a double-bind: become a victim and die or become a winner and perpetuate the cycle of victimization. Gaylard describes this dilemma as the central conflict of any reality show but posits it as a conflict with capitalism: "embrace capitalist survival whole-heartedly and ... deceive and betray, or ... take an ethical standpoint via another value system, and thereby lose the game." Similarly, Jérôme Bourdon connects reality television to a victim culture in that "being a victim and telling about it in public space [the show] is now a strategy both for identity construction (individual and collective) and for gaining rights in public space"; however, these programs, he claims, do not permit one to maintain victim status. Instead, "the victim must demonstrate an ability to overcome victimization, to become a 'winner,' sometimes through exploiting what made [them] a victim" to win sympathy with the show's producers or audience and thus remain on the show (73). Within the context of a reality competition show, such a move comes at a price because becoming a winner means eliminating other players who also may be victims but do not get a chance to tell their stories because the winner has silenced them (73). Viewed in this light, the Hunger Games serves as a synecdoche for the broader oppression citizens face at the hands of the state.

The Hunger Games makes this victimization visual and attempts to transform it into political power. When the Capitol exerts its power on the citizens, one "touches the three middle fingers of their left hand to their lips" and raise them in the air (*Hunger Games* 24). Because the Capitol controls not only all means of communication but also all methods of surveillance, silence constitutes "the boldest form of dissent they can manage." Their silence says, "[They] do not agree. [They] do not condone. All of this is wrong" (24). While this silent protest may not appear to accomplish much for the oppressed, Baudrillard suggests it may be the only effective protest one has in an image culture. The "absence of a response can no longer be understood at all as a strategy of power, but as a counterstrategy of the masses themselves when they encounter power" ("Implosion" 84).

Collins adopts this dynamic for Katniss's political awakening in *The Hunger Games*, in which Katniss turns the death of Rue, another tribute, into a media event that broadcasts their powerlessness. Collins describes her thoughts shifting from anger at her opponents in the Games who killed Rue toward an anger at the Capitol itself. "Rue's death has forced me to confront my own fury against the cruelty, the injustice they inflict upon us," she says, and her feeling of "impotence" allows Katniss to discover the power of the image as a political tool (*Hunger Games* 236). "I want to do something, right here, right now," she says, "to shame them, to make them accountable, to show the Capitol that whatever they do or force us to do there is a part of every tribute they can't own. That Rue was more than a piece in their Games. And so am I" (236–37). Katniss creates a makeshift funeral for Rue, arranging flowers around her that cover her wounds and surround her with bright, vivid colors that reveal her as a child unjustly killed. "They'll have to show it" on television, she notes (237). In building a memorial to Rue, Katniss creates a media event, an image, an act that has heretofore been the sole privilege of the Capitol. Where the Capitol's mediation dehumanizes the people of the districts, Katniss's act turns Rue into a person, making visible to viewers what the Capitol has been using the Hunger Games to hide for seventy-four years: the state is killing people and packaging that murder as entertainment.

In creating an image, though, Collins demonstrates that silence need not be voiceless. Katniss's makeshift funeral for Rue and the whistle that served as their secret signal in the Games become the rallying cries and catalyzing symbols for uprisings in the districts. After this scene, Katniss behaves less like an individual in the Games and more like a spokesperson. When she receives

Katniss steps into her spotlight.

a gift from District 11 in thanks for memorializing Rue, Katniss "step[s] into the last falling rays of sunlight" and addresses the camera to express her gratitude (239). In stepping into a light and speaking into the camera to thank her sponsors, Katniss effectively takes over as host of The Hunger Games. Rue's death awakens Katniss to the control that she has over the Games and what the Capitol broadcasts, and because the Games are the mechanism of the state's power, that means Katniss also exerts power over the state itself.

This power becomes most apparent in the climax to *The Hunger Games*. Earlier in the novel, when Katniss and her fellow District 12 tribute Peeta's budding romance made for good television, the Gamemakers announced that they would allow two people to win, so long as they were from the same district; however, when Katniss and Peeta are the only two tributes left breathing, the Capitol, displeased with Katniss's defiant actions, reverses its ruling, forcing either Katniss of Peeta to kill the other. These rule changes serve the same function as The Hunger Games themselves: to demonstrate the power that the Capitol has over the lives of its citizens. Like the state, the Gamemakers can change the rules and save lives, or they can change them and take lives. Katniss and Peeta subvert the Capitol's dominance with a rule change of their own by forming a suicide pact live on-air, plotting to take their lives by eating poisonous berries rather than killing each other. Collins's consumption metaphor becomes clear: in eating what the state feeds them, citizens consume their own death.

The Hunger Games cannot end without a winner, and so this suicide pact saves their lives: the Capitol pronounces them the winners of the Games before they can eat the berries, proving that only deaths sanctioned and carried out by the state are allowed. In choosing how and when they die, Katniss and Peeta "not only deny the Capitol the captured life of a victor, they also deny it their deaths," transforming a commonly accepted "reconfirmation of the Capitol's power" into "an act of refusal" (Fisher, "Precarious Dystopias" 30). Katniss and Peeta's pact breaks down the workings of the show and forces it (and the state that controls it) to play by their rules, demonstrating that whoever controls the game also controls the government. The Gamemakers and the Capitol turn out to be players as well, and they can be forced into making moves by not following their rules. By doing it on live television, Katniss and Peeta show the world that the Capitol's interests can be defied without immediate retribution, thus "converting fatalism into insurrection" that marks a "reinvention of solidarity" that the Capitol has suppressed (Fisher, "Precarious Dystopias" 30, 33). As President Snow rightly fears, "If a girl from District 12, of all places, can defy the Capitol and walk away unharmed, what is to stop [others] from doing the same?" (*Catching Fire* 21). Their action "increases displacement in the games" and has a strong "effect on the balance of power" (Lyotard 16). Their "unexpected 'move'" in the Games "suppl[ies] the system with that increased performativity" in the form of uprisings in the districts, proving that when one challenges the game, one also challenges the state (Lyotard 15).

Each strike against the Capitol's grip on the people begins with an attack on the game show that symbolizes it because Panem is an image-based culture. The 75th Hunger Games in *Catching Fire* ends with Katniss and the other victors banding together to subvert the show from within, with Katniss leading an assault on the most menacing contestant in the Games: the Game itself. She fires an arrow into the sky/screen, causing an electrical malfunction that makes the Capitol's power, both literally and figuratively, go out. With the Games fully defeated at the end of *Catching Fire*, the uprising can now attack the Capitol directly, bringing the arena to the booby-trapped streets of power, with former tributes navigating the game space hoping to arrive at the cornucopia of government control.

Collins's choice to have a game show as the main exemplar of state media manipulation and a disobedient game-show contestant as the symbol of the revolution shows the degree to which power perpetuates itself via the image. In a hypermediated image culture in which governments exert control over the image, resistance movements believe they must do the same if they desire any chance at success. Thus, the revolution that occupies the action of *Catching Fire* and *Mockingjay*, Collins's follow-ups to *The Hunger Games*, is fought more with broadcast signals than with guns. However, Collins's series convincingly argues, as does Jean Baudrillard, that battles waged at the level of the image flood more information into a system, which leads to an implosion of meaning rather than a distillation of it. Like the Capitol, the rebellion's manipulation of the media sows the seeds of its own destruction until it becomes the very thing it aims to destroy: a totalitarian state that conscripts citizens in a power game for control of their lives. For Collins, there is no escaping the Games because the Games are power itself. There is always another round of play.

Katniss Everdeen serves as the foremost symbol of the rebellion, but the mockingjay also comes to represent the resistance because the creature, like the people it represents, began its life as a tool of the Capitol that adapted and "thrive[d] in a new form" that could destroy its oppressive creator (*Catching Fire* 92). Katniss protests being reduced to a two-dimensional celebrity image of the revolution, to little success. Her defiance becomes a "fashion sensation" in the Capitol, with the mockingjay appearing on belt buckles, brooches, and tattoos (78). Katniss objects to the commodification of the rebellion. "Real rebels don't put a secret symbol on something as durable as jewelry," she complains, "they put it on a wafer of bread that can be eaten in a second if necessary" (190). While her complaint does resemble a hipster complaining about a band gone mainstream, rebellion against a consumption-based state is incompatible with consumer goods because these accessories strengthen the very culture they want deposed. Revolution becomes just another product in the marketplace, effectively consuming itself in the process of commodification. This detail acts as a miniature "implosion of meaning" that foreshadows the ways in which the resistance, in adopting the methods of the Capitol, will fail in establishing a new society free from image-based oppression and the games that attend it.

Initially, however, Collins instills readers with hope that the more aware one becomes of the mechanics of image production, the more cracks in power's façade they can see and reveal. Twill, a dissident from District 8, shows Katniss a "live" video feed from District 13, the district allegedly obliterated by the Capitol during the Dark Days. Close inspection of this "live" video reveals the same mockingjay flying in the background of the charred, barren landscape of District 13 every time the Capitol broadcasts it. This detail transforms the story of District 13 from fact to fiction, making it a show produced by the Capitol to control the population just like The Hunger Games. Collins combines several symbols and themes into this moment: the evidence that proves the feed's fraudulence is also the symbol of the resistance, which shows that when the powerless gain access to the means of broadcasting and image manipulation, they become revolutionaries against image-based oppression.

The rebels wage war with what they call "Airtime Assaults," pirate broadcasts that hijack the Capitol's signal and expose the reality behind the Capitol's lies via short propaganda spots, or "propos." The rebellion flooding the airwaves with the conflicting information of their propo is "directly destructive of [the Capitol's] meaning and signification" in two ways: their information in the propo proposes an alternative to the Capitol's version of the truth, and their taking

Mockingjay's barrage of visual data.

control of the signal weakens the authority of the Capitol's future broadcasts and assertions of power (Baudrillard, "Implosion" 79). However, rather than establishing truth, these propos call truth into question by presenting an alternate version of Panem's reality that, as a broadcast image, appears as authentic as the Capitol's imagery. These broadcasts may "assault" the Capitol's televisual stronghold, but they also distract viewers from the real.

This misdirection is intentional on the part of the rebellion because they use one assault to provide cover for a rescue team as it infiltrates the Capitol to free Peeta. Francis Lawrence's staging and editing of this "Airtime Assault" in the film *Mockingjay: Part 1* (2014) represents a Baudrillardian implosion of meaning colliding with an act of resistance. The montage privileges cinematic space by having the camera simultaneously present the "live feed" from the raid, the rebel's propaganda, and the rebels controlling both from their headquarters in District 13. Lawrence cuts from banks of monitors showing the feed from the rescue team's helmets and the propo being broadcast, to shots of Katniss (Jennifer Lawrence), Plutarch Heavensbee (Philip Seymour Hoffman), and Alma Coin (Julianne Moore) watching from the control room, to the computer screens where the broadcast signal is hacked, to shots of the rescue team infiltrating the Capitol, all while the audio from the propo plays under every shot in the sequence. While the television signal can only present one feed to viewers in the film, the cinematic space can present every feed. As viewers, both the rebels and the audience are bombarded with imagery and audio from a variety of sources until one can do little but become captive to the screen, helpless to alter the outcome of any of the feeds and uncertain as to which image represents the truth. In fact, viewers are not even sure which image to look at.

The Hunger Games shows "mass media on the side of power in the manipulation of the masses" to the extent that power and media represent the same entity; however, Collins's work also shows the media engaging in "the liquidation of meaning." Unlike Baudrillard, though, this liquidation is not "on the side of the masses" (Baudrillard, "Implosion" 84). Even though they are the ones producing the counterstrike against power, the rebels' strike merely transfers oppression and image-based deception to another entity. Thus, *The Hunger Games* shows an implosion of media and message. In pumping more images into the system, the rebellion is not producing truth but obscuring it until the revolution ends in the "total entropy" of the rebellion and the Capitol becoming virtually indistinguishable (Baudrillard, "Implosion" 80).

Mockingjay reveals Collins's suspicious attitude toward power because even though The Hunger Games may no longer exist, the power they represent never goes away. Collins equates the new-and-improved state that the resistance imagines with the state it seeks to replace in that both play games with human lives to advance its agenda. Readers get hints of their similarity before Katniss even travels to District 13. At the end of *Catching Fire*, Katniss discovers that her seemingly autonomous acts of rebellion against the Capitol were actually part of an elaborate scheme orchestrated by Gamemaker Plutarch Heavensbee, who has been secretly working for the resistance all along. Instead of being free, Katniss's every move has been controlled by a Gamemaker; she has been "used without consent, without knowledge" by a political group for the purposes of them gaining power over others (*Catching Fire* 385).

In becoming part of the revolution, Katniss merely moves from one game to another, and the bulk of *Mockingjay* concerns her realizing that the rebellion she symbolizes is the same as the government it nominally opposes. Groomed by Heavensbee to be the Mockingjay in the flesh, "the symbol of the revolution ... the actual leader, the face, the voice, the embodiment of the revolution. The person who the districts ... can count on to blaze the path to victory," Katniss has more in common with the star of a new reality show than the leader of a resistance movement (*Mockingjay* 10). To serve as "the actual leader, the face, the voice, the embodiment of the revolution," Katniss must submit to "a whole team of people to make [her] over, dress [her], write [her] speeches, orchestrate [her] appearances" (10, 11). She travels through the districts "suited up in [her] Mockingjay outfit, with [her] bow slung over [her] shoulder and an earpiece ...just in case a good opportunity for a propo arises" (206). As an armed correspondent, Katniss spends every moment poised to become part of a war, a television show, or both, making her the star tribute in the rebellion's version of The Hunger Games, always ready to "spontaneously" produce rebellious content. She is pure image, pure surface, pure symbol. Despite her lack of image consciousness, Katniss is hyperaware of when she could be being watched, always noting cameras, which she alternately calls "buzzards" and "insectlike," are likely to be (*Hunger Games* 16, 40). Even when someone does not act like a movie star, a surveillance state trains its subjects to think like one. There is little difference between The Hunger Games and the entire country: both are under continual surveillance, and both are kept compliant by the threat of deadly violence. The Hunger Games is Panem in miniature. The map is the territory.

Similarly, the resistance movement in District 13 is a mirror version of the Capitol, strictly governed by an anti-consumerist, anti-materialist, thoroughly regimented life in which fashion and makeup are outlawed, people are only allowed to eat "enough calories to take [them] to the next meal," and "waste is practically a criminal activity" (*Mockingjay* 35, 18). Where the Capitol is a garish world of excess in the films, District 13 has no color at all in the *Mockingjay* films. Its gunmetal gray and dirt brown color scheme makes the desaturated world of District 12 look lush by comparison. Further, the space the rebels inhabit demonstrates how much their shadow government resembles their enemy's: they operate in an underground compound originally created as "a clandestine refuge for government leaders in a time of war" (17). On one level this choice of setting exemplifies a strong sense of irony because, like the Games themselves, the space that is created to preserve Panem's government winds up being the space the rebellion uses to tear it down; on another level, though, Collins's irony is much more cutting because this resistance movement's mimicry of the Capitol's methods does in fact preserve its power in a time of war.

By the end of *The Hunger Games* series, the revolution that Collins seemed to be dreaming of the whole time proves itself to be corrupt before it is even realized. The spartan policies of District 13 merely foreshadow a larger approach to control that Coin and Heavensbee intend to enact. When the revolution comes to fruition in *Mockingjay*, some in the new government want to kill "those who held Capitol citizenship," which equates to game show contestants gaining power over the show and subjecting the producers and the audience to the game. (368). President Coin's compromise turns out to be just that: she wants to renew The Hunger Games for a 76th season, "a final, symbolic Hunger Games," with the tributes coming from "the children directly related to those who held the most power" (369). The show must go on because the Games are the state's expression of power.

Katniss revolts against these methods of power, believing that "it benefits no one to live in a world" that "sacrifices its children's lives to settle its differences" (*Mockingjay* 377). This notion explains why Katniss's only act of political violence is not assassinating President Snow, which was her goal for the bulk of the series, but the newly empowered President Coin. Katniss's assassination of Coin strikes more directly at corrupt power than killing Snow would. Because Snow has been deposed, killing him would no longer be a revolutionary act;

in doing so, Katniss would be on the side of Coin's authoritarian state and its score-settling. Killing Coin takes aim at state power with the hopes of overthrowing it permanently; however, Collins does not provide readers with much assurance that Katniss's act accomplishes more than cancelling The Hunger Games for the time being. From beginning to end, reader surrogate Katniss Everdeen only has the illusion of being an independent operator. In actuality, she has always been a pawn in someone else's game, playing a role in a game that ensures a stable transfer of power. Even after killing Coin and supposedly delivering the revolution from implosion, she still must pretend to be an enemy of the state, living under the assumption that she will receive a pardon once the state stabilizes, which, given all the evidence, may never occur. Like the last tribute standing at the end of The Hunger Games, Katniss ends the series sequestered in a sort of Victor's Village. She is a winner. The state still controls her fate. The odds are as in her favor as they have always been.

Collins ends her series without much sense of hope for a state free from authoritarian, image-based control. She not only does not imagine a world outside the endless repetition of brutal game shows and oppressive state power, she does not seem convinced that one is even possible. Now that the revolution is over, Gamemaker Plutarch Heavensbee turns his attention to producing Katniss's show trial and a singing program. The Games, it seems, never end because the culture demands to be provided with content, which the state happily obliges and uses to advance its own agenda, or at least distract citizens from it.

The failure of the revolution in *The Hunger Games* confirms Baudrillard's claim that "it is useless to dream of revolution through content, useless to dream of a revelation through form, because the medium and the real are now in a single nebula whose truth is indecipherable" ("Implosion" 83). All power is corrupt for Collins because power is simply a game that permits one group of people to play with the lives of a larger group, with the hosts and the contestants serving as the only variables. The game show becomes an apt metaphor for her ideas because like tributes, contestants must submit to the will of the game or risk not being able to play. One could accuse Collins of having a failure of imagination for ending the series without much positive change; however, her ending does follow Baudrillard's claim that "there is no alternative to this, no logical resolution" when "the media carry meaning and countermeaning" in which they deliver "the simulation internal to the system and the simulation that destroys the system" ("Implosion" 84). There is, in effect, no outside, not even in District 13, which is and always was a shadow of the state above-ground, just waiting for the opportune moment to rise up and take its turn hosting the Games.

CATEGORY

THE PRESSURE APPLIED BY THE SYSTEM

A similar dynamic appears in Peter Watkins's 1969 film *The Gladiators*, where direct, violent resistance no longer poses a threat to autocratic power but becomes the means by which power sustains its dominance. Shot in his trademark quasi-documentary style that combines vérité cinematography with editorializing montage and voiceover, Watkins's film chronicles the 256th International "Peace Games," a simulated military conflict (sponsored by a pasta company) in which twenty soldiers representing various members of the UN and leading Communist countries compete to reach the control room first (Arthur 59). These Peace Games exist, the voiceover explains, to "maintain international peace and internal security ... and to reaffirm faith in the dignity and worth of the human being" by "channel[ing]" and sating each country's "aggressive drives" for militarized conflict and to stoke nationalistic pride in the viewers of this immensely popular broadcast (Gomez 87). Simply put, the ritual of the game show simulates the ritual of war; the militarized nations of the world fight each other in the game to avoid global annihilation, or so they claim (Arthur 62).

The Peace Games may be a military exercise, and the film may open with an elaborate flag-raising ceremony, but the generals are not the ones in charge. They function primarily as an audience in the film, snacking on hors d'oeuvres and pasta while they watch the game play out from a lush Swedish mansion, far from the control room. The real headquarters for the Peace Games resides in a computer named Ideological Correction and Rapid Unification System (ICARUS), which, like the Gamemakers in *The Hunger Games*, controls everything: it changes the weather, it electrifies doors, it even alters the contestants' mental and emotional states at the push of a button. Watkins allows the audience to hear the sub-audible pulses that can trigger anything from changes in weather to more abstract shifts such as "Achilles heel," "existential threat," or "slow-motion murder" at will. These beeps represent "the pressure applied by the system" on the players "to ensure that we all play the game as hard as we can."

In truth, as in *The Hunger Games*, everything in *The Gladiators* succumbs to "the pressure applied by the system"—soldiers, generals, countries, even revolutionaries determined to tear the system apart. As Collins does with Katniss Everdeen, Watkins shows how resistance figures attempting to seize the means of broadcast production not only ensure the preservation of the image culture that they claim to be terminating, but how this hunger for control over the image

The audience of generals far from the control room.

The generals enjoy hors d'oeuvres.

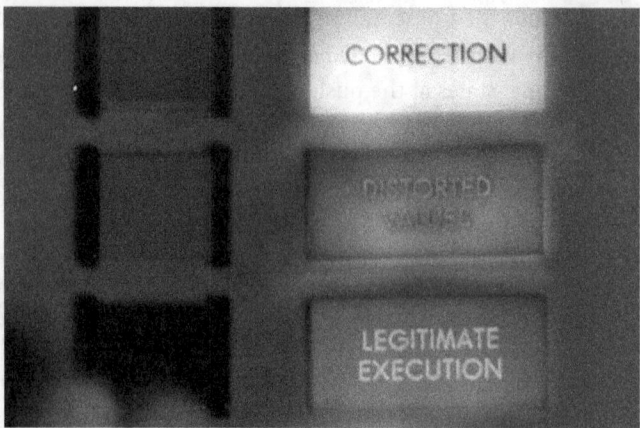
The ICARUS control system.

A rebel in the control room?

negates genuinely revolutionary energies. The film leads the audience to believe that B-3, a French student on the Allies team played by Jean-Pierre Delamour, is a revolutionary fighter. This angry young man of Mai '68 delivers strident denunciations of the system, proclaiming his determination to bring about a violent and permanent end to the Peace Games by storming the control room, demolishing ICARUS, and establishing a new form of government. However, B-3 is not in fact a subversive. He may be unaware of it, but he plays perhaps the most vital role in the success of the game and the stability of the existing world order, which viewers gradually discover through the absolute calm every authority greets him with. His opposition to the game is simply part of the game, an obvious and direct form of opposition that the game anticipates and depends on. His rebellion is not against the system: it is part of the system's means of control. A feature, not a bug. Therefore, B-3's entrance into the control room makes perfect sense: he is part of the machine, and his role does not impede the Peace Games but strengthens them because, regardless of his idealistic statements to the contrary, he does not seek to end the repressive power of the state but to wield it, to occupy the other side of the screen.

Another force of resistance appears in *The Gladiators*, but, unlike B-3, it constitutes a threat so urgent that the game must stop to neutralize it immediately. B-6, a man on the Allies team played by J. Z. Kennedy, falls in love with C-2, a woman from the Chinese team played by Pik Sen Lim who has been captured by the Allies. Together, they attempt to escape the game. The metaphorical implications of this relationship are not hard to see: when opposing nations interact outside the confines of armed conflict, they will develop a sense of empathy and solidarity that will drive them out of the cycle of antagonism and militarization. Unlike the behavior of B-3, which merely duplicates violent conflict, B-6 and C-2's relationship constitutes the truly revolutionary, subversive threat in to the prevailing order in *The Gladiators* precisely because it rejects the rules of both the Peace Games and the game of Cold War politics; there can be no winner if one rejects competition and aggression in favor of collaboration and empathy. While subverting the rules is often thought of as an aggressive act, refusing to play by the rules can be peaceful when the rules themselves encourage violence.

The final sequence of the film illustrates how the state would rather abandon its own military objectives and cancel the game than allow "counter-revolutionary" and "subversive young perverts" to play freely and determine their own outcome. The generals attempt to shirk the burden of killing B-6 and C-2 by switching ICARUS into automatic mode, which triggers a malfunction in the machine that rains bombs down on most of the game space and jeopardizes the future of the Peace Games. The automatic, or natural, outcome of the Peace Games is complete annihilation. Fortunately for the officers, B-3 infiltrates the control room during this breakdown and restarts the ICARUS machine, unknowingly bringing back online the system he sought to destroy and ensuring that B-6 and C-2 are captured, beaten, and presumably killed. B-3's moves, no matter how revolutionary he perceives them to be, are not unexpected, so they cannot inject fresh energy into the system by "increas[ing] displacement in the games" and "supply[ing] the system with that increased performativity"; they simply keep the gears turning as usual (Lyotard 16, 21). Through B-3, Watkins illuminates an idea latent in *The Hunger Games* and explicit in Baudrillard: "Revolutionary movements can never succeed if they fight the system on its own terms" (Gomez 98).

The Gladiators ultimately shows how the state uses violent games and ersatz uprisings to keep transformative revolution at bay. The same emotions that compel players to play or destroy the game are the same ones the state stokes in its citizens to maintain its grip on power—hostility, nationalism, othering, etc. Despite B-3's assertions that his system will be more equitable, Captain Davidsson, the ICARUS technician played by Hans Bendrik, dismisses his idealism as ignorance: "The Machine uses all of us," he tells B-3 at the film's end. "Your system or someone else's. They're all the same." *The Gladiators* suggests that most people, even self-proclaimed subversives such as B-3, submit to the pressures applied by the system because it, like the ICARUS machine, controls them unconsciously via the subaudible "pulses" in the culture that allow them to act under the impression that they are autonomous individuals with political agency, when those beliefs are in fact created, anticipated, and neutralized by the system. The Peace Games accurately simulate how the state governs: this reality-based game demonstrates that the state is far less concerned with ideology than with "a pathological need for control" that keeps the world eternally on the brink to concentrate power within the military (Arthur 62). The governments do not host the games to ward off global thermonuclear war but, as Joseph A. Gomez argues, "to perpetuate a climate of world hate, distrust, and aggressive antagonism in order to maintain their own nationalistic systems and value structures" (93). The end of the film supports this claim when rising nations such as Nigeria and India do not take a stand against the imperialism of the West; instead, they collaborate because they want to know that they have arrived on the world stage, to be recognized as players in the game.

Similarly, the get-rich-quick wish fulfilment of game shows only validates and intensifies the capitalist ethos by extolling the consumer market as the only source of happiness and self-actualization. Players do not seek to beat a game show but to win by satisfying its needs; any genuine expression of agency on the part of a player would grind the game to a halt until that player could be ejected. As in the Peace Games, the message of a game show is never that there is a more satisfying, equitable alternative elsewhere, just that the only way to win is to keep playing, keep fueling the same system responsible for the conflict one plays the game to resolve. Rather than provide viewers with a way out of this oppressive cycle, the games fill contestants and viewers with an illusory freedom that ensures all participants will "play the game as hard as we can" and get, in the words of Watkins himself, "safely nowhere" (Gomez 98).

CATEGORY

SEEING IS BELIEVING

Although these works are effective in their criticism of the symbiotic relationship between the media and the state in controlling people's lives, they largely leave out a crucial player that allows this dynamic to continue: the audience. Even though they feature televised executions, these works focus remarkably little on the mechanics of broadcasting and viewing. Collins's choice to have *The Hunger Games* series narrated from the point of view of Katniss Everdeen limits the amount of information about the look and tone of the broadcast viewers receive because Katniss is seldom a spectator. The fealty of the directors of *The Hunger Games* films to the source material extends so far that one can view all four *Hunger Games* films and still not have much sense of what a broadcast of the Games actually looks like to a viewer. In focusing his attention onto the military brass watching the Peace Games in *The Gladiators*, Watkins overlooks the complicit role of the media and the audience in preserving bourgeois comfort. Watkins's style may, as Joseph Gomez argues, "start a process of thinking in the audience about the nature of all television programs"; however, in never seeing who watches the broadcast or what that broadcast even looks like apart from one on-camera field correspondent, a viewer has no sense of how closely the world in which they sit watching *The Gladiators* resembles the dystopian world that *The Gladiators* presents (95). As a result, the viewer's anger remains inertly directed at the people who play the game and not as those whose watching sustains it. Omitting the audience from the world of the story allows viewers to identify with the protagonists of the film—oppressed, lower class, defiant, not entertained—and ignore the truth: the reality viewers inhabit as consumers aligns them far more closely with the invisible spectators of these brutal games—privileged, compliant, and definitely entertained.

Thankfully, Stephen King's Richard Bachman novel *The Running Man* (1982) and Paul Michael Glaser's 1987 film adaptation devote considerable attention to the audience's role as spectators. Although the details differ, the game show in each work is similar: *The Running Man* is a manhunt in which a contestant runs from a team of executioners while a fascinated public eagerly roots for the runner's gory demise. In the novel, contestants volunteer and earn money for each hour they evade capture, with a grand prize of "one billion New Dollars" if they remain at-large for thirty days (King 67). There is no set: the Hunters pursue the contestant across the entire country. Everyday citizens are both the studio audience and potential contestants who could win $100 for "a verified sighting" and $1,000 for "a sighting which results in a kill" (88). The network continually broadcasts runner Ben Richards's whereabouts and encourages the public to track him down and assist the state in killing him, which turns the show into "a fourth-estate hit squad," a "vigilante" program packages policing as entertainment (Texter 50, 52).

Glaser's film extends the policing metaphor of the novel to the entire criminal justice system. The contestants in the film are convicts who compete for fabulous prizes such as "a trial by jury, a suspended sentence, or maybe a full pardon." The Hunters here are called Stalkers, and they hunt the runners through a ruined urban landscape that is "400 square blocks of danger, destruction, demolition, and death." The show is produced by ICS "in association with the Department of Justice" and taped in front of a live studio audience. Together, King's novel and Glaser's film create "worlds of bureaucratic voyeurism, totalitarian control, and video-bred violence" that demonstrate the American bourgeoisie's complicity in creating and perpetuating the conditions that give rise to a program such as *The Running Man* (Doherty, "Video" 71; Texter 53). If these works want

The Running Man's enthusiastic crowd.

Damon Killian (Richard Dawson) presents the next Hunter to an excited audience.

The Running Man's bloodthirsty audience.

readers and viewers to see the game show as a metaphor for state power, their inclusion of the audience forces readers and viewers to accept that watching the show equates to voting for the state's agenda.

Where *The Hunger Games* employs a series of distancing devices to keep the audience from feeling the connection between its world and theirs too immediately—renaming America Panem, outrageous costumes, overdetermined names, Nazi iconography—both versions of *The Running Man* try to hit as close to home as possible. Even though both works are set decades into the future, the world is very much contemporary. These reminders prevent audiences from getting sucked into the story because they frequently call on readers and viewers to interrogate the degree to which they already inhabit the dystopia of the story. Ironically enough, after several false starts, Ben Affleck and Matt Damon turned King's conception of *The Running Man* into the streaming show *The Runner*, where a "runner" would be tracked across America by "agents" who would be aided by "the greatest resource on the planet—the American public," who could join in the hunt by signing up online as bounty-hunters (Texter 68). The show launched in 2016, one year ahead of the 2017-set film.

King's novel critiques the failure of a democratic capitalist government based in consumption, creating a world where providing outstanding entertainment overshadows providing basic services to people. Wendy Brown shows how the partnership between neoliberalism and neoconservatism weakened the public's understanding of a democratic government that serves all by "producing a governed citizen who looks to find solutions in products, not political processes" (705). The chapters where Ben Richards signs up to be a contestant on one of the big-money game shows represent what Texter describes as King's "Marxist-oriented interrogation of the American superstructure," where the suffering of the poor and neglected becomes the catalyst for first-rate entertainment (45). Game shows are so popular in King's 2025 that the Free-Vee network dedicates an entire building to it, the biggest skyscraper in town. The Network Games Building rises so high that its "top [is] half buried in cloud and smog cover" (9). Free-Vee's game shows such as *Treadmill to Bucks*, *Swim the Crocodiles*, and *Dig Your Grave* are little more than elaborate torture scenarios and snuff television. *Treadmill to Bucks*, for instance makes "chronic heart, liver, or lung patients" chat with the host while walking on an accelerating treadmill, winning ten dollars per minute and receiving $50 for each trivia questions they answer correctly (2). There is no prize for winning because contestants are not expected to survive; the cash is for the loved ones they leave behind after they drop dead.

Ironically, Richards encounters free, top-notch health care inside the Network Games Building, even though everyone chosen to appear on game show will likely be dead within a fortnight. Richards thinks about how such care would cure his daughter's illness and make it unnecessary for him to volunteer to be murdered live on television or for his wife to turn tricks. This scene resembles a moment in *The Hunger Games* when Katniss receives an ointment in the arena that heals her burns almost instantly. It appears that such rapid, life-saving care exists in these worlds, but the government only provides it to its wealthiest citizens and the poor who are willing to act as entertainment for them. The Network even prints its own money in the form of "Games Certificates" that are not only "redeemable for dollars" but are better than cash because "a reputable doctor will accept them as legal tender, while a quack will not" (71–72). The best cared-for animals are the ones headed to the slaughter.

Rather than repair a broken democracy, its ruins become part of the game show's apparatus. Each medical test in the game show's intake procedure occurs in a voting booth, making being on a game show the new way citizens participate in democracy. Richards even gives a urine sample in a voting booth, giving new meaning to the notion of pissing one's vote away. His final step involves stating that he has no "relatives who have been arrested on charges of crimes against the government or against the Network" and signing a "loyalty oath" and a "Games Commission release form" (28). The body of another contestant killed in the games gets "displayed in the rotunda of the Kansas statehouse" (207). With these details, King confirms not only that government and entertainment are the same, but that going against the Network, which is capitalized, is a greater crime than going against the government, which is not.

Although alarmists frequently argue that violent programming creates more violence in the streets, *The Running Man* becomes the government's best deterrent against an uprising. In the novel, a character named Bradley rants to Richards that the Network uses these programs to narcotize the country: they "gave us the Free-Vee to keep us off the streets so we can breathe ourselves to death without making any trouble" (170–71). Or, as Killian states in the film, "You want people in front of the sets instead of on picket lines. You can't get there with reruns of *Gilligan's Island*." Douglas W. Texter shows how this dynamic works as a hybrid of an Althusserian Ideological State Apparatus and a Repressive State Apparatus in that it employs the language of game shows and war journalism to fabricate "a working-class, dangerous Other" whose execution will simultaneously stoke middle-class suburbanites' fears of urban crime while also "assuaging" them (49). Dan Killian, the executive producer of *The Running Man*, demonstrates how the program fulfills repressive government functions such as social cleansing and turning citizens into informants. The show, he says, "is one of the surest ways the Network has of getting rid of embryo troublemakers." "People won't be in the bars and hotels or gathering in the cold in front of appliance stores rooting for you to get away," he tells

Richards. "They want to see you wiped out, and they'll help if they can. The more messy the better" (66–67). Even though Richards has not committed a crime, the show turns the audience against him by manipulating photos of him, making "his eyes deeper, his forehead a little lower, his cheeks more shadowed" until he looks like "the angel of urban death … the uptown apartment dweller's boogeyman" (91). (Similarly in the film, the network reedits footage of Richards to make it appear that he led, rather than attempted to stop, a massacre.) The crowd's hateful reaction traps the innocent, violated Richards into "projecting exactly the aura of hate and defiance that they wanted him to project" (92–93). The affluent audience has their villain and the lower-class man has his enemy; there is no room for dialogue or compromise between them, and the conflict can only end with one of them being silenced. Thus, the show fulfills two vital social functions for the repressive government: "captur[ing] both middle-class imaginations and working-class bodies" (Texter 45). In that sense, as an enemy of the state and the temporary star of a hit television show, Ben Richards becomes both a product and a producer. Similar to Katniss, he must file video of himself each day or he loses prize money, supplying his executioners with fresh content that could also lead to him being located and killed. When he tries to make his content more political as he becomes more radicalized, his audio mysteriously drops out and returns with someone else's voice mimicking Richards and painting him as a crazy political radical, which only further incriminates him in the eyes of a public who eagerly awaits his murder.

King implicates the audience in *The Running Man*'s convergence of entertainment and politics through Richards's encounter with Amelia Williams, an average viewer whom he takes as a hostage. This confrontation resembles a hated reality-show contestant facing off with "the folks at home" on a reunion episode; however, unlike that scenario, it is not as satisfying to hear the audience talk back to the show. King cleverly has led readers to identify with bitter, beleaguered family man Richards, even though his financial circumstances are far from those of the middle-class reader. King's harsh portrayal of a middle-class audience member startles the reader; however, his depiction of her as smug and judgmental mimics the way the average reality television viewer speaks about cast members they do not like. This turn in the novel challenges the reader's identification and forces them to reevaluate their position in the structure of not only the novel but the American world of comfort it critiques.

King includes the audience within his work to critique their complacency, writing that the "lack of desperation" in the eyes of audience members like Amelia Williams makes them all appear "oddly incomplete, like pictures with holes for eyes or a jigsaw puzzle with a minor piece missing" (284). Richards tells Williams that after he is dead she "can go back to [her] nice split-level duplex and light up a Doke and get stoned and love the way your new silverware sparkles in the highboy. No one fighting rats with broomhandles in your neighborhood or shitting by the back stoop because the toilet doesn't work" (263). Instead of listening to the content of his description of poverty, her only response is to call him "disgusting" and complain that he "talk[s] dirty" (263). Where Richards is dirty and poor, the narrator remarks that Williams is one of the "beautiful chosen ones" who "exist[s] up where the air was rare," an existence that keeps her glued to the television and prevents her from "see[ing] the big picture, the one that runs twenty-four hours a day on channel one," which is known as the real world (264). This interaction casts new light on Killian's advice to Richards early in the novel. Killian tells him that to avoid capture for as long as possible, he should "stay low" and "close to [his] own people" (97, 96). While "low" initially seems to mean inconspicuous, the class distinctions are undeniable. Killian and the show want to ensure that the audience and the spectator never have to interact with each other because interacting would lead to them not only recognizing their shared humanity but the audience reckoning with how much their comfort depends on (and derives from) the suffering of others.

Just as appearing on the show radicalizes Richards, who previously "had shunned causes with contempt and disgust" because causes "were for pig-simple suckers and people with too much time and money on their hands," Williams's encounter with Richards shows her that the institutions that television has told her are protecting her interests do not care for her when she is not watching television (198). She learns she is as disposable as Richards to them after the police shoot at her in an attempt to get Richards. After this moment, King writes that "the mask of the well-to-do young *hausfrau* on her way back from the market now hung in tatters and shreds" (271). This notion also largely explains why so many of these works omit the audience from their narratives; including them would diminish the entertainment value of the work and prod the audience to ask tough questions of themselves that are easier to gloss over in favor of violent spectacle. Richards's encounter with Amelia Williams shows that *The Running Man* merely intensifies the same rigidly stratified social classes that give rise to people from Richards's social class being viewed as disposable objects of entertainment. Any interaction between these two separate groups of people ends up turning them both against the show and the government that encourages the affluent to view the impoverished as "dirty" criminals who deserve the abject lives they lead.

Paul Michael Glaser's film adaptation of King's novel uses the Amelia Williams confrontation as inspiration for the structure of the film itself. While Ben Richards does not interact with an audience member to the same degree that his counterpart in the novel does, viewers of *The Running Man* do: themselves.

Running Man host Richard Dawson.

Texter convincingly argues how the film adaptation "rip[s] away the relentless interrogation of material conditions offered by the novel" and "neutralize[s] it ... transforming it into the very thing it predicted and criticized" (63, 62). His reading of the novel is first rate and his criticism of the film is valid; however, his reading obscures the film's problematizing of spectatorship and the degree to which it shows that all aspects of American life have been absorbed by game show logic and aesthetics. Granted, this notion is not the novel's, but the film's indictment of American society is as withering as the one found in King's novel. In fact, the glee with which it depicts this world makes its criticism even more biting than King's bleak dystopia, which still envisions the possibility of not watching television. In the film, the people of America are too distracted by violent entertainment to even see what is happening to them, and the film encourages its audience to recognize themselves in *The Running Man*.

The film's casting makes its world mirror reality, especially the brilliant decision to cast former *Family Feud* host Richard Dawson in the role of Killian, who hosts *The Running Man* in the film. Dawson replicates his game-show-host schtick so effortlessly that one can easily overlook the nuances of such a knowingly self-aware performance that allows cinema audiences to think that they are watching a familiar game show on television at home. Thomas Doherty observes how Dawson brings the smarmier parts of his television persona to the role of Killian and leans on these predatory qualities for the behind-the-scenes interactions that require him to be an especially nefarious network producer and political operative, thus bringing the audience's game-show affiliations off the studio set and into the political realm ("Video" 76). No matter whether

The Running Man Home Game.

Killian is giving away fabulous prizes or speaking to the President's agent or arranging for a contestant's death, audiences see a game-show host.

Today's audiences may not know who Dawson is at all, but the film's other casting choices resonate even more strongly today. *The Running Man* depicts the fusion of government and entertainment in ways that even the film could not foresee. Two of its stars, former bodybuilder Arnold Schwarzenegger, who plays Ben Richards, and former pro wrestler Jesse "The Body" Ventura, who plays a Stalker named Captain Freedom, go on to become governors of California and Minnesota, respectively. Although casting bodybuilders and wrestlers may have limited the film's gravity in 1987, the fact that these figures go on to hold state office only proves the film's assertion that entertainment overpowers politics. While the film likely regarded Ronald Reagan as the pinnacle of politics and entertainment converging, its response to Reagan winds up predicting a future even more spectacular than an actor-turned-president. The fact that both Schwarzenegger and Ventura had been out of political office for several years by 2017, and the president in 2017 was a former game show host and producer, makes the film's political forecast less farfetched and more conservative. (At the risk of making the connections even more dizzying, Arnold Schwarzenegger briefly took over as host of *Celebrity Apprentice* after Donald Trump's inauguration.)

The opening prologue may state that "television is controlled by the State," but the film clearly depicts that the deal is the other way around. Showbiz has swallowed democratic life to the extent that one cannot distinguish the language of television from the language of politics (Doherty, "Video" 76). The Justice

"I'll be back"?

Department has an "Entertainment Division" that supplies *The Running Man*'s convict contestants with "court-appointed theatrical agents" and dresses them in jumpsuits sponsored by Adidas. As host of the show, Killian is a government employee who also endorses products in commercials, effectively making those products government-approved. Even the president of the United States has an agent. Unlike most films in this book, *The Running Man* adopts "the look and language of authentic television," complete with commercial breaks and promos for other game shows until the film is indistinguishable from a television show; it refuses to "elevate the cinematic spectator over his video counterpart" (76). Instead, the film continually reminds the viewer of the rhythms of television, "implicating itself and its audience into the spectator's passive complicity" (76). Doherty shows how, even though they cheer for different players, "the frothing on-screen studio audience" differs little from a crowd coming to see an Arnold Schwarzenegger action film: both want to see their hero dispatch as many people in as many different ways as possible (77). The studio audience may not compete on the show in the traditional sense, but "you don't have to be a menace to society to be a winner." Audience members get to participate in the convicts' execution by choosing their favorite Stalker to dispatch the contestants. For their efforts, they get *The Running Man* Home Game. The film does not explain what playing the game at home would entail, but it does not really need to: viewers of the film, most of whom watch the film in the comfort of their own home on video or cable, already know. The film *is* the Home Game. Like in *The Hunger Games*, there is no such thing as being off the show. There is only running.

Even though it strays from the plot of its source material, the structure of Glaser's film subtly suggests that life in 2017 plays out like a game show whether one watches television or not. In the film's first action sequence, Richards escapes from prison when other convicts hack into and disable the security system during a staged fight with the guards. Killian "discovers" Richards for *The Running Man* through the surveillance-camera footage of this event, making this jailbreak Richards's audition for the show. Richards's episode of *The Running Man* plays as a rerun of this sequence because both involve convicts using a fight with guards (the Stalkers) as a distraction so they can seize control of a broadcast signal and escape from their fatally repressive environment while the cameras record everything. After Richards repeats the same process in *The Running Man*, he again breaks out of the studio to run in the wider world as a fugitive from justice. Schwarzenegger's trademark catchphrase "I'll be back" becomes a death sentence in this regard: viewers will always be back because the show never ends.

Despite such a dire situation, both versions of *The Running Man* wholeheartedly believe that the airwaves can be a source of truth if placed in the right hands. In the novel, Richards declares, "It's the Free-Vee that gives the Network the clout that it has. If you see it on the Free-Vee, it must be true," which leads subversives to believe that broadcasting is the answer: one "could blow the [Network] outta the water with ten minutes talktime on the Free-Vee. Tell em. Show em" (298, 171). Similarly, the other two runners in the film are political subversives trying to access a network uplink within the arena of *The Running Man* to broadcast messages about the Network's misdeeds for the resistance. Like the rebellion in *The Hunger Games*, the revolutionaries in *The Running Man* assume control of the signal to broadcast propos of their own that expose Killian's lies and exonerate Richards of his crimes. The film shows audiences immediately accepting and believing this new information. As the network's slogan goes, "Seeing is believing"—the truth simply becomes whatever was broadcast last. However, viewers of these films cannot be so convinced that more information leads to more understanding because Baudrillard has shown that conflicting versions of "the truth" only call the idea of truth into question.

The Hunger Games and *The Running Man* equate challenging and defeating the game show with challenging and defeating the state because in a mediated society, whoever controls the images controls the country. However, neither work can imagine a world without media—they are, after all, media themselves—which leaves audience members simply trading one form of image-based control for another. Actual freedom does not seem to be something that these works or their audiences can see. After all, seeing requires spectation, which makes viewers part of the studio audience and allows the show to go on. No one in these works wants to stop watching television: they just want to control what people watch. They do not seek to destroy the Network and what it represents, only to run it.

A contestant cannot win on *The Running Man* because winning the game means triumphing over the state, which would set a dangerous precedent and make the show into less of a repressive tool of pacification and more of an inspirational tool of revolution. Rather than let people see Richards succeed, the show tries to absorb him, thus maintaining their control over the airwaves and the people who view them. In each work, the network offers Richards a position as the main hunter/stalker. Expectedly, Richards rejects these offers. In the novel, he chooses to die by crashing a plane into the Network Games Building, firmly demonstrating his "ultimate solidarity with the working class and his rejection of co-optation by the ruling elite" (Texter 57). He may destroy the Network Games building and everyone in it, but he also destroys himself, which is what the game wants in the first place. The resolution that King imagines is one of mutual destruction: destroying the game may destroy the state, but it will take the resistance down in flames with it in a "tremendous" explosion that "light[s] up the night sky like the wrath of God" and "rain[s] fire twenty blocks away," proving that violence and destruction are still the biggest spectacle in town (412).

Richards's refusal in the film is a more traditional showdown between the hero and the villain. Richards straps him into the pod that sends runners into the game as Killian pleads, "Americans love television. They love a game." Richards dispatches Killian by saying, "I haven't been in TV as long as you, but I'm a quick learner, and I'm going to give the people what I think they want" and launching him into the game, where his capsule crashes into a cement wall and explodes. As clever as Richard's reply may be, it is also fraught with contradictions. He may be killing the host of the show, but in reversing their roles, he has become the host, perpetuating the show he seeks to destroy by giving the people what he thinks they want: more violence. The destruction of *The Running Man* becomes just another episode of the show; however, unlike Texter claims, this outcome does not neutralize the film's or the source material's critique. After all, Richards is right about what the people want: the audience does want to see him kill Killian. That is the climax the entire film has been headed toward, and it is what the people left their homes (and televisions) to see. In knowingly embracing its status as an image-based consumer product, the film shows how everything—criminal justice, politics, human relationships, even life and death—is now an image-based consumer product that plays out according to the logic of game shows. Reality television is indeed the map to reality's territory, and this realization invites the audience to ask itself why entertainment aimed at them must end this way. Why is it what the people want? With its emphasis on the studio audience and their reactions to the suffering of innocent people, the film compels the audience "to consider implicitly just what kind of political system would allow its youngest and most vulnerable citizens to be made into such grotesqueries" (Texter 61).

Even though the book and the film do not present much choice between "total destruction" or "complete assimilation," they do alert audiences to "the bourgeoisie's anxiety" about the existence of a lower class amidst all their material comfort (Texter 62). The works show how, instead of confronting the system that fosters such class disparity, media normalizes it in a "postmodern archaic" that transforms human suffering and abjection into entertainment. One could argue that the irony the works use to alert audiences "feeds rather than challenges capitalist realism" by "perform[ing] our anti-capitalism for us, allowing us to continue to consume with impunity" (Fisher, *Capitalist Realism* 12). However, the lack of a satisfying resolution to these works makes that claim harder to endorse. In their failure to gratify the audience's desire for a successful overthrow of an oppressive state fully, the works elicit scrutiny, not passivity, inviting the audience to interrogate why and how the characters' efforts fail and what obstacles impede political change in American culture.

Although it does feature a healthy dose of the kind of didacticism one might expect from a young-adult novel, Collins's explanation for renaming the nation Panem delivers a damning and pointed critique of American culture to her impressionable readers. The name comes from "*panem et circenses*," meaning that "in return for full bellies and entertainment," people will gladly give up their political agency, if only to no longer be hungry for entertainment (*Mockingjay* 223). Katniss and the other tributes are entertainment for a gluttonous state, its bread *and* its circus. The rebellion also uses Katniss as bread for the hungry in the form of her image and as circus through propos that inspire and entertain the rebels. As long as audiences resemble the kind depicted in these works, "fickle, stupid beings with poor memories and a great gift for self-destruction," then they will remain tributes, runners trapped in a cycle of spectation in which the odds are never in their favor (379).

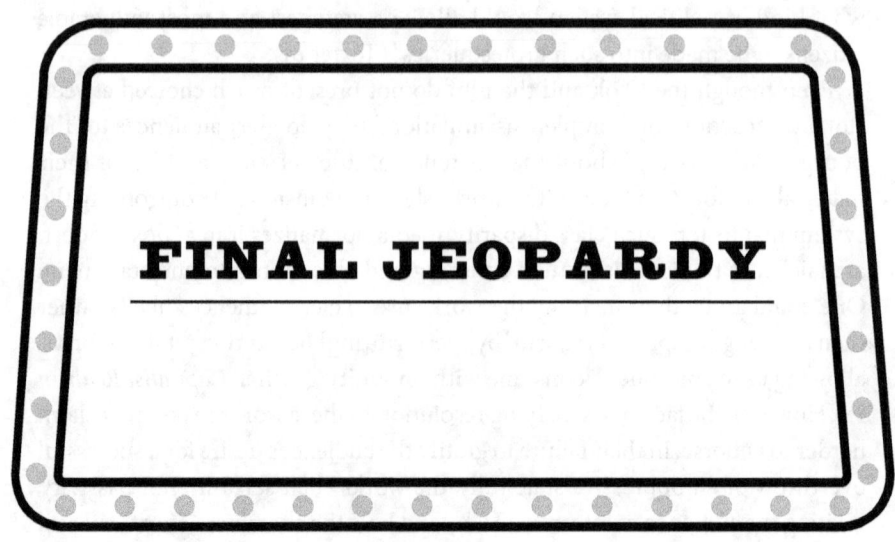

FINAL JEOPARDY

I'VE STARTED, SO I'LL FINISH.

When I began this project, Donald Trump was not a candidate for public office. As of this writing, he is the 45th president of the United States. By the time this book makes it to its current reader, there is no telling what will be the case: America could be back to its regularly scheduled programming, or it could be celebrating the Fourth Hunger Games. Derek Thompson called television in 2018 "politics by other means," but with a game show host in the White House scheduling all his major Presidential announcements for prime time (and teasing them for days in advance on Twitter), I wonder why he feels the need to separate the two.

Trump's presidency marks the apotheosis of what Douglas Kellner calls "spectator politics." Kellner observes in *Media Spectacle* that since the election of John F. Kennedy, "presidencies in the United States are staged and presented to the public in cinematic terms, using media spectacle to sell the policies, person, and image of the president to a vast and diverse public" (160). Trump's adaptation of spectator politics to suit the rhythms of twenty-four-hour television and social media cycles ultimately demonstrates how spectator politics limits a participatory democracy by reducing the role of the citizen from active participant in the process of better government to a passive spectator who, in choosing a candidate, selects the spectacle that best aligns with the programs they already consume (Kellner, *Media Spectacle* 160, 177). Jeet Heer pushes Kellner's claim to the limit when he describes President Trump as "the culmination of late capitalism."

In the same way that reality television shows brought the game show format out of the studio and into real environments, Trump's candidacy and presidency have incorporated and normalized the rhythms and aesthetics of the game show into American life to a degree that even the wildest satires failed to imagine. Comparing the primary season and the campaigns to a reality competition program once seemed alarmist and farfetched but is now almost too trite and obvious to mention. Since Trump's inauguration, the daily rounds of outrageous reversals, distractions, lies, scandals, investigations, firings, resignations, and indictments more closely resemble an episode of *Survivor* or, dare I say it, *The Apprentice*, than good government. Trump even hired a former *Apprentice* contestant, Omarosa Manigault, to serve in the White House as Assistant to the President and Director of Communications for the Office of Public Liason, who then went on to appear as a contestant on *Celebrity Big Brother* after being fired from her post.

The daily constitutional crisis that is the Trump administration has also introduced bits of arcane political trivia once of interest only to constitutional scholars—the emoluments clause, the Twenty-Fifth Amendment, campaign finance laws, the Hatch Act, Presidential pardons, financial disclosures, the structure and personnel of heretofore unremembered government agencies, congressional committees, etc.—into everyday discourse (and breaking news notifications on smartphones everywhere). Trump's is truly the trivial presidency, both with regards to the amount of new bits of data citizens must absorb and retain and in its assault on truth and meaning that reduces unflattering assertions of fact and value to "fake news" and "alternative facts." On a quiz show, if a person has the answers, they can topple even the mightiest of competitors. Now, when the right answers no longer have the power to level the playing field, citizens are left with a situation in which the winners are those lucky enough to be already wealthy and powerful, the one preexisting condition that never gets denied. Game shows exist to provide the vicarious experience of watching people's fortunes change in a way that reality does not permit. In electing a game-show host to the highest office in the land, America truly became The Land of the Game Show.

America, is this your final answer?

If the last few paragraphs smack of hyperbole, consider what has happened to the game show in the Age of Trump, which has already responded with games that acknowledge the sense of desperation and futility running throughout the culture. Gone are the big bucks and the fabulous prizes of yesteryear. On one of the most-discussed new game shows, TruTV's *Paid Off*, contestants play to pay off their student loan debt. With prizes like that, even the winners go home empty-handed, but that is the new normal everywhere: just getting by is the grand prize. On the game show of today, Ian Bogost writes, "everyone claws for table scraps" ("HQ"). The paltry prizes on HQ Trivia, the most popular game show today, make a win on *Paid Off* look like a windfall. HQ Trivia makes winners split its $2,000 prize among themselves, with individual winnings seldom topping $15, which is less lucrative than winning a free bar tab at pub trivia. These games transform "the game show's promise of small-scale wealth" into the "promise of a pittance for the few" (Bogost, "HQ"). Similarities to the American Dream are entirely coincidental and not the intention of the game's creators.

Paid Off tacitly acknowledges the indignity of contestants lining up for the life-changing experience of getting back to zero. It may not be the first show to feature debt-free living as a prize—there was *Debt* in the 1990s, where contestants played to have their credit card debt paid off—but the difference here is that student-loan debt does not result from frivolous living or addictive behavior. In fact, it is often promoted as so-called "good debt," and many student loans are even financed by the federal government. In response to this situation, one of the show's conventions gives players the opportunity to flip off Congress; however, the show makes this gesture of defiance as self-defeating as it is futile. First of all, contestants wear an oven mitt when extending the bird to their representatives, so their anger is censored by the very outlet claiming to provide them with a platform to air their grievances. Even though such an attack would likely have limited impact to begin with, the show's "standards and practices" ensure that it never reaches its intended target. Second, appearing on a game show to seek debt relief already surrenders one's faith that engaging in representative democracy will improve one's life. The show may perform gestures of its own toward the injustices of the system, but it ultimately contributes to them by creating a "game show-lottery shadow government" in which "entertainment is labor, pay, and citizenship all at once" (Thompson; Bogost, "HQ"). This "social-media welfare state" delivers a weaker, less effectual version of policies and services that would be done by the state in any other country in the developed world and for fewer people (Thompson). Rather than combat income inequality or the rot eating away at America, these shows have monetized it, turning "desperation into the basis of entertainment" (Bogost, "HQ").

Even though this book did not begin as an attempt to answer how the game show provides insight on how to navigate Trump's America, its argument implicitly seeks to address that by examining how writers and filmmakers use the game show in their work. Instead of looking at *The Apprentice* to understand the current moment, one should examine another game show host and chief executive who shares the current existential bewilderment over how to live when one's fantasy has turned monstrous and taken over reality. He also

Barris's foiled desert escape.

shares Trump's vulgarity and penchant for spreading utter bullshit: Chuck Barris. In his sole directorial effort, *The Gong Show Movie* (1980), Barris plays Chuck Barris, who cannot get a moment's peace because, from the moment he leaves his home, people hound him to let them audition for *The Gong Show*. Although *The Gong Show* was already off the air when the film was produced, it lives on in the film, confirming that it does not necessarily need to be on the air to dominate the culture's imagination. Barris, not surprisingly, questions the purpose of his life as a producer of trash TV in the film and wishes to bang the gong on the virus he has unleashed on the world, but not before giving cinema audiences a peek at *Gong Show* outtakes the networks deemed "too hot for TV." This indulgence-wrapped-in-an-apology provides Barris the opportunity to simultaneously atone for the sin of lowering the decency level of American entertainment while continuing to commit it.

For the film's climax, Barris flees to "the middle of the biggest desert in the whole world" to get away from the horror he has created; however, even there he cannot escape. The moment he sits down in the sand, a helicopter arrives, followed by the cast of the film and the USC marching band, all of whom, via a large musical number, beg him to return to television. He is, it seems, trapped. So he gives in and loses himself in the unending pageant. Despite his oft-stated desires to the contrary, Barris proves himself unable (or unwilling) to let go of what he has created, even as it terrorizes him. After all, what else is he going to do? Where else can he go? He is not *apart* from the chaos; he is *a part* of it.

One might be inclined to dismiss Barris's choice as relevant only to him. He of course can embrace an oblivion of bullshit and abject spectacle because he is a creature of that system. What about the average American shouldering the anxiety, anger, and uncertainty of living under the Trump administration? Several works of fiction compare game show participation with participatory democracy. Donald Barthelme's story "A Shower of Gold," Max Apple's short story "Noon," and Philip K. Dick's novel *Solar Lottery* suggest that average Americans may be no different from Chuck Barris or Donald Trump because, like them, they too are creatures of the system conceived in, raised in, trapped in the Land of the Game Show. These works offer three alternative approaches to living in the Land of the Game Show, contending that, while no one may be able to escape the game, they do get to decide how they play it.

A precarious existence brings Hank Peterson to the game show *Who Am I?* in Barthelme's 1963 story. Peterson, a struggling artist in need of cash, views appearing on a game show as "unavoidable" as long as he "want[s] to eat," but one quickly sees that his precarious existence is more, well, existential and that the show aims to help him resolve his crisis of faith (Barthelme 8). The questions Hank fields during his audition interview reveal the show's philosophical leanings: "Are you absurd?" "Do you encounter your own existence as gratuitous?" "Are you *interested* in absurdity?" (7, 8). Hardly the standard contestant questionnaire. Hank claims not to believe in absurdity and spends more of his time in the story fretting over whether appearing on television is "slightly disgraceful" rather than viewing his existence, on or off television, as "problematic," indicative of "something more elegant: nausea" (9, 8, 9). Like Barris's character in the film, Hank spends his time trying to ward off absurdity in his own life, to escape it instead of being interested in it, to bracket it off in art or dreams or, in the case of Barris, *The Gong Show*. Both learn quickly, however, the futility of these efforts to avoid the absurd because "*you* may not be interested in absurdity," the interviewer tells Hank, "but absurdity is interested in *you*" (8).

Just as Barris (or any other artist) cannot ignore the success of his creation, the nature of existence in the media age can only be blocked out for so long before it intrudes into one's day-to-day life. Each encounter he has in the story challenges his perceptions of the world and demands he take an interest in the absurd. His art dealer believes Hank's "romantic impulse . . . estranges [him] from those possibilities for authentic selfhood that inhere in the present century" (9). In one of his dreams, the President bursts into his studio on a sleigh pulled by twelve Secret Service agents, smashes Hank's art, and tells him that his diseased liver is a sign that he is "making progress" and "thinking" (10). His Nietzsche- and Pascal-quoting barber tells Hank that he needs to "break out of the hell of solipsism," while a cat-piano player berates him for not viewing his choices as part of "a gigantic conspiracy" in which "things are done to [him]" rather than his own (10). Through his anxiety and nausea over appearing on *Who Am I?*, Hank discovers that absurdity and existential crisis constitute the modern condition; not believing in them or refusing to take an active interest in them amounts to not being alive. "How can you be alienated without first having been connected?" Hank asks *Who Am I?*'s studio audience epiphanically (16). If his apprehension over appearing on the show evinces his alienation, then engaging in the game qualifies as connecting with the mediated world in all its absurdity.

Hank's monologue at the close of the story can be read as his rebirth *into* absurdity, in which Hank both asks and answers the central question of the show and life: who am I?

> Don't be reconciled. Turn off your television sets, . . . cash in your life insurance, indulge in a mindless optimism. . . . Think back and remember how it was. . . . My mother was a royal virgin . . . and my father was a shower of gold. My childhood was pastoral and energetic and rich in experiences which developed my character. As a young man I was noble in reason, infinite in faculty, in form express and admirable, and in apprehension . . . (15–16)

As he speaks, Hank becomes one with the absurdity of television, focusing on nothing but "the little red light" above the camera, never breaking eye contact with it even as it leaps from one camera to another "in an attempt to throw him off balance" (16). In appearing on television, Hank is no longer "alone in a featureless, anonymous landscape, in fear and trembling and sickness unto death" but immersed in a world where "possibilities nevertheless proliferate and escalate all around us and there are opportunities for beginning again" (8, 15). Accepting the absurd allows him to finally accept himself and everyone else without guilt. Barthelme's story posits that instead of bemoaning where one's condition and the circumstances that brought them to it, they too can lean in to them and, in doing so, gain vital knowledge about their situation that can help to steer them out of it and into a more enlightened, less absurd state of being.

Perhaps. However, as Max Apple's 1976 story "Noon" suggests, Barthelme's solace in leaning into the absurdity of the modern condition could easily become a fatal despair that bears a striking resemblance to today. Apple fills each moment of his story with the encroaching sense that existence is wedded to television in a marriage that endures beyond the limits of death. There is just no escaping the game show in "Noon." Even if someone kills it, the show will go on because it is always live. Hank Peterson's bliss in "A Shower of Gold" derives from embracing a life in which a game show is the gateway to truth; Cook, the main character of "Noon," lashes out against such blissful absurdity by killing Larry Love, the host of the *Let's Make a Deal*-esque *Trade or Betrayed*, during a live broadcast. Apple's story adopts the form of Cook's confession to his bewildered defense attorney, in which he characterizes his violent act as retaliation against media, capitalism, politics, and his own conception.

Barthelme and Apple connect the game show to politics by comparing their game show hosts to presidents, a comparison more sobering today than when these stories first appeared. In "A Shower of Gold," Hank thinks the host of *Who Am I?* "resemble[s] the President and [does] not look at all friendly" (14). Apple makes his political connections much more explicit. Larry Love may not resemble a political figure physically, but Apple's allusions to presidents throughout the text imply that Love's murder constitutes an assassination. According to a Minneapolis astrologer that Cook consults, Love's chart resembles Abraham Lincoln's so much that "the match is identical," and Apple describes Love's dead body lying on the ground as "Lincolnesque" (143, 148). An assassination requires an assassin, and Cook's mention that his rifle cost "three times the price of the Italian rifle that got John Kennedy" casts him in the role of the Angry Lone Nut Assassin *à la* Oswald or Booth opposite Love's Lincoln. This parallel becomes even more apparent considering that the murder takes place in a theatrical space, with the set of *Trade or Betrayed* serving as a modern-day Ford's Theatre (143).

Following this logic invites disturbing comparisons between Cook and real-life game show viewers simultaneously enchanted by and obsessed with the thing they hate. Cook had to kill Larry Love, he claims, because Love was "Satan," "one of the seven deadly sins, the electric version of Horatio Alger," "the culmination of television" (142, 134, 141). The first two details certainly echo the rantings of a deranged assassin, but this last detail gives Cook's fatal grudge a critical edge more in line with Baudrillard and Jameson than Oswald and Booth. The rest of the story largely supports Cook's characterization of his act as a political strike against "the culmination of television." Like many people in this heavily mediated age, Cook experiences a dependence on and hostility towards television because there is not a moment in Cook's life where he does not coexist with a screen. Television dominates his labor: there is "a TV blaring all the time" in the drugstore where he worked his first job, and his security guard post at a department store required him to watch customers on "a seven-inch closed-circuit screen" as he "switch[es] channels" from one department to another (138, 137). His encyclopedic knowledge of other daytime television programs and game show hosts suggests that he watches even more television when he is away from work. His environment encourages Cook to be a passive viewer to the extent that he cannot conceive of an existence apart from television. His identity as a passive viewer drives him to think of himself as a televisual image. He begins his story by asking his attorney and us to think of him as an embodied televised image, "two hundred and sixty-three lines of broken light per second scattered through twenty-one years" (133). The consumer becomes what he consumes.

His statements are not the exaggerations they appear to be: he identifies so strongly with television because he was practically conceived on television; it is where his life originates. When his parents were married on *Bride and Groom* in 1952, his mother was two weeks' pregnant with him, making him "a member of the *Bride and Groom* cast," a detail Cook offers as "part of his defense" (135). His murderous actions become his attempt to emancipate himself from an existence that keeps him as tethered to an image as an embryo is to its mother. Such a violent separation has mortal consequences for both parties, and even after Love's murder, Cook, like Barris, searches for a way back into the womb of the media, proposing to his lawyer that he tape his confession so that "we can put the little Sony on the Bible" or sell it for "a TV series based on [his] life" (137). No matter how much one declares that they want to divorce themselves from a mediated life, they have difficulty imagining what such a life looks like, let alone how they would live it.

Death may loom over "Noon," but Apple loads the final confrontation between Cook and Love with matrimonial language, making the murder not only an assassination but a marriage ceremony between contestant and host, between the audience and the game show. Cook's murder of Love mimics a wedding ceremony. When Love, the bachelor host, has Cook approach him from the crowd, he asks Cook, who is dressed as a cornucopia, to remove his hat "so he can see [his] face" as though it were a veil and "looks into [Cook's] eyes the way Ken and Edith [Cook] must have gazed at one another" during their wedding (146). These details portray the scene as both his wedding and a reenactment of his parents' televised wedding, which also constituted his televisual conception. The moment before the shooting, Tina, the silent female co-host, rather than forever hold her peace, speaks now, telling Cook "Shoot." Tina's command slowly builds to the entire audience, until everyone repeats it "just the way they called out 'the money' or 'the box' earlier" on the show (147). Love's murder becomes the entertainment, the spectacle, the prize, the kiss that culminates the matrimonial rite. Even Larry Love "forms 'shoot' with his lips as if he's cheating at charades," and Cook says, "holding him tight as a lover, I do" (147). "Shoot" and "I do" act as an exchange of vows, with Cook's shot ending the ritual and forming a bond between viewer and host which no man can put asunder, the true "culmination of television." In a clever closing detail, Apple mentions that *Trade or Betrayed* is followed by *The Newlywed Game*. As it should be. America is wedded to the game show in a spectacle of violence and excess. Everyone may, like Cook, Larry Love, Hank Peterson, and Chuck Barris, yearn

Barris's broken Gong.

to be free of the game, but the show continues. *Trade or Betrayed* finishes the episode with a new host, suggesting that not even an act of violence can free America from the grip of the game but further binds it to it.

Apple's story depicts the futility and absurdity of attempting to liberate culture from the influence of the game show through violence because an escape does not exist; not even killing the host will illuminate a pathway out of the studio. However, *The Gong Show Movie* features a telling moment that might showcase another alternative, a solution that lies not on the screen but in viewers. The scene, which, like over one third of the film, repurposes *Gong Show* material, shows Barris attempting to segue from one setpiece to the other, only the large "Gong" sign in the center of the set refuses to disappear. Barris calls out to stagehands, but the "Gong" remains in place, taunting Barris in its immobility. Barris bangs the "Gong" with his cane for emphasis, only to discover that the sign is not solid, and his cane crashes right through it. Barris is not amused, and proceeds to whack the sign repeatedly, demolishing it. As amusing of a gaffe as the scene is, it contains an interesting and instructive moral. As in the rest of the film, Barris wants to move on from a moment that no longer has any use for him, so he follows the rules of the show and hits the "Gong," literally and figuratively. Only there has been some glitch in the system, and the rules no follow their own logic. However, this glitch becomes extremely useful because it reveals to Barris, the studio audience, and all the viewers at home, that this system, no matter how oppressive and indestructible it may appear, is not real. Like the sign, its power is paper thin. Barris stands helpless on the set waiting for the show to remove itself from his life, not realizing he hosts the show and can sound his own gong whenever he chooses. Instead, he returns to hosting the show in a resigned, exhausted embrace of oblivion. This is where the moral for the viewer comes in: one's response to the unpredictability of the current system need not be so acquiescent. Like Barris, audiences do not acknowledge that no one else will deliver them from the moment they feel trapped in. No one is going to come and take anyone off the stage or escort anyone to the winner's circle. No one is in charge of the game but the viewers themselves.

Philip K. Dick's 1955 novel *Solar Lottery* illustrates these ideas. The year is 2203, and the game show has taken over the known universe. Solutions to "problem[s] of production" in the twentieth century spawned "problem[s] of consumption," with more consumer goods being produced than people could consume (12). Enter the quiz shows, to "[prop] up the economy" with "elaborate give-away devices that [dispense] tons of glittering merchandise" to people for whom such luxury items are financially out of reach (12). Giving away consumer items eventually loses its allure, however, which leads to the Quizzes giving away "more realistic items: power and prestige," until the grand prize is to become Quizmaster, the person who runs not only the Quiz but also, it appears, the entire universe (12). This kind of prize may not be as farfetched as it seems. Reality competition shows such as *The Next Food Network Star* or *HGTV Star* (formerly *HGTV Design Star*) already have done away with traditional prizes in favor of giving winning contestants their own television programs to host.

The novel's crisis in consumption sparks a crisis of confidence in the fabric of society that may have a familiar ring to it:

> people lost faith in natural law itself. Nothing seemed stable or fixed; the universe was a sliding flux. Nobody knew what came next. Nobody could count on anything. Statistical prediction became popular ... the very concept of cause and effect died out. People lost faith in the belief that they could control their environment; all that remained was probable sequence: good odds in a universe of random chance. (18)

Citizens in Dick's novel cope with their despair by espousing "the theory of Minimax ... a kind of stoic withdrawal, a nonparticipation in the aimless swirl in which people struggled" (13). Rather than attempting to win, "the M-game player sat waiting for the game to end" (13). Unlike Barthelme's Peterson or Apple's Cook, these characters do not embrace absurdity or attack it but let it have its way with the world, stripping themselves of their power to alter the course of events that affect their daily lives and placing all their agency at the whims of chance.

This refusal to engage becomes the foundation of politics and government, to the extent that the Quizmaster is chosen by a bottle that twitches to a different person's number at random intervals. If the Quizmaster's term does not end with another twitch of the bottle, it can end in death if one of the "public assassins" breaks through the "telepathic corps" that guards the Quizmaster and kills them for a grand prize of one million gold dollars (29). This hunting of the Quizmaster, called the Challenge Convention, is televised and wagered on, making the constant changeover in power into serialized entertainment. Each Quizmaster has ruled for an average of two weeks, not much longer than the reign of an exceptional game-show contestant. The rationale is that this process protects citizens "from incompetents, from fools and madmen" because "nobody can gain power and hold it; nobody knows what his status will be next year, next week. Nobody can plan to be a dictator ... we're completely safe: no despots and no crackpots" (38). The tradeoff, however, hardly represents an improvement: citizens may not be under the thumb of a tyrant, but they also have no sense of stability under which to imagine a future. As Americans have noticed during this administration in which no one, not even the leaders themselves, knows what comes next, a nation governed by constant turnover and reversals does not bless citizens with peace of mind: without any sense of what comes next, life becomes "a constant gamble, an unceasing lottery" in which volatility becomes a twisted form of stability (39). Where some Trump supporters, and, to be fair, the bulk of the news media, welcomed his unscripted remarks and behavior as refreshingly authentic and entertaining in a candidate, citizens are seeing how unsettling it is for a leader or host to be making the show up as he goes with no editing room standing by to make sense of the raw footage.

To inject some semblance of constancy into their lives, people in the world of *Solar Lottery* adopt loyalty oaths to people and positions, but these oaths shackle them to the random fortunes of others and fails to grant them agency over the direction of their lives. Ted Benteley, Dick's protagonist, suffers such a fate when he pledges a loyalty oath to a Quizmaster the moment before the bottle casts him out of office. As the efficiency of the system falls apart over the course of the novel, Benteley dreams of a utopian world, one in which people pledge their loyalty to "an ideal," something "bigger than any man or group of men" (85, 84). The world he dreams of is of course modern America, but few people in the novel share his aspirations. Another character counters that being loyal to "an abstraction" constitutes "superstition," that "it's people who are real" and deserving of fealty, "not institutions and offices" (84). When "everything else in the universe has collapsed," she says, "the only thing that's left is people ... what is there, beyond people? What is there you can depend on" apart from the loyalty "between protector and serf, between a man and his mistress" (84, 85). In other words, if people want something to count on, they must relinquish control over their lives and submit to the will of a superior.

The appeal of believing in other people quickly diminishes when such thinking ends in serfdom. Benteley's response to what one should depend on, however simplistic or obvious, also carries profound weight: "depend on yourself" (84). Pledging oneself to an ideal does not bind one to another person or thing. Rather, it binds one further to themselves because one commits to an ethos that guides and informs but does not dictate one's choices; the responsibility still resides within the individual. For Benteley, such a choice is "the cement that keeps this whole thing from collapsing" because it requires individuals to believe in things greater than "cynicism, luxury and poverty, indifference" and "brilliant criminals working for powerful criminals" and take action to give reality the extreme makeover it needs (85).

Solar Lottery stands out among Dick's other work because it ends on a rare note of optimism in which characters turn the game against itself and forge a new direction free from the whims of chance. Through a series of schemes and reversals orchestrated by Leon Cartwright, the current Quizmaster working to reconceive a society free from Quizzes, Benteley becomes the next Quizmaster, which means the loyalty oath he took at the beginning of the novel now binds him to himself. "I'm probably the first person who was ever under oath to himself," he says. "I'm both protector and serf at the same time. I have the power of life and death over myself" (192). Cartwright responds, "That might catch on. It sounds like a good kind of oath, to me. You take full responsibility for protection and for carrying out the work. You have nobody to answer to but your own—conscience" (192–93). Dick's solution runs the risk of appearing overly simplistic or even downright hokey; however, it is preferable when one considers the alternatives offered by Bartheleme and Apple. When "the rules are fixed so [one] can't win," it is the ideal time to assert one's agency and assume control over their lives, to "draw up new rules and play by them," making themselves Quizmaster of their own game (191).

The American system resembles a rigged quiz show more and more each day in which government and business conspire to consolidate wealth and power, and citizens must decide how they wish to handle it. They can "hold [their] nose[s] and pretend it isn't there" or even gleefully embrace its absurdity like Bartheleme's protagonist, hoping that the show will select them as a winner, or they can strike against it in an apocalyptic rush toward death as Cook does in Max Apple's story, but none of these options presents a desirable or inhabitable world (179). Pretending everything is fine changes little, and "tearing down isn't enough" to free anyone from the game show's grasp (179). As Benteley says, "Something has got to go up in its place; something has to be built," and citizens "have to do something that alters things" from their current untenable situation that is "rotten, corrupt" and "ready to fall on its face" (179). *Solar Lottery* and, to a lesser degree, Chuckie Baby's *Gong Show* gaffe dimly illuminate ways citizens can alter the perception of themselves as powerless and become the hosts of their own experience.

As truthful as Dick's vision may be, its individualized, empowered optimism fails to hold up under even the gentlest critical scrutiny. It becomes difficult to unequivocally endorse something as sentimental and pat as "depend on yourself" as a viable solution to the current political moment, or any other moment, for that matter. The sentiment may appear optimistic on the surface, but it quickly can take on the appearance of abandoning collective efforts in exchange for stepping into yet another isolation booth, only this time one of one's own design. Therein lies the dilemma. On the one hand, as examination of the works in this book has shown, there does not appear to be a viable way out of the hypermediated landscape that does not itself fall victim to the nefarious strategies it purports to combat; on the other hand, critique's tendency to identify the blind spots and flaws in any proposed solution enables problems to persist by making belief itself politically untenable. Leaving the Land of the Game Show is naïve at best, impossible at worst, whereas choosing not to play at all seems destined for failure or only the most limited, temporary kind of success. Any constructive path forward would need to offer readers something to sign on to without abandoning the critical gaze necessary to avoid slipping into a new-and-improved version of the same situation one desires to escape.

Jonathan Lethem's 2013 novel *Dissident Gardens* may not appear to offer much solace in its chronicle of generations of leftists failing to realize the better world they imagine, but it uses the game show and a series of game-show encounters to build to a moment that, no matter how small and unexceptional it may be, presents an unsentimental model of an active, generative resistance rooted in memory and communal practices repurposed for an individualized era. Neither naïve nor utopian, Lethem's novel takes a position jaded enough to see that the game of American life is rigged but sincere enough to believe that knowledge and memory can subvert the game's control over individual lives.

Lethem's multi-generational saga touches on nearly every round of this book: its narrative traces the connections and fates of a family that opposes oppressive state power (a few even give their lives in the struggle), each member of this family battles with its legacy in their attempt to establish a unique and original self, and throughout all of it, Lethem dramatizes the catalyzing role that memory plays in resolving or complicating each of these conflicts. While only one chapter, "Cities in Crisis," directly involves a game show, each character's story contains a crisis point of its own that could be construed as a game-show encounter. The novel opens with matriarch Rose's interrogation before the leaders of her local chapter of the American Communist Party, which results in her being expelled for having an affair with a married African American police officer. Miriam, Rose's rebellious daughter, embarrasses herself during a disastrous appearance on *The Who, What, or Where Game*, and her inability to navigate a later confrontation among the revolutionaries in Nicaragua costs her and her husband Tommy their lives. Rose's cousin Lenny Angrush has an equally embarrassing encounter in the front office of a new major-league baseball team when he petitions them to adopt a name and a theme song with a proletarian bent (they decide to call themselves the Mets instead). Cicero Lookins, son of Rose's cop lover, has his chess prowess tested (and dismissed) by Lenny, and he repeatedly tests the students in his early-morning seminar before he dismisses them and their intellects. Finally, the novel ends with Miriam's son Sergius, who searches for information about the family he never knew, immersed in a defiant encounter with a TSA officer. In these encounters, one character is quizzed by an authoritarian representative of an institution—the American Communist Party, the United States government, the academy, the game show. The hosts of the game-show encounters may pose questions, but the tone of their delivery makes it clear that what they say is "a command, not a question," blurring the line between host and interrogator, contestant and suspect, game and trial, and each character's fortune turns on how he or she performs in this encounter (Lethem 3). Through the fates of each of these characters, Lethem's family saga considers and rejects various forms of resistance to and critiques of power and identity before ending the novel with a vision of a way forward.

Lee Konstantinou concludes his book *Cool Characters: Irony and American Fiction* with a discussion of *Dissident Gardens* and its vision of a political future in an era where corporate co-optation and ironic resistance are the norm, if not accomplices in advancing a neoliberal agenda. The novel, which Konstantinou characterizes as a "postironic Bildungsroman," positions the Occupier as the figure whose memory of the activism of the past and skepticism of the futility of taking action in the present allows them to envision a future that their present position inhabits (275). Lethem's appeal to Occupy Wall Street, which comes in the form of Sergius's relationship with Lydia, one of America's last occupiers, allows him to embrace what Konstantinou calls "prefigural causality" (275). To achieve this state, Konstantinou argues, "one must traverse from a state of political naivety through a phase of cynicism or postmodern irony, arriving finally at a state of postironic political commitment" (275). Lethem populates his novel with characters occupying different points on that spectrum to allow the reader to see the strengths and limits of each position before accepting "postironic political commitment" as the most viable direction forward, with the final scene of the novel representing Sergius's (and the reader's) initiation into a state of postironic belief (275).

Like Barthelme, Apple, and Dick, Lethem explicitly connects game-show hosts to political figures in his description of Art James, host of *The Who, What, or Where Game*. James's appearance and demeanor, in addition to being well dressed, well spoken, and vaguely Midwestern, "is characterized above all by its successful sublimation of the disarranging trauma" of World War II. Lethem calls this type simply "the host." This host figure can not only host "nearly anything," but this type "has colonized the public imagination to such a degree" that New York's mayor, and all similar political figures by extension, "is, effectively, a 'host'" (112). Throughout this description, the host's purpose is embodying and promoting a repression that sublimates trauma in pursuit of an orderly status quo undisturbed by contemporary geopolitical upheaval. The other hosts in the novel operate in much the same way, tamping down the activists in Rose's extended family, stamping out their cells one member at a time until each figure is completely isolated and alone.

Matthew Luter cautions against concluding that the failure of these characters to realize their political dreams means that their visions are tainted or problematic. Rather, Lethem uses their failures to illustrate the enormous challenges progressives face in contemporary culture and the prices that they must pay for working to remake reality according to one's political vision (111). To dramatize the complexity of any attempt to change the modern world, Lethem places an activist on a game show and has another character, Sergius, embrace activism in a game-show encounter with a TSA agent. Juxtaposed, these two scenes offer contrasting visions of self-defeating or self-actualizing responses to the legacy of political engagement and leftist politics.

In her appearance on *The Who, What, or Where Game*, which Lethem bases on an actual broadcast of the program, Miriam crumbles under the weight of her own oppositional irony, which renders her unable to employ her voluminous amount of knowledge for any productive end, politically or monetarily (Luter 109). Miriam appears on the show in the first place because she thinks of herself "as a whiz at games and puzzles, genius taker of standardized tests and filler-out of standardized forms, master of negotiation with bureaucracies both of the New York civic infrastructure and of the Organized Left, and above all a dervish at one-on-one interlocutive repartee, *at always having the answers, always clearing the hurdle*" (122). The repetitive use of words connoting excellence such as "whiz," "genius," "master," and "dervish" emphasize the extent to which Miriam's intellect represents the core of her identity and fuels her sense of superiority to the "standardized" "bureaucracies" and institutions that claim power over her life. Characters such as Miriam and Cicero pride themselves on what they know or, more accurately, how they can use what they know to expose what others, especially others in positions of power, do not know. Being able to debunk accepted truths and ideologies as lies, to strip away "the veil of sustaining fiction that drove the world," demonstrates to others that they possess "secret knowledge" (65, 63). Armed with this secret knowledge, they can win any battle of wits. However, this same "secret knowledge" hinders their ability to reject the allure of irony and cynicism because of the power they receive from such poses.

Miriam's appearance on *The Who, What, or Where Game*, along with Cicero's undergraduate seminars and verbal sparring match with Lydia and Sergius, illustrates the political impotence of this irony-fueled "secret knowledge." Lethem links Miriam's failures as a game-show contestant to her failures as an activist through a flashback during the game to the moment when she was rejected by a CORE recruiter. One of the categories, "Spanish Expressions," also anticipates her future failure in Nicaragua by revealing that, in "a rebuke to Rose," Miriam refused to learn Spanish, a refusal that will ultimately contribute to her murder (120). These details recontextualize Miriam's secret knowledge as mere arrogance, the ironist's destructive brand of smug self-satisfaction. Her "talent for worldly implication" that suggests "she knew more than what she knew" may appeal to Cicero, who shares her desire for "secret knowledge," but it falters under the gentle pressure of a quiz show, the secret of her knowledge being that it is but mere "implication" (71).

Leftism frequently gets portrayed as a trivial pursuit of its own, especially after the fall of the Soviet Union, but Lethem's novel demonstrates how rapidly corporate culture defuses the threat of the left by co-opting its most superficial attributes. Miriam arrives at 30 Rockefeller Center to discover that her hipper-than-thou countercultural detachment, turbocharged by the marijuana she smoked before reporting to the studio, has already been aped by "dressed-up freaks" working at NBC who managed to have "*turned on* without *dropping out*" (108). These "go-getter[s] ... in wry quote marks" want to look cool but also want straight jobs "carry[ing] the city's tasks forward," so they turn leftism into a hip-but-benign costume with no political teeth (108). The episode ends with the narrator alleging that "the show has been scripted as a delayed rebuke to" the "skinny hippie[s]," showing them that their aesthetic may have "exfoliated its vibe outward, encompassing the whole island overnight," but without its attending beliefs (129, 108). The rebuke is ultimately effective, as Miriam repeatedly misses questions "whose answer[s] [are] her very birthright" before she "goes sullenly *unprotesting*" from the set of the show (119; emphasis added). Miriam engages in some acts of defiance on the show, but these acts are mostly thoughtless, such as her incredulously asking Art James, "That's my question?" after he asks her a question that has nothing to do with "Cities in Crisis," or at least her interpretation of those terms (she goes on to get the question wrong) (118). The narrator takes great care to mention that each of her rebellious actions "will be edited out" and will not "appear when the program is broadcast," emphasizing the futility of Miriam's ironic protests by demonstrating how easily they can be silenced (118). Much like the oven mitt that contestants don on *Paid Off* prior to extending the bird toward the Capitol, Miriam's revolution will not be televised.

Sergius's game-show encounter with a TSA agent in the novel's final pages synthesizes *Dissident Gardens*'s various perspectives on political action and presents a vision for navigating game-show encounters in the Age of Trump. According to the agent, Sergius is "automatically flagged" for two reasons: accompanying a woman to the airport while having no travel plans himself, and the "incongruent time signature" between his entering the airport and his arrival with her at the airline kiosk (364). Sergius is reluctant to answer the agent's questions truthfully because the truth is incredibly personal: his "time signature" is "incongruent" because he and Lydia were having sex in the airport bathroom. The agent's overly formal questioning and Orwellian terminology builds until Sergius brazenly insults the agent and tells him "we did it, right in your pokey little Jetport. You got me, you caught one" (366). The novel ends with Sergius being asked to put his hands on the interrogation table.

If a confrontation with a TSA agent seems like the furthest thing from a game show, consider Ian Bogost's description of the design of the HQ Trivia app. According to Bogost, the ten-second timeframe players have to answer questions, combined with the "pulsating, bright-colored blobs" of animation, the "hypnotic" music, and the endless stream of vitriolic or nonsensical user comments flooding the bottom of the screen during play, bypasses the rational sectors of one's mind in what amounts to a startling re-creation of the inundation of data that comprises post-9/11 life. Bogost concretely unpacks the ideology inherent in the app's interface: these deliberately chosen features stress that "sensation is more important than thought" and "intuition wins out over reason." Such an ideology values truthiness over truth and replaces virtue with instinct, with thoughtless compliance serving as the highest of all virtues (Bogost, "HQ"). This so-called harmless distraction anticipates a future where each moment can suddenly turn into a political quiz show, where "tests of knowledge amount to tests of loyalty, erupting on screens clutched by citizens at all times, demanding instant, correct responses" (Bogost, "HQ"). Citizens would need to ensure that their instincts align with the quizmaster in this brave new world of the game show because they will have "no time for thought, [only] the terror of hopeful conformity to natural tendency" (Bogost, "HQ").

Lethem's novel does not need a space-age trivia app to inhabit this world, nor does the average American. A TSA agent may come off as a "mundane" figure; however, the agent's ubiquity and function as a representative of "the American national security state" fills the mundanity of their individual role with menace (Konstantinou 285). After all, no matter how ineffectual or banal an agent may seem, everyone acknowledges that compliance is the only option because resistance could quickly alter one's travel plans permanently. In the isolation booth of the interrogation room, Sergius faces exactly the kind of loyalty quiz Bogost describes in which his allegiance to the ruling order is being quizzed and time for thought will not be provided.

Previously in the novel, Sergius's practice of resistance to a violent, mediated world proved iconic but ultimately empty. He acquires legendary status at his local arcade with his unconventional approach to playing a video game called Time Pilot. The rules of the game require the player to advance through levels and score points by shooting enemy fighters; however, Sergius refuses to shoot and instead avoids all contact, becoming a true Time Pilot by stretching one quarter for over an hour until the bad guys occupy all available space to move. In political terms, Sergius occupies Time Pilot until he is forced out. While he never wins the game, he also "never ha[s] to die" (306). His defiance changes the rules of the game as well as its meaning, but this victory is short-lived and inconsequential to say the least, because just as "the lamb who lies down with the beasts is devoured," "the Time Pilot who never fires a shot remains stuck at level one, until his enemies thicken to blot out the very air he requires to breathe" (317). Though it may not ultimately amount to anything, this episode serves as a staging ground for the more meaningful confrontation Sergius has with the TSA agent who wants him to comply with a set of rules as rigid as those of Time Pilot.

As he does with Time Pilot, Sergius declines to play by the TSA agent's rules, or even use his language. The bulk of their encounter operates as a verbal sparring match, a literal language game where both parties attempt to get the other to accept their definitions. When challenged, the agent frequently asks Sergius to respond "in [his] own words," or to "put it in [his] own language" or "offer a term in place of [his]" (364, 365). Sergius demurs, first jokingly asking, "Who else's words would I use," then refusing to offer terms of his own and eventually attacking the agent's language, stating, "What's that supposed to mean?" and, "Is that some kind of code word?" (364, 365). In rejecting the agent's language, first humorously and then aggressively, Sergius refuses to acknowledge the agent's legitimacy and the legitimacy of his query, hindering the path of the agent's inquiry in much the same way that he obstructed the objectives of Time Pilot.

The argument turns on the agent's use of the phrase "fellow traveler" to describe Lydia. Sergius's exploration into his family history has made him hyperaware of the charged Cold War meaning of that phrase, and the TSA agent's use of it alerts Sergius to the political nature of their conversation. While the agent is likely unaware of the legacy of the phrase "fellow traveler" in American history, this phrase quickly morphs the argument from a conversation about Sergius's travel plans and timeline into a discussion of his identity and lineage in which Sergius defines both Lydia and, more importantly, himself not as travelers but as Occupiers. Although the Occupy movement is nearly defunct at the time of this exchange, Lydia reorients Sergius's understanding of what it means to Occupy after they make love in the bathroom: according to her, Occupy is "wherever you are, right now" because it is "a way of being. Just living differently" (360). This inclusive, flexible language game contrasts with the TSA agent's rigid language game that offers Sergius no room for alternative meanings, possibilities, or realities. With these clever language games Sergius gets involved in, Lethem traces a line in which "fellow traveler" leads to "Occupier," connecting the legacy of the American left from Rose's time period to Sergius's. This connection makes Sergius a Time Pilot once again, except this time he does not arrive in the present empty-handed: he brings his grandmother Rose's political commitment back with him.

In *Capitalist Realism*, Mark Fisher describes two kinds of reality at play in reality television shows such as *Big Brother* that encourage audience participation: the contestants' "unscripted behavior" and the audience's "unpredictable responses," both of which influence and reinforce each other in a sort of feedback loop (48). Audience participation entices viewers to watch a program because it gives them the feeling of having a role in the show's development, but in participating, the audience ratifies the game's rules, governance, and vision of reality. No one may be able to predict which contestant viewers will vote to remove, but viewers will vote for someone, which makes their response predictable enough for the show to move forward. Fisher argues that the "you decide" slogan of *Big Brother* is an "empty seat of power" in which our "desires and preferences are returned to us, no longer as ours, but as the desires of the big Other" (48, 49). However, what works on *Big Brother* need not be what works in the world. "*You tell me*," Sergius's final statement in the novel, broadens the conception of what an "unpredictable response" looks like (Lethem 366). "You tell me" achieves the disruptive result that Miriam's "that's my question" failed to do. One is incredulous and petulant, the other determined and autonomous. By changing the rules of the language game, Sergius subverts the interrogation and positions himself as the author of the script, the host of the game.

Konstantinou reads the novel's final line, "A cell of one, beating like a heart," as Sergius viewing himself as a "collective subject" (285). Sergius's defiance, unlike Miriam's, is generative, reviving the spirit of Rose's political engagement, and his assertion that he is occupying rather than traveling suggests that this kind of commitment will not disappear into the past the way the activism of his parents did. In the room with the TSA agent, he claims his "radical inheritance" that is Rose's legacy and becomes "a student of *no*" by crafting a refusal in the face of authority that is "no longer merely the *no* of [his] inheritance, the *no* of [his] forebears" but rather "a *no* of [his] own personal devising" (Konstantinou 281; Lethem 141). Sergius, then, becomes not only the Occupier but the Synthesizer and Fulfiller of the political energies of the novel's other, less successful activist-protagonists (Konstantinou 285).

Sergius's breakthrough would not be possible without his encounter with Lydia in the bathroom stall. Bathroom stalls are made to be occupied by only one person and designated for personal, private activities. They are isolation booths. Sergius and Lydia's occupation of this space for private, communal activity, and Sergius's subsequent actions, subvert its intended design and fill it with the potential for collective action. Their lovemaking enacts Rose's vision of her politics as "exist[ing] in the space between one person and another, secret sympathies of the body. Alliances among those enduring the world" (272). Sergius, or anyone else, discovering such an alliance in a bathroom stall may seem unlikely, but, as Rose notes, "you found this where you found it, suddenly and without warning" (272). In fact, their alliance gains importance from occurring in a bathroom because such a setting suggests no one is alone in the struggle, no matter how isolated they may feel. Sergius's "final state of postironic political commitment" is not born in isolation but in congress with another; it is a collective action, a transfer of "secret sympathies" between two bodies "enduring the world." From this transfer comes not only Sergius's sudden defiance of governmental authority and the novel's sudden end, but a "renewal of postironic political engagement, a new political hope," the realization of Rose's vision (Konstantinou 281). Sergius's actions at the airport allow him, to quote Jodi Dean on Occupy Wall Street, to "imagine and enact a new subject that is collective and in doing so appear differently to [himself]" (213). Sergius not only becomes "visible before the law" at the end of the novel but to himself as well (Lethem 366). Where Miriam's visibility on the game show embarrasses and silences her, Sergius's galvanizes him, making the "mystery" of his life instantly coherent, connecting him not only to memory and legacy but to the future that his present actions prefigure.

Lethem's description of Sergius as existing "in this crucial indefinite place, this undisclosed location, severed from the life of the planet yet not aloft" echoes not only his description of Miriam as "untethered" after her appearance on *The Who, What, or Where Game* but also Robert Olen Butler's description of Gabrielle and Vinh parasailing in "The American Couple" (Lethem 366, 129). There are crucial differences, however. Where Butler's phrasing expresses a yearning for one to be "separated from [one's] body" and being freed from having "to worry about anything on the planet Earth anymore," Lethem's language builds to Sergius having "arrived at last" (Butler 165, 192). This "arrival" suggests the kind of movement from naivety and irony that Konstantinou sees as leading one to postironic detachment. Where Miriam becomes "untethered" from "her legacy under Rose Zimmer's nurture" as a result of her appearance on the game show, Sergius experiences being simultaneously "grounded" and "unrooted" in his resistance to the TSA, making him free to occupy whatever he chooses (Lethem 110; Konstantinou 285). Like Wallace's "Little Expressionless Animals," Lethem's novel ends the moment before this wave of defiance and memory "meet[s] what it moves toward," remaining a prefigural moment full of potential (Wallace, "LEA" 42).

In *Dissident Gardens*, Cicero paraphrases Doris Lessing to argue that "the deep fate of each human being is to begin with their mother and father as the whole of reality and to have to forge a journey to break into the wider world"; however, Lethem positions Sergius's epiphany as the result of a journey back to his ancestors (201). Sergius's plot follows Lessing's ideas to a point because he does "break into the wider world" by allowing his parents and "atmosphere" of their debilitating irony to "[drift] off to space"; however, this "wider world" steers him toward the belief and commitment of Rose (290). If the major question of both *Dissident Gardens* and this final category is "what form our new collective subjectivity should take," then Lethem directs us, surprisingly, toward memory and legacy as guides toward this "new collective subjectivity," claiming "you remembered what you kept" (Konstantinou 273; Lethem 290).

And so this book ends in a similar place to where it began with *Radio Days* by talking about the game show and memory. Konstantinou also sees memory as crucial to any future-oriented "oppositional ethos" because "transcending political cynicism" "require[s] a historical sense of the changing political fortunes of countercultural irony" (288). Miriam's defiant performance on the game show enacts a politics of forgetting that severs its connection to the past with the intent to make a new future. However, her actions accomplish nothing because, as Lenny reflects to himself early in the novel, our "detachment from history" is what has made life resemble "a patient that had survived a hideous and life-threatening surgery" (101). For Luter, "*Dissident Gardens* emphasizes the ways that the most earnest attempts to effect change can go wrong if approached with unsophisticated romanticism" (111). Much like *Magnolia*, *Dissident Gardens* demands that individuals must first "wise up" to the realities of the world around them before they set out to make the world anew, or otherwise they will be embarrassed and destroyed by their own naivete like Tommy Gogan and Lenny Angrush. However, mere cynicism will also embarrass and destroy them, as it does for Miriam and Cicero. Sergius's behavior performs what Timothy Robins calls "a counter-memory" to the "dominant memory" represented by the "historical apparatuses" of "media and heritage institutions" (211, 204). One's identity, one's legacy and relationship to the past, becomes "a resource for resistance and change" rather than an obstacle to it (212). One need not "shed religion and history" in order to prepare "for the radiant future" because such "detachment from history" and memory limits one's ability to confront and oppose the oppression of the present (Lethem 121). In a situation where the ruling powers continually insist on scripting their own version of reality, truth, and the past, memory becomes an oppositional force; forgetting merely enables.

If, as Konstantinou alleges, one must devote themselves to dismantling the "structures, practices, and institutions" that gave rise to this seemingly inescapable consumer world of hypermediation, then the game show serves as a valuable example of how entrenched and ubiquitous these structures are; however, in its familiarity, ubiquity, and adaptability, the game show also serves as a valuable, useful symbol for articulating how these structures, practices, and institutions operate and for communicating opposition to them. "Even the most debased corporate inventions" might be useful, including the game show (288). Especially when the opponent is a game show host.

Lethem's model of Occupiers celebrates collective memory over individual knowledge, and one can see how citizens in the Land of the Game Show are already deploying trivia and memory to occupy the role of host in the Age of Trump. Whether memory-based resistance comes in the form of citizens organizing marches and counter-protests online, using Trump's old tweets against him to highlight self-serving lies and inconsistent policies, historians posting long-form, evidence-based refutations of conservative ideologues' historically specious or disingenuous claims on social media, or calmly and unwaveringly advocating a Democratic Socialist platform that refuses to apologize for its vision of the country, citizens are using media to occupy the discourse on the fate of America. Plenty of Americans are also using these tools to destroy democratic ideals; however, their use has often amplified opposition to their views and served to mobilize citizens who might otherwise have stayed silent to reject them.

Of course, no single instance of these things will be enough to transform the system; however, these actions do constitute a practice that can carry over to a post-Trump world. Where divisive politics seek to make each concerned citizen feel like a disillusioned loner, these collective practices awaken individuals to a postironic form of political belief that keeps each "cell of one beating like a heart." As much as the American narrative, exemplified by the game show, wishes to champion the primacy of the individual in every endeavor, the work lying before the country is much too imposing for one to adopt a "depend on yourself" ethos. Everyone needs to cooperate. As every unstoppable pub-quiz team has demonstrated to a crowd of envious opponents, "a group of people, each with a specialty, might best one smart loner" (Bogost, "HQ").

What these artists have shown through their work with game shows is the truth regarding where entertainment culture has gotten Americans as individuals, a community, and a nation. However, as final as these prospects may seem, everyone is, like Sergius at the end of the novel, still in the opening round. The results are still to come, and the people's to control. If everyone can accept these truths, no matter how dispiriting or uncomfortable they may be, they can not only begin to see the consequences, but deal with them and, if everyone is bold enough to press their luck, improve them.

ACKNOWLEDGMENTS

NO ONE COMPLETES WORK LIKE THIS ONE ALONE, AND I have been ridiculously fortunate to know so many generous and intelligent people who have guided me and this book over the past four years. This space cannot fully express the extent or depth of my gratitude, but I hope it can serve as a start for when I thank them at greater length in person.

Metairie Park Country Day School is the most supportive school one could ask for. Carolyn Chandler and Matt Neely recognized the importance of this project to me and my teaching and never hesitated to provide me with the resources I needed to produce this work. Howard Hunter and Dr. Bill LeCorte created and sustained the Faculty Fellows program, which gave me the space, time, and finances to shape this book in its early stages. Howard, you coach scholars as hard and as well as you fight for them, and I could not have a better person in my corner than you. Betsy Petersen listened to my bountiful delights and my even more bountiful complaints, always responding with, "It's just so cool!" My colleagues at Country Day continually showed up at readings and presentations, and you all should know that your interest and enthusiasm did not just help me meet my deadlines: they sustained me. Liam Campbell, Lucas Miller, Jen Sciortino, Erin Walker, and Chris Young have put up with me more than anyone should, and the book is better for it.

Loyola University New Orleans continues to give me far more than I have given it over the past twenty years. John Biguenet and Chris Schaberg nudged me early and often to write a book. John always helped me appreciate how important it was, and Chris always made it sound just easy enough to keep me from giving up. Without your contacts and encouragement, this book would not be here. Chris also helped me find the fun in the book when it needed it most. Chris Chambers, David Estes, Melanie McKay, and Marcus Smith pushed me as a young scholar, and their encouragement convinced me that my ideas were worth sharing. The staff at the Monroe Library at Loyola University New Orleans tracked down any and every obscure article, book, and film I asked for.

Thanks are also long overdue for:

David Hering, for telling me "yeah, there's a book there" on a drizzly afternoon in 2015 in Normal, Illinois.

Mary Holland, for championing the book when it was barely a proposal and me when I was barely a scholar.

Conley Wouters, for some great notes on the earliest drafts of Rounds Two and Three.

Amina Cain and Ariana Kelly, for inviting me to present an early draft of Round Two at Betalevel's Errata Salon.

Rob Short, for helping me find my way into the isolation booth.

Josh Epstein, for some powerful feedback and encouragement at the buzzer.

Zachary Atchley, for his speedy and devoted research assistance. This is only the start of your thanks. I'll be using your hard work for years to come.

Katie Keene, Mary Heath, Jordan Nettles, Shane Gong Stewart, and the rest of the staff at the University Press of Mississippi, for their enthusiasm for this project and their careful guidance through each step of the process.

Robert Jefferson Norrell, for his fantastic copyediting.

Matthew Luter has forgotten more about game shows than I will ever know, and his steadily fervent support from day one has led to something far more valuable, enlightening, and enduring than this book: a treasured friendship. Thank you for carefully considering every half-baked inkling of an idea I have had over these four years. Most of all, thank you for giving me the mantra that has carried me through the roughest patches of this project: "This is a book that does not exist but should."

Thanks are also in order for the unsung heroes of the academic publishing process: the anonymous peer reviewers whose generous and insightful feedback brought depth, nuance, and sophistication to this work. Someday I hope to return the favor. Until then, I remain in your debt.

Finally, no amount of words or deeds can convey my gratitude and love for my biggest supporters: my parents, my wife Amelia, and my best research assistants: my pop-quiz kids Malcolm, Ezra, and Hawthorne. The right answers in this book are all yours.

BIBLIOGRAPHY

Alexander, Alison. "The Meaning of Television in the American Family." *Television and the American Family*, edited by Jennings Bryant and J. Alison Bryant. 2nd ed. Lawrence Erlbaum Associates, 2001, pp. 273–87.

Alters, Diane F. "The Family in U.S. History and Culture." *Media, Home, and Family*, by Lynn Scholfield Clark, Diane F. Alters, Joseph G. Champ, Lee Hood, and Stewart M. Hoover. Routledge, 2004, pp. 51–66.

Anderson, Kent. *Television Fraud: The History and Implications of the Quiz Show Scandals*. Greenwood Press, 1978.

Anderson, Paul Thomas. Interview by Marc Maron. *WTF with Marc Maron*, 5 January 2015, http://www.wtfpod.com/podcast/episodes/episode_565_-_paul_thomas_anderson?rq=paul%20thomas%20anderson. Accessed 15 January 2015.

Apple, Max. "Noon." *The Oranging of America*. Bantam, 1978, pp. 131–48.

Arthur, Paul. "The Troublemaker." *Film Comment*, vol. 40, no. 3, 2004, pp. 58–60, 62–65. https://search.proquest.com/docview/210288636?accountid=41521. Accessed 14 May 2018.

Attanasio, Paul. "Radio Days." *Washington Post*, 30 January 1987, www.washingtonpost.com/wp-srv/style/longterm/movies/videos/radiodayspgattanasio_a0ad93.htm. Accessed 23 April 2016.

Baldwin, James and Raoul Peck. *I Am Not Your Negro*. Vintage, 2017.

Barris, Chuck. *Confessions of a Dangerous Mind: An Unauthorized Autobiography*. Miramax Books, 2002.

Barthelme, Donald. "A Shower of Gold." *Sixty Stories*. Penguin, 2003, pp. 7–16.

Barthes, Roland. *A Lover's Discourse: Fragments*. Translated by Richard Howard. Hill and Wang, 1978.

Baudrillard, Jean. *The Ecstasy of Communication*. Translated by Bernard and Caroline Schutze. Semiotext(e), 2012.

Baudrillard, Jean. "Hypermarket and Hypercommodity." *Simulacra and Simulation*. Translated by Sheila Faria Glaser. University of Michigan Press, 2010, pp. 75–78.

Baudrillard, Jean. "The Implosion of Meaning in the Media." *Simulacra and Simulation*. Translated by Sheila Faria Glaser. University of Michigan Press, 2010, pp. 79–86.

Blake, Richard A. *Street Smart: The New York of Lumet, Allen, Scorsese, and Lee*. University Press of Kentucky, 2005.

Blake, Richard A. *Woody Allen: Profane and Sacred*. The Scarecrow Press, 1995.

Bogost, Ian. "HQ Trivia Is a Harbinger of Dystopia." *TheAtlantic.com*, 22 December 2017, www.theatlantic.com/technology/archive/2017/12/hq-trivia-future-dystopia/549071/. Accessed 15 July 2018.

Bogost, Ian. "Videogames and Ideological Frames." *Popular Communication*, vol. 4, no. 3, 2006, pp. 165–83.

Boswell, Marshall. *Understanding David Foster Wallace*. University of South Carolina Press, 2003.

Bourdon, Jérôme. "Self-Despotism: Reality Television and the New Subject of Politics." *Framework: The Journal of Cinema and Media*, vol. 49, no. 1, 2008, pp. 66–82. www.jstor.org/stable/41552512. Accessed 28 October 2015.

Brown, Wendy. "American Nightmare: Neoliberalism, Neoconservatism, and De-Democratization." *Political Theory*, vol. 34, no. 6, 2006, pp. 690–714. www.jstor.org/stable/20452506. Accessed 19 June 2018.

Butler, Robert Olen. "The American Couple." *A Good Scent from a Strange Mountain*. Penguin, 1993, pp. 155–234.

Carter, Cynthia. "Nuclear Family Fall-Out: Postmodern Family Culture and the Media." *Theorizing Culture: An Interdisciplinary Critique after Postmodernism*, edited by Barbara Adam and Stuart Allen. New York University Press, 1995, pp. 187–200.

Collins, Suzanne. *Catching Fire*. Scholastic, 2013.

Collins, Suzanne. *Mockingjay*. Scholastic, 2010.

Collins, Suzanne. *The Hunger Games*. Scholastic, 2009.

Confessions of a Dangerous Mind. Directed by George Clooney, performances by Sam Rockwell, Julia Roberts, Drew Barrymore, and George Clooney. Miramax, 2002.

Congdon, David. "Reconsidering Apocalyptic Cinema: Pauline Apocalyptic and Paul Thomas Anderson." *Journal of Religion and Popular Culture*, vol. 24, no. 3, 2012, pp. 405–18. https://search.proquest.com/docview/1270648918?accountid=41521. Accessed 30 January 2015.

Cooper, Alan. *Philip Roth and the Jews*. State University of New York Press, 1996.

Courtright, Paul. "Life as a Game Show: Reading Slumdog Millionaire." *Religion Dispatches*, 19 June 2009, religiondispatches.org/life-as-a-game-show-reading-islumdog-millionairei/. Accessed 28 October 2015.

Cross, Gary. *An All-Consuming Century: Why Commercialism Won in Modern America*. Columbia University Press, 2000.

Cross, Gary. *Consumed Nostalgia: Memory in the Age of Fast Capitalism*. Columbia University Press, 2015.

Dean, Jodi. *The Communist Horizon*. Verso, 2012.

DeWitt, Helen. *Lightning Rods*. New Directions, 2011.

DeYoung, Cliff, and Jessica Harper. "Bitchin' in the Kitchen." *Shock Treatment Original Motion Picture Soundtrack*. Rhino, 1994. music.amazon.com/albums/B00DZLR0MI/CATALOG?do=play&ie=UTF8&qid=1533660596&albumAsin=B00DZLR0MI.

De Young, Cliff, Jessica Harper, Ruby Wax, Charles Gray, and Chorus. "Anyhow, Anyhow." *Shock Treatment Original Motion Picture Soundtrack*. Rhino, 1994. music.amazon.com/albums/B00DZLR0MI/CATALOG?do=play&ie=UTF8&qid=1533660596&albumAsin=B00DZLR0MI.

Dick, Philip K. *Solar Lottery*. Mariner, 2012.

Dickinson, Emily. "I'm Nobody! Who Are you?" *The Collected Poems of Emily Dickinson*. Barnes and Noble, 1993, pp. 17.

Dillman, Joanne C. "Twelve Characters in Search of a Televisual Text; Magnolia; Masquerading as Soap Opera." *Journal of Popular Film & Television*, vol. 33, no. 3, 2005, pp. 143. https://search.proquest.com/docview/199402388?accountid=41521. Accessed 30 Janurary 2015.

Doherty, Thomas. "Sex, Half-Truths and Videotape: Auto Focus and Confessions of a Dangerous Mind." *Cinéaste*, vol. 28, no. 2, 2003, pp. 10–13. JSTOR, www.jstor.org/stable/41689572. Accessed 26 October 2015.

Doherty, Thomas. "Video, Science Fiction, and the Cinema of Surveillance." *Journal of the Fantastic in the Arts*, vol. 2, no. 2 (6), 1989, pp. 69–79. www.jstor.org/stable/43309585. Accessed 26 October 2015.

Englund, Axel. "Intermedial Topography and Metaphorical Interaction." *Media Borders, Multimodality and Intermediality*, edited by Lars Ellestrom. Palgrave Macmillan, 2010, pp. 69–80.

Everything You Always Wanted to Know about Sex* (*But Were Afraid to Ask). Directed by Woody Allen, performances by Woody Allen, Gene Wilder, Louise Lasser, Burt Reynolds, and Lynn Redgrave. United Artists, 1972.

Fischer, Lucy. "Mr. Dummar Goes to Town: An Analysis of Melvin and Howard." *Film Quarterly*, vol. 36, no. 1, 1982, pp. 32–40. www.jstor.org/stable/3697183. Accessed 26 October 2015.

Fisher, Mark. *Capitalist Realism: Is There No Alternative?* Zero Books, 2009.

Fisher, Mark. "Precarious Dystopias: *The Hunger Games, In Time*, and *Never Let Me Go*." *Film Quarterly*, vol. 65, no. 4, 2012, pp. 27–33. www.jstor.org/stable/10.1525/fq.2012.65.4.27. Accessed 14 May 2018.

Fiske, John. *Television Culture*. 2nd ed. Routledge, 2011.

Fiske, John. *Understanding Popular Culture*. Routledge, 1989.

Fox, Julian. *Woody: Movies from Manhattan*. Overlook, 1996.

Friedlander, Whitney. "Are We in the New Golden Age of Game Shows?" *Paste*, 22 June 2017, www.pastemagazine.com/articles/2017/06/are-we-in-the-new-golden-age-of-game-shows.html. Accessed 3 August 2017.

Friedman, Jonathan. "Narcissism, Roots and Postmodernity: The Construction of Selfhood in the Global Crisis." *Modernity and Identity*, edited by Scott Lash and Jonathan Friedman. Blackwell, 1992, pp. 331–66.

Gaylard, Gerald. "Postmodern Archaic: The Return of the Real in Digital Virtuality." *Postmodern Culture*, vol. 15, no. 1, 2004. https://search.proquest.com/docview/1428991034?accountid=41521. Accessed 26 August 2017.

Giles, Paul. "Sentimental Posthumanism: David Foster Wallace." *Twentieth Century Literature*, vol. 53, no. 3, 2007, pp. 327–44. www.jstor.org/stable/20479816. Accessed 30 January 2015.

The Gladiators (a.k.a. *Gladiatorerna*). Directed by Peter Watkins, performances by Arthur Pentelow, Kenneth Lo, Jean-Pierre Delamour, and Keith Bradfield. New Line, 1969.

Gomez, Joseph A. *Peter Watkins*. Twayne Publishers, 1979.

The Gong Show Movie. Directed by Chuck Barris, performances by Chuck Barris, Robin Altman, and Jaye P. Morgan. Universal, 1980.

Hampton, Howard. "Instant Authenticity." *Film Comment*, vol. 39, no. 4, 2003, pp. 25–27. www.jstor.org/stable/43455989. Accessed 26 October 2015.

Harper, Jessica. "In My Own Way." *Shock Treatment Original Motion Picture Soundtrack*. Rhino, 1994. music.amazon.com/albums/B00DZLROMI/CATALOG?do=play&ie=UTF8&qid=1533660596&albumAsin=B00DZLROMI.

Harper, Jessica, and Cliff De Young. "Looking for Trade." *Shock Treatment Original Motion Picture Soundtrack*. Rhino, 1994. music.amazon.com/albums/B00DZLROMI/CATALOG?do=play&ie=UTF8&qid=1533660596&albumAsin=B00DZLROMI.

Hassan, Ihab. "Almost the Voice of Silence: The Later Novelettes of J. D. Salinger." *Wisconsin Studies in Contemporary Literature*, vol. 4, no. 1, 1963, pp. 5–20. www.jstor.org/stable/1207180. Accessed 30 January 2015.

Hayes-Brady, Clare. *The Unspeakable Failures of David Foster Wallace: Language, Identity, and Resistance*. Bloomsbury, 2017.

Heer, Jeet. "America's First Postmodern President." *New Republic*, 8 July 2017, newrepublic.com/article/143730/americas-first-postmodern-president. Accessed 24 July 2017.

Hering, David. *David Foster Wallace: Fiction and Form*. Bloomsbury, 2017.

Hoerschelmann, Olaf. *Rules of the Game: Quiz Shows and American Culture*. State University of New York Press, 2006.

Hoffmann-Axthelm, Dieter. "Identity and Reality: The End of the Philosophical Immigration Officer." *Modernity and Identity*, edited by Scott Lash and Jonathan Friedman. Blackwell, 1992, pp. 196–217.

Holbrook, Morris B. *Daytime Television Game Shows and the Celebration of Merchandise: The Price Is Right*. Bowling Green State Press, 1993.

Holland, Mary K. *Succeeding Postmodernism: Language and Humanism in Contemporary American Literature*. Bloomsbury, 2013.

Holmes, Su. *The Quiz Show*. Edinburgh University Press, 2008.

Horton, Robert. "Radio Days." *What a Feeling!: A Critic's Diary of a Flabbergasting Movie Decade*, 27 May 2011. eightiesmovies.wordpress.com/2011/05/27/radio-days/. Accessed 24 April 2016.

The Hunger Games. Directed by Gary Ross, performances by Jennifer Lawrence, Liam Hemsworth, Josh Hutcherson, Donald Sutherland, and Lenny Kravitz. Lionsgate, 2012.

The Hunger Games: Catching Fire. Directed by Francis Lawrence, performances by Jennifer Lawrence, Liam Hemsworth, Josh Hutcherson, Donald Sutherland, and Philip Seymour Hoffman. Lionsgate, 2013.

The Hunger Games: Mockingjay—Part 1. Directed by Francis Lawrence, performances by Jennifer Lawrence, Liam Hemsworth, Josh Hutcherson, Donald Sutherland, and Elizabeth Banks. Lionsgate, 2014.

I Am Not Your Negro. Directed by Raoul Peck, performances by James Baldwin and Samuel L. Jackson. Magnolia, 2016.

Jameson, Fredric. *Postmodernism, or, The Cultural Logic of Late Capitalism*. Duke University Press, 2005.

Jeffrey, Paul. "Hard Eight and the Isolated Actor." *Senses of Cinema*, vol. 74, 2015. sensesofcinema.com/2015/cteq/hard-eight-and-the-isolated-actor/. Accessed 4 April 2015.

Jenkins, Henry. "Why Fiske—Still Matters." *Television Culture*, by John Fiske, 2011, 2nd ed. Routledge, 2011, pp. xv–xli.

Jones, Kent. "Kent Jones Tours P.T. Anderson's Magnolia." *Film Comment*, vol. 36, no. 1, 2000, pp. 38–39. https://search.proquest.com/docview/210267104?accountid=41521. Accessed 30 January 2015.

Kellner, Douglas. *Media Spectacle*. Routledge, 2003.

Kellner, Douglas. "Popular Culture and the Construction of Postmodern Identities." *Modernity and Identity*, edited by Scott Lash and Jonathan Friedman. Blackwell, 1992, pp. 141–77.

King, Stephen. *The Running Man*. Pocket Books, 2016.

Kleeman, Alexandra. *You Too Can Have a Body Like Mine*. Harper Perennial, 2016.

Koehler, Robert. "Slumdog Millionaire." *Cinéaste*, vol. 34, no. 2, 2009, pp. 75–77. www.jstor.org/stable/41690771. Accessed 28 October 2015.

Konstantinou, Lee. *Cool Characters: Irony and American Fiction*. Harvard University Press, 2016.

Krater, Tully. *Game Show*. Amazon Digital, 2013.

Kunzru, Hari. "Afterword to 'Little Expressionless Animals.'" *The David Foster Wallace Reader*. Little, Brown, 2014, pp. 98–99.

Lane, Christina. *Magnolia*. Wiley-Blackwell, 2011.

Laplanche, Jean, and Jean-Bertrand Pontalis. "Fantasy and the Origins of Sexuality." *Reading French Psychoanalysis*, edited by Sara Flanders and Alain Gibeault Dana Birksted-Breen. Routledge, 2010, pp. 310–37.

LaRocca, David. "Unauthorized Autobiography: Truth and Fact in Confessions of a Dangerous Mind." *The Philosophy of Charlie Kaufman*, edited by David LaRocca. University of Kentucky Press, 2011, pp. 89–108.

Laymon, Kiese. *Long Division*. Bolden, 2013.

Lee, Sander H. *Woody Allen's Angst: Philosophical Commentaries on His Serious Films*. McFarland, 1997.

Lethem, Jonathan. *Dissident Gardens*. Vintage, 2014.

Ljungberg, Christina. "Intermedial Strategies in Multimedia Art." *Media Borders, Multimodality and Intermediality*, edited by Lars Ellestrom. Palgrave Macmillan, 2010, pp. 81–95.

Luter, Matthew. *Understanding Jonathan Lethem*. Columbia: University of South Carolina Press, 2015.

Lyotard, Jean-François. *The Postmodern Condition: A Report on Knowledge*. Translated by Geoff Bennington and Brian Massumi. University of Minnesota Press, 1984.

Lyotard, Jean-Francois, and Jean-Loup Thebaud. *Just Gaming*. Translated by Wlad Godzich, University of Minnesota Press, 2008.

Magnolia. Directed by Paul Thomas Anderson, performances by John C. Reilly, Jason Robards, Julianne Moore, Tom Cruise, Philip Seymour Hoffman. New Line, 1999.

Mann, Aimee. "Wise Up." *Music from the Motion Picture Magnolia*. Reprise, 1999.

McCall, Jason. "The Past is Not Dead: Time and Race in Kiese Laymon's *Long Division*." *Los Angeles Review of Books*, 20 November 2013. lareviewofbooks.org/article/the-past-is-not-dead-time-and-race-in-kiese-laymons-long-division/. Accessed 7 July 2018.

Melvin and Howard. Directed by Jonathan Demme, performances by Paul Le Mat, Mary Steenburgen, and Jason Robards. Universal, 1980.

Merchant, Anya. *Limitless Game Show*. Amazon Digital, 2014.

Minow, Newton N. "Television and the Public Interest." *Federal Communications Law Journal*, vol. 55, no.3, 2003, pp. 395–406. www.repository.law.indiana.edu/fclj/vol55/iss3/4/. Accessed 13 December 2016.

Morreale, Joanne. "Faking It and the Transformation of Personal Identity." *Makeover Television: Realities Remodelled*, edited by Dana Heller. I.B. Tauris, 2007, pp. 95–106.

O'Brien, Geoffrey. "A Drifter and His Master." *Stolen Glimpses, Captive Shadows: Writing on Film, 2002–2013*. Counterpoint, 2013, pp. 291–300.

Olson, Randal. "100 Years of Marriage and Divorce in 1 Chart." 15 June 2015, www.randalolson.com/2015/06/15/144-years-of-marriage-and-divorce-in-1-chart/. Accessed 14 July 2018.

Ozersky, Dick. "Mass Media: THE CONTENT-FREE MEDIUM." *ETC: A Review of General Semantics*, vol. 35, no. 1, 1978, pp. 86–89. www.jstor.org/stable/42575309. Accessed 26 October 2015.

Palahniuk, Chuck. *Invisible Monsters: Remix*. Norton, 2012.

Palmer, Gareth. "Extreme Makeover: Home Edition: An American Fairy Tale." *Makeover Television: Realities Remodelled*, edited by Dana Heller. I.B. Tauris, 2007, pp. 165–76.

Pipher, Mary. *Reviving Ophelia: Saving the Selves of Adolescent Girls*. Ballantine, 1994.

Quiz Show. Directed by Robert Redford, performances by Rob Morrow, Ralph Fiennes, John Turturro, David Paymer, and Hank Azaria. Hollywood Pictures, 1994.

Radio Days. Directed by Woody Allen, performances by Seth Green, Michael Tucker, and Dianne Wiest. Orion, 1987.

Rajewsky, Irina O. "Border Talks: The Problematic Status of Media Borders in the Current Debate about Intermediality." *Media Borders, Multimodality and Intermediality*, edited by Lars Ellestrom. Palgrave Macmillan, 2010, pp. 51–68.

Redden, Guy. "Makeover Morality and Consumer Culture." *Makeover Television: Realities Remodelled*, edited by Dana Heller. I.B. Tauris, 2007, pp. 150–64.

"Review: 'Radio Days.'" *Variety*, 31 December 1986. variety.com/1986/film/reviews/radio-days-1200427140/. Accessed 23 April 2016.

Robins, Timothy. "Remembering the Future: The Cultural Study of Memory." *Theorizing Culture: An Interdisciplinary Critique after Postmodernism*, edited by Barbara Adam and Stuart Allen. New York University Press, 1995, pp. 201–13.

Roth, Philip. *Zuckerman Unbound*. Vintage, 1995.

The Running Man. Directed by Paul Michael Glaser, performances by Arnold Schwarzenegger, Jesse Ventura, Maria Conchita Alonso, Yaphet Kotto, and Richard Dawson. TriStar, 1987.

Salinger, J. D. "Raise High the Roof Beam, Carpenters." *Raise High the Roof Beam, Carpenters and Seymour, an Introduction*. Little, Brown, 1991, pp. 3–92.

Salinger, J. D. "Zooey." *Franny and Zooey*. Little, Brown, 1991, pp. 45–202.

Schickel, Richard. *Woody Allen: A Life in Film*. Ivan R. Dee, 2003.

Schwartz, Arthur. "For Seymour: With Love and Judgment." *Wisconsin Studies in Contemporary Literature*, vol. 4, no. 1, 1963, pp. 88–99. www.jstor.org/stable/1207187. Accessed 30 January 2015.

Severs, Jeffrey. *David Foster Wallace's Balancing Books: Fictions of Value*. Columbia University Press, 2017.

Shock Treatment. Directed by Jim Sharman, performances by Jessica Harper, Cliff De Young, Jim Sharman, and Patricia Quinn. Fox. 1981.

Sippl, Dianne. "Tomorrow Is My Birthday: Placing Apocalypse in Millennial Cinema." *Cineaction*, no. 53, 2000, pp. 2–21.

Slumdog Millionaire. Directed by Danny Boyle, performances by Dev Patel, Anil Kapoor, Frieda Pinto, and Madhur Mittal. Fox Searchlight, 2008.

Smith, Carlton, and Deborah Paes De Barros. "Singing in the (Post-Apocalyptic) Rain: Some High/Low Notes on Post/Postmodernism and Contemporary American Fiction." *American Studies International*, vol. 33, no. 1, 1995, pp. 1–18. www.jstor.org/stable/41280844. Accessed 30 January 2015.

Sparks, Colin. "The Media and the State." *Media Studies: A Reader*, edited by Paul Morris and Sue Thornham, Edinburgh University Press, 1996, pp. 84–90.

Sperb, Jason. *Blossoms and Blood: Postmodern Media Culture in the Films of Paul Thomas Anderson*. University of Texas Press, 2013.

Stacey, Judith. *Brave New Families: Stories of Domestic Upheaval in Late Twentieth Century America*. Basic Books, 1990.

Stay Tuned. Directed by Peter Hyams, performances by John Ritter, Pam Dawber, and Jeffrey Jones. Warner, 1992.

Table No. 21. Directed by Aditya Datt, performances by Paresh Rawal, Rajeev Khandewal, and Tina Desai. Eros International, 2013.

Taylor, Ella. *Prime-Time Families: Television Culture in Postwar America*. University of California Press, 1989.

Tegmark, Mats. "Constructions of Transcultural Subjectivity: Going Beyond Nationalism and Ethnicity in A Good Scent from a Strange Mountain." *Transcultural Identities in Contemporary Literature*, edited by Irene Gilsenan Nordin, Julie Hansen, and Carmen Zamorano Llena. Rodopi, 2013, pp. 93–112.

Texter, Douglas W. "'A Funny Thing Happened on the Way to the Dystopia': The Culture Industry's Neutralization of Stephen King's *The Running Man.*" *Utopian Studies*, vol. 18, no. 1, 2007, pp. 43–72. www.jstor.org/stable/20719846. Accessed 26 October 2015.

Thompson, Derek. "The Most American Television Show of 2018." *TheAtlantic.com*, 12 July 2018, www.theatlantic.com/entertainment/archive/2018/07/win-a-game-show-pay-off-your-student-debt/564980. Accessed 17 July 2018.

Tichi, Cecelia. *Electronic Hearth: Creating an American Television Culture.* Oxford University Press, 1991.Toles, George. *Paul Thomas Anderson.* University of Illinois Press, 2016.

Tulloch, John. "Gradgrind's Heirs: The Presentation of 'Knowledge' in British Quiz Shows." *Screen Education*, Summer 1976, pp. 3–13.

Tyree, J. M. "Against the Clock: *Slumdog Millionaire* and *The Curious Case of Benjamin Button.*" *Film Quarterly*, vol. 62, no. 4, 2009, pp. 34–38. www.jstor.org/stable/10.1525/fq.2009.62.4.34. Accessed 26 October 2015.

Udovitch, Mim. "The Epic Obsessions of Paul Thomas Anderson." *Rolling Stone*, no. 833, February 2000, pp. 46–49+. https://search.proquest.com/docview/220171809?accountid=41521. Accessed 30 January 2015.

Wallace, David Foster. "E Unibus Pluram: Television and U. S. Fiction." *A Supposedly Fun Thing I'll Never Do Again: Essays and Arguments.* Back Bay, 1998, pp. 21–82.

Wallace, David Foster. "An Expanded Interview with David Foster Wallace." *Conversations with David Foster Wallace*, by Larry McCaffrey, edited by Stephen J. Burn. University Press of Mississippi, 2012, pp. 21–52.

Wallace, David Foster. "Little Expressionless Animals." *Girl with Curious Hair.* W. W. Norton, 1989. 1–42. Print.

Weber, Myles. "Reading Salinger's Silence." *New England Review*, vol. 26, no. 2, 2005, pp. 118–41, 266. https://search.proquest.com/docview/234366966?accountid=41521. Accessed 30 January 2015.

White Men Can't Jump. Directed by Ron Shelton, performances by Woody Harrelson, Wesley Snipes, Rosie Perez, and Kadeem Hardison. Fox, 1992.

Wernblad, Annette. *Brooklyn Is Not Expanding: Woody Allen's Comic Universe.* Fairleigh Dickinson University Press, 1992.

Whitfield, Stephen J. "Quiz Show." *American Jewish History*, vol. 84, no. 2, 1996, pp. 129–35. https://search.proquest.com/docview/1001901637?accountid=41521. Accessed 11 February 2018.

Whitman, Walt. "Song of Myself." *Leaves of Grass.* Barnes and Noble, 1993, pp. 25–76.

Who Wants to Be an Erotic Billionaire? Directed by John Bacchus, John Paul Fedele, Joe Ned, and Michael Raso; performances by Julian Wells, Vivica Taylor, Bethany Lott, and Allison Slinger. E. I. Independent, 2002.

INDEX

Page references in *italics* indicate an illustration.

absurdity, 216–17
Affleck, Ben, 202
Alexander, Alison, 135–36
Allen, Fred, 6
Allen, Woody: *Everything You Always Wanted to Know about Sex*, 114; *Manhattan*, 22. See also *Radio Days*
Alters, Diane F., 130
Amarcord (Fellini), 22
Amazing Race, The, 174–75
"American Couple, The" (Butler), 32, 80–85, 231–32
American Dream, 10–13, 42, 53–54, 57–58, 130, 214. *See also* meritocracy; upward mobility
American Family, An, 174
American Graffiti, 24
American Ninja Warrior, 17
Anderson, Kent, 35, 37, 61
Anderson, Paul Thomas, 4, 132–34. See also *Magnolia*
apocalyptic events, 167–68
Apple, Max, 33; "Noon," 216–20, 223
Apprentice, The, 7, 174–75, 213–14
Arlen, Michael J., 124
Attanasio, Paul, 22, 45
audience, 199–211; in *The Gladiators*, 199–200; in *The Hunger Games* series, 199, 202, 209, 211; in *The Running Man*, 200, *201*, 202, 204–11
authenticity. *See* self
autobiography, 88

Bachelor, The, 17, 94–95
Baldwin, James, *I Am Not Your Negro*, 11–13, 16
Ballhaus, Michael, 46, 48
Barris, Chuck, 33; as CIA hitman, 39, 86, 88; *Confessions of a Dangerous Mind*, 32, 38, 85–88, 90–91; criticism of shows by, 7; *The Dating Game*, 10, 86–88, 93–94, 96, 118; *The Gong Show*, 12–13, 86–89; *The Gong Show Movie*, 214–16, *215*, 220, 220–21; influence of, 85–86; *The Newlywed Game*, 21–22, 86, 105, 221
Barros, Deborah Paes de, 144
Barthelme, Donald, 33; "A Shower of Gold," 216–18, 223
Barthes, Roland, 97–99, 103–4, 109–10, 123, 127–29
Baudrillard, Jean, 218; on battles via images, 189; on the body as an assemblage of parts, 121; on ecstatic forms, 95, 110, 115–16; on meaning in the media, 179, 192; on negative satellites of the city, 185; on prostitution and pornography, 96; on revolutionary movements, 198; on secrets, 128; on seduction, 104, 128; on silent protest, 187; on tests, 180–81; on truth telling, 95
Beat Shazaam, 17
Bergman, Ingmar, 22
Big Brother, 13, 17, 174–76, 230
Black, Max, 19
Black Jeopardy! sketch (*Saturday Night Live*), 71
Blake, Richard A., 23, 27

Blind Date, 94
Bogost, Ian, 15–16, 214, 228–29, 234
Boswell, Marshall, 144–46, 149–50, 153
Bourdon, Jérôme, 175–76, 186
Boyle, Danny. See *Slumdog Millionaire*
bridges, symbolism of, 83
Broom of the System, The (Wallace), 152
Brown, Wendy, 179, 202
Butler, Robert Olen, "The American Couple," 32, 80–85, 231–32

call-in programs, 24–25
Catcher in the Rye, The (Salinger), 138
CBS, 34–35
Celebrity Big Brother, 213
Celebrity Rehab, 174
charity shows, 64
Chinatown, 24
Clooney, George, *Confessions of a Dangerous Mind*, 32, 38, 85–91
Collins, Suzanne. See *Hunger Games* series, *The*
commodity spectacle, 9, 69–70
Condemned, The, 176
Confessions of a Dangerous Mind (Barris), 32, 38, 85–88, 90–91
Confessions of a Dangerous Mind (Clooney), 32, 38, 85–91
Conformist, The, 24
Congdon, David, 165–68
consumerism: Americans' relationship to society affected by, 8; definition of, 8; of game shows, 8–11; and heterosexuality/heteronormativity, 10, 94, 96, 109–10, 113–14; knowledge affected by, 8; vs. the Protestant work ethic, 10
Convy, Bert, 133
Cross, Gary, 8–10, 20, 23–24, 26
culture: American dominance in game shows, 71–74 (*see also* "American Couple, The"; *Long Division*; *Zuckerman Unbound*); capitalist, and reality shows, 175–76, 179, 181–82, 186, 211; and knowledge, 71; of media, as isolating, 31–32; pace of, 23; popular, studies of, 3–4, 15–16; as revealed by game shows, 14

Damon, Matt, 202
Danielewski, Mark, 131; *House of Leaves*, 132, 134–35, 154
Das Millionenspiel, 176
Dating Game, The, 10, 86–88, 93–94, 96, 118
dating shows, 17, 93–98
Datt, Aditya, *Table No. 21*, 103–5, 107
Dawson, Richard, 206, 206–7
Deal or No Deal, 12–13, 174
Dean, Jodi, 231
death and totalitarianism, 32–33, 174–211. See also *Hunger Games* series, *The*; *Running Man, The*
Debt, 214
debt relief, 213–14
Demme, Jonathan, *Melvin and Howard*, 32, 55, 57–63, 59, 62, 70
Despair (Nabokov), 87–88
De Witt, Helen, *Lightning Rods*, 32, 115, 123–28
Dick, Philip K., 33; *Solar Lottery*, 176, 216, 221–24
Dillman, Joanne Clarke, 157–58, 164
DiPalma, Carlo, 24, 29
directors, styles used by, 157
Dissident Gardens (Lethem), 224–33
divorce rates, 94
Doherty, Thomas, 86, 89, 179, 206, 208
Double Dare, 13, 99–100

ElimiDate, 94
ellipsis, symbolism of, 80
Endgame, 176
Englund, Axel, 19
erotica, 32, 111–15, 120–22, 124–26
"*E Unibus Pluram*: Television and U. S. Fiction" (Wallace), 171
Everything You Always Wanted to Know about Sex (W. Allen), 114
existential crisis, 216–17
Extreme Makeover, 17, 131

family, 130–73; as diverse/fluid, 131; in the Glass Family saga, 32, 133, 136–43; vs. global village, 133; in *House of Leaves*, 132, 134–35, 154, 171; in *Infinite Jest*, 131–32, 143, 155, 172; nuclear, 105, 130–31; overview of,

32; as a system of meaning and relationships, 135–36. See also *Franny and Zooey*; "Little Expressionless Animals"; *Magnolia*
Family Challenge, 131
Family Double Dare, 131
Family Feud, 21, 131, 206
Father Knows Best, 131
Fear Factor, 174–75
Federal Communications Commission v. American Broadcasting Co., Inc., The, 34
Fellini, Federico, *Amarcord*, 22
5th Wheel, The, 94
Fischer, Lucy, 57, 60–62
Fisher, Mark, 177, 230
Fiske, John: on the American Dream, 10; on carnivalesque, 11; on culture, 16, 175; on the education system, 55–56; on game shows as making sense of the world, 16, 30; on play, 177–78; on the political potential of game shows, 14; on quiz-show knowledge, 21; on rags-to-riches narratives, 10; on ritual in game shows, 10–11, 55; on vertical intertextuality, 17
Fox, Julian, 27–28
Franny and Zooey (Salinger), 132; acting/performance in, 138–41; Buddy character, 140–42; on connection, 150, 152; disconnection in, 138; Franny character, 138–40, 142–43, 168, 172; on knowledge, 138; Les character, 138; on mass media as a catalyst for connection, 137, 141–42; Parable of the Fat Lady, 139–42, 166; on religious study/transcendence, 141–42; Seymour character, 137, 140–42; wise-child complex in, 136–39; Zooey character, 138–43, 172
French New Wave, 157
Friedman, Jonathan, 77
Fujimoto, Tak, 57

"Game Show" (Krater), 112, 124
game shows: in the Age of Trump, 213–16, 228 (see also *Dissident Gardens*; "Noon"; "Shower of Gold, A"); American culture's dominance in, 71–74 (*see also* "American Couple, The"; *Long Division*; *Zuckerman Unbound*); call-in programs, 24–25; capitalism promoted via, 9–11; as carnivalesque, 10–11; consumerism of, 8–11; criticism of, 5–8, 11–14; and danger (*see* death and totalitarianism); death- and torture-based, depictions of, 176–77; debt-relief, 213–14; and the education system, 55–56; as erotic spaces, 32, 111–15, 120–22, 124–26; female audience for, 8; in fiction and film, 16–18; as genre, 17; genres, texts, and media mixed in, 17; heteronormativity of, 10 (*see also* heterosexuality/heteronormativity); as imitating real life, 16–17, 20–21; as language games, 20, 36, 71; legalization of, 34; luck's role in, 10; as metaphor for state power, 176–77, 201–2; as narrative devices, 16, 18, 20; and participatory democracy, 216; popularity of, 174; as pornography, 96 (*see also* intimacy; romantic relationships); postmodern, 56; primetime vs. daytime, 7–8, 35; prizes on, 8–9, 35, 213–14; race/ethnicity addressed in, 71–72, 85 (*see also* "American Couple, The"; *Long Division*; *Zuckerman Unbound*); reputation of (*see* quiz-show scandals); and ritual, 10–11, 13–14, 55; and romantic discourse (*see* romantic relationships); scholarship on, 4–6, 14–15; and the self (*see* self); significance of, 30; success/revival of, 13, 33; in television programs, 31; trivia of, 22. *See also specific types and shows*
Gaylard, Gerald, 175–76, 181–82, 186
Giles, Paul, 143, 148
Gladiators, The (Watkins), 178, *196–97*, *197–200*
Glaser, Paul Michael, *The Running Man*, 200, *201*, *202–10*, *206–8*
Glass Family saga (Salinger), 32, 132–36, 137–43. See also *Franny and Zooey*
Gomez, Joseph A., 199–200
Gong Show, The, 12–13, 86–89
Gong Show Movie, The (Barris), 214–16, *215*, *220*, 220–21
Goodwin, Richard, 49. See also *Quiz Show* (Redford)

Griffin, Merv, 132–33. *See also under* "Little Expressionless Animals"

"Hanging Tree, The," 185
Hassan, Ihab, 140–41
Hayes-Brady, Clare, 145–46
Heer, Jeet, 212
Hering, David, 144, 146–47, 168
heterosexuality/heteronormativity, 10, 94–96, 103, 106–7, 109–10, 113–14, 131
HGTV Star, 221
Hickey, Neil, 6
Hoerschelmann, Olaf: on the American Dream, 10; on dating shows, 94; on family, 131; on frivolity of game shows, 175; on game shows as conduits for meaning, 30; on meritocratic-norm reversals in game shows, 11; *The Rules of the Game*, 11, 14–15; on torture quiz shows, 175
Hoffmann-Axthelm, Dieter, 40, 64, 69, 86
Holbrook, Morris B., 6, 9–10, 14
Holland, Mary K., 131–35, 143–44, 146, 154–55, 171–73
Hollywood Game Night, 16
Holmes, Su, 10–11, 14–15, 30, 60, 174–75, 178–79; *The Quiz Show*, 10, 14–15
Holocaust films, 184
Horton, Robert, 22
House of Leaves (Danielewski), 132, 134–35, 154
HQ Trivia app, 13, 214, 228
Hunger Games series, *The* (Collins), 176, 180–95; annual games as terror by the state, 185; audience in, 199, 202, 209, 211; binge-and-purge culture of games, 184; capitalism modeled in, 182; *Catching Fire*, 182–84, 189–90, 192; choice absent in, 178; cinematography of, 191; contestants as food in games, 183–84; dangers of citizenship in, 33; description of/rationale for games, 181–82; end of, 194; Gamemakers' control of games, 183; health care in, 203; *The Hunger Games*, 182, 184–85, *185*; Katniss and Peeta's romance and suicide pact, 188–89; Katniss character, 181, 184–85, 187–94, *188*, 211; memorialization of games, 183; *Mockingjay*, 185, 189–93, *191*, 211; mockingjay symbolism in, 190, 192; national identity in, 181; Nazi aesthetics of, 184–85, *185–86*; Panem, 182, 184–85, 189, 211; President Coin character, 193–94; President Snow character, *186*, 189; rebellion in, 189–94, 198, 211; resistance movement in District 13, 193–94; Rue's death, 187–88; rule changes in games, 188; silent protest in, 187; surveillance of games, 187, 193; television coverage of games, 182–83, 187–89, *188*; tests in, 180–81; as a total screen, 180–81; victimization in games, 185–87; wilderness setting and technology in, 182
Hyams, Peter, *Stay Tuned*, 103, 105–8, 119, 122

I Am Not Your Negro (Peck and Baldwin), 11–13, 16
identity. *See* self
Infinite Jest (Wallace), 131–32, 143, 155, 172
information-based society, 8–9
intermediality, 18–21, 31, 37, 134–35
intimacy, 31, 89; as authenticity, 117; as a commodity, 96–97, 110; erotica, 32, 111–15, 120–22, 124–26; and knowledge, 97–104, 111–14, 126–28; and patriarchy, 106–7, 113; and recognition, 117–19, 123–28; as trivialized by game shows, 93; and truth telling/transparency, 95, 103–6; as unattainable, 96–97, 110
isolation booths, *37*, 37–38, 56–57

Jackson, Samuel L., 12–13
Jameson, Fredric, 23–24, 218
Jenkins, Henry, 16
Jeopardy!: academic vs. everyday knowledge on, 21; in "Little Expressionless Animals," 132–33, 145, 147, 151–52, 172; success of, 13; in *White Men Can't Jump*, 99–102, *100*
Jerry Springer Show, The, 12
Jews, 72–77

Kellner, Douglas: on the commodity spectacle, 9, 69–70; on cultural rituals, 13–14; on the logic of capital, 59; on prizes for knowledge, 8–9; on selfhood, 35–36,

38–39, 49, 85; on spectator politics, 212; on video games, 15
Kennedy, John F., 212
King, Stephen. See *Running Man, The*
Kleeman, Alexandra, *You Too Can Have a Body Like Mine*, 32, 110, 115–24, 127
Klum, Heidi, 174
knowledge: academic vs. everyday, 21; and American culture, 71; consumerism's effects on, 8; factual vs. human, 21; imparted by nursery rhymes, 30; and intimacy, 97–104, 111–14, 126–28; and memory, 30; and power, 180; prizes for, 8–9; and self, 36–39, 45, 64, 92
Koehler, Robert, 68–69
Konstantinou, Lee, 225, 230, 232–33
Krater, Tully, "Game Show," 112, 124
Kunzru, Hari, 146, 150

Lane, Christina, 157–58, 160–61, 164, 168, 170
language games, 20, 36–37, 71, 169, 179, 230
Laplance, Jean, 126
LaRocca, David, 88, 91
Lasch, Christopher, 144
Lawrence, Francis, 191
Laymon, Kiese, *Long Division*, 32, 77–80, 101, 113
leftism, 227
Lessing, Doris, 232
Lethem, Jonathan, 33; *Dissident Gardens*, 224–33
Let's Make a Deal, 112
Lévi-Strauss, Claude, 10
Lightning Rods (De Witt), 32, 115, 123–28
"Limitless Game Show" (Merchant), 114–15
"Little Expressionless Animals" (Wallace), 132–33; on connection, 149–53; on familial societal problems, 143–44; family trees in, 143; Faye character, 148–51; on fiction vs. television, 152–53; final scene, 168, 172; fluid boundaries in, 144–46, 151–54; game shows' insincerity in, 32; Griffin in, 133, 143, 145, 147, 151, 172; *Jeopardy!* in, 132–33, 145, 147, 151–52, 172; Julie character, 146–52, 172; on knowledge and stages of love, 149; on knowledge and wisdom, 134; Lunt character, 151–53, 172; on mass media as a catalyst for connection, 134–36; overconnection in, 143; Sajak in, 133; spectation/trauma scenes, 144, 146, 150–51; Trebek in, 133, 147–48, 150, 152; TV addict character, 148
Live!, 176
logic of capital, 59
Long Division (Laymon), 32, 77–80, 101, 113
love. *See* intimacy; romantic relationships
Luter, Matthew, 226, 232
Lyotard, Jean-François: on institutional discourses, 98; on intermedial metaphor, 20; on knowledge, 8, 30, 92, 180; on language games, 20, 36, 179; on selfhood, 36, 92; on social bonds, 179

"Mack the Knife" (Weill and Brecht), 41–42, 91
Mad Men, 5–6
Magnolia (P. T. Anderson), 132; abuse and neglect in, 158, 161–63, 167; Big Earl Partridge logo, 156–57, 157, 164; cancer metaphor in, 133, 156, 161, 167–68; child characters, 161–63; cinema's dominance in, 168–69; coda, 167–68, 169, 170–73; connection and disconnection in, 134–36, 154, 160, 165, 167–68, 170; credits, 159, 164; faith in, 167–68; families in, 154–56; fathers/masculinity in, 133, 156, 158, 160–61, 164, 166–67, 172–73; game shows' insincerity in, 32, 171; Gwenovier's interview, 164–65, 169; identity crises in, 161; irony in, 170; on knowledge and wisdom, 134; loneliness in, 154–55, 165, 170; main story, 159, 167; preamble, 158–59; rain of frogs in, 156, 159–60, 162, 166–67, 172; "Seduce and Destroy," 160–61, 170; soundtrack, 159, 165–66, 173; Stanley's rebellion and monologue, 163–66; structure and design of, 155–58, 164; television critiqued in, 156, 163–64; television's dominance in, 157–58, 162, 168; *What Do Kids Know?*, 133, 155–56, 161–65, 170; wise-child complex in, 161
Major Bowes' Original Amateur Hour, 7
makeover shows, 56, 58, 62, 86, 91

Manhattan (W. Allen), 22
Manigault, Omarosa, 213
Mann, Aimee, 159, 173
Mantle, Anthony Dodd, 65
Man vs. Wild, 17
Marty, 43
mass media as threatening American life, 40–41. *See also* television
masturbatory fantasy, 126
Match Game, The, 13
McCall, Jason, 80
media: film (*see specific films*); meaning in, 179, 191–92; radio, 30; the state's relationship with, 176–77, 179–80, 189, 200 (see also *Gladiators, The*; *Hunger Games* series, *The*). *See also* television
Melvin and Howard (Demme), 32, 55, 57–63, 59, 62, 70
memory, 22–30, 224, 232–33
Merchant, Anya, "Limitless Game Show," 114–15
meritocracy, 11, 39, 53, 56. *See also* American Dream; upward mobility
Minahan, Daniel, *Series 7: The Contenders*, 176
Minow, Newton, 6–7
Modern Family, 5–6
Morreale, Joanne, 56, 70, 85–86, 91

NAB (National Association of Broadcasters), 6–7
Nabokov, Vladimir, *Despair*, 87–88
Name That Tune, 17
National Association of Broadcasters (NAB), 6–7
NBC, 34
neoliberalism, 177, 202
New Deal ideology, 24–25, 27
New Hollywood, 157
Newlywed Game, The, 21–22, 86, 105, 221
Next Food Network Star, The, 221
"Noon" (Apple), 216–20, 223
nostalgia, 23–24, 26, 30

O'Brien, Geoffrey, 154
O'Brien, Richard, *Shock Treatment*, 32, 103, 107–10, *108*, 118, 122, 127

Occupy movement, 230
"One" (Three Dog Night), 159
On the Waterfront, 43–44

Pabst, G. W., 91
Paid Off, 213–14, 228
Palahniuk, Chuck, 21
Pale King, The (Wallace), 152
Peck, Raoul, *I Am Not Your Negro*, 11–13, 16
Pipher, Mary, 118
Pontalis, Jean-Bertrand, 126
popular culture, 3–4, 15–16
pornography, 96, 111–16, 119–26
Portnoy's Complaint (Roth), 74
presidencies in the United States, 212. *See also under* Trump, Donald J.
Press Your Luck, 13
Price Is Right, The, 7–8, 10, 12–13, 21, 93
"Prize of Peril, The" (Sheckley), 176
Professor Quiz, 7
Protestant work ethic, 10, 60

Q & A (Swarup), 63
Queen for a Day, 56
Quiz Show (Redford), 32, 70, 85; Charles Van Doren character, 42–43, 45–46, *47–48*, 48–49, 51, 54–55, 72–73; cinematic vs. televisual language in, 49, 60; cinematography of, 45–46, 48, 51–52, *51–52*; Columbia campus scene, 46, 48, 54; congressional hearing scenes, 44, 49–51, 63–64, 72; cynicism in, 53–54; Enright character, 43, 48, 52; ethnicity in, 72–73; final scene, 51–53, *53*; Goodwin character, 42, 48–52, *50*, 54–55, 72–73; isolation booth in, 42; Jewish characters, 72; "Mack the Knife" used in, 41–42, 53, 91; Mark Van Doren character, 45; on mass media, 40–41; opening scenes, 41–43; phone booth scene, *48*, 48–49, 54; players vs. audience in, 50–51; projection room scene, 49–50, *51*; Queens neighborhood scene, 54; script, 45, 49; sealed envelope of questions in, 41–42, *42*; selfhood in, 38, 40–44, 55; Snodgrass character, 44, 49; social class, 54–55; Stempel character, 42–45, 51, 54, 72–73; wrong quiz answers in, 43–44

Quiz Show, The (Holmes), 10, 14–15
quiz shows: aesthetics of, 14–15; and coherence vs. fragmentation, 56; first, 7; highbrow vs. lowbrow, 7–8; Hoerschelmann on, 11, 14; knowledge categories on, 21–22; made over as game shows, 35; popularity of, 7, 14–15, 34
quiz-show scandals (1950s), 41, 74; cancellations following allegations, 35; effect on quiz shows, 32, 35, 93; effects on television, 7, 35, 53; first allegations of fixing, 35; popular reaction to, 53; *The $64,000 Question*, 34–35, 93; sponsors' pressure to rig shows, 34–35; Supreme Court ruling on jackpot prizes, 34. See also *Quiz Show* (Redford); *Twenty-One*

racial imagination, 11–12
radio, 30
Radio Days (W. Allen), 22–30; cinematography of, 24, 29; critical reception of, 22–23; final scene, 27–28, *28*; and the Glass Family saga, 136; as homage to *Amarcord*, 22; on impermanence, 23, 26, 28; nostalgia/memory in, 22–30; quiz show scene, first, 24–26, *26*, 30; quiz show scene, second, 26–27; trivia in, 28–30; whiz kid scene, 136
rags-to-riches narratives, 10, 61, 63
Rajewsky, Irina O., 18–19
Rapping, Elayne, 6
Reagan, Ronald, 207
reality shows, 174–211; and capitalist culture, 175–76, 179, 181–82, 186, 211; choice absent in, 178; competition-based (gamedocs), 13, 174–75 (see also *Big Brother*; *Survivor*); criticism of, 7; gameplay and politics in, 177–78; humiliation, pain, and aggression in, 175; influence of, 174; realism in, 179–80; spontaneity in, 176; submission to rules in, 176; types of reality in, 230; victim culture of, 186–87; as voyeuristic, 176. See also *specific shows*
Real World, The, 17, 174
Redden, Guy, 58, 62
Redford, Robert. See *Quiz Show* (Redford)
remediation. See intermediality

Riefenstahl, Leni, 184
Rocky Horror Picture Show, The, 107, 109–10
Rogan, Joe, 174
romantic relationships, 93–129; and dating shows, 93–98; and game-show vs. romantic discourse, 32, 96–99, 104, 107, 109; and heterosexuality/heteronormativity, 10, 94–96, 103, 106–7, 109–10, 113–14, 131; marriage, 94–95, 103–10; and truth telling, 95, 103–6. See also intimacy
Ross, Gary, 184
Roth, Philip: *Portnoy's Complaint*, 74; *Zuckerman Unbound*, 32, 73–78
Rules of the Game, The (Hoerschelmann), 11, 14–15
Runner, The, 202
Running Man, The (Glaser), 200, *201*, 202–11, *206–8*
Running Man, The (King), 176; audience in, 200, *201*, 202, 204–5; choice absent in, 178; dangers of citizenship in, 33; democratic government critiqued by, 202–5; vs. the film adaptation, 205–6; Free-Vee's game shows in, 202–3, 209; health care in, 202–3; Killian character, 203–10; as metaphor for policing, 200; Richards character, 200, 202–5, 207–10; social class in, 204–5, 211; Williams character, 204–5
RuPaul, 174

Sajak, Pat, 133
Salinger, J. D., 4, 132; on authenticity, 134; *The Catcher in the Rye*, 138; Glass Family saga, 32, 132–33, 136–43 (see also *Franny and Zooey*); influence on Wallace, 133; performance in works of, 138–39
Saturday Night Live, 71
"Save Me," 173
Schindler's List, 184
Schwartz, Arthur, 138
Schwarzenegger, Arnold, 207–9, *208*
self, 34–92; authentic, 37–39, 41–42, 45, 85; as fluid, 85–91 (see also *Confessions of a Dangerous Mind*); and knowledge, 36–39, 45, 64, 92; and language games, 36–37, 71; in makeover shows, 56, 58, 86, 91; modern

vs. postmodern, 35–40, 49, 55, 59, 90–91; passport examination to prove identity, 64; in *Quiz Show*, 38, 40–44, 55; rigged games as threats to, 32 (see also *Quiz Show* [Redford]); in *Slumdog Millionaire*, 63–64, 67–70; as spectacle, 39
Series 7: The Contenders (Minahan), 176
sex/sexuality. See erotica; heterosexuality/heteronormativity; pornography; romantic relationships
Sharman, Jim, *Shock Treatment*, 32, 103, 107–10, *108*, 118, 122, 127
Sheckley, Robert, "The Prize of Peril," 176
Shelton, Ron, *White Men Can't Jump*, 32, 99, *100*, 101–3, *102*, 111, 113, 128
Shock Treatment (O'Brien and Sharman), 32, 103, 107–10, *108*, 118, 122, 127
Shop 'Til You Drop, 131
"Shower of Gold, A" (Barthelme), 216–18, 223
Siegel, Newton Thomas, 86–87
Singled Out, 94
Sippl, Diane, 161
$64,000 Question, The, 34–35, 93
Slumdog Millionaire (Boyle): Bachchan scene, 66–67; Bollywood dance scene, 69, *70*; cinematography of, 65; on exploitative capital, 67–68; final scene, 67; as intermedial metaphor, 18–20; Jamal character, 63–70, *67*; Jamal's motives, 67–68; Latika character, 67; as a makeover show, 63; opening scene, 63, 65; police interrogation scenes, 65–66, 68; Pram character, 66; quiz show narrative in, 63–64; as a rags-to-riches narrative, 63; on rigged games, 32; Salim character, 66–67; selfhood in, 63–64, 67–70; social class in, 55, 63–64, 66–71; and *Who Wants to Be a Millionaire?*, 18–19, 63; "written" destiny/fatalism in, 63–64, 68–70, 77, 80
Smith, Carlton, 144
Solar Lottery (Dick), 176, 216, 221–24
Sparks, Colin, 177
spectator politics, 212
Speer, Albert, 184
Sperb, Jason, 161
sponsor-controlled programming, 35, 38

Sputnik, 41, 56
Stacey, Judith, 131, 135–36
Stay Tuned (Hyams), 103, 105–8, 119, 122
Stewart, Susan, 24
Strike It Rich, 56
Sunday Express, 6
Supermarket Sweep, 10, 93, 96
surveillance, 176, 179, 187, 193, 209
Survivor, 13, 17, 174–75, 181–82, 213
Swarup, Vikas, *Q & A*, 63

Table No. 21 (Datt), 103–5, 107
Take It or Leave It, 34
Taylor, Ella, 130
Tegmark, Mats, 80–81
television: as babysitter, 144; as cancerous, 133, 135–36, 156, 161, 167–68; vs. cinema, 168–69, 173; commercial breaks on, 35, 38; criticism of, 6–7; live, popularity of, 34; masculinity threatened by, 106–7; power to connect people, 134; quiz-show scandals' effects on, 7, 35, 53. See also game shows; reality shows
Temptation Island, 95
Texter, Douglas W., 202–3, 206, 210
"This Is Water" (Wallace), 152
Thompson, Derek, 212
Tichi, Cecelia, 107, 124
Tic-Tac-Dough, 34–35
Time, 35
title card, 160, *160*
Toles, George, 173
To Tell the Truth, 13, 51
Trebek, Alex, 133
trivia vs. meaning, 26
Trump, Donald J.: as game-show host, 7, 174; game shows in the age of, 213–16, 228 (see also *Dissident Gardens*; "Noon"; "Shower of Gold, A"); as president, 7, 207, 212–16, 222, 228, 233; vulgarity of, 215–16
Twenty-One: Charles Van Doren as a contestant on, 40; isolation booth, 37, *37*; as rigged, 37, 40–41, 93 (see also *Quiz Show* [Redford]); set of, 7; sponsors' pressure to rig, 34–35
Tyree, J. M., 68

Uncle Jim's Question Bee, 7
upward mobility, 55–59, 61, 68–69. *See also* American Dream; *Melvin and Howard*; meritocracy

Van Doren, Charles, 40, 49. See also *Quiz Show* (Redford)
Ventura, Jesse ("The Body"), 207
vertical intertextuality, 17
video games, 15–16
Vox Pop, 7, 21–22

Wall, The, 13, 17
Wallace, David Foster, 4; on authenticity, 134; *The Broom of the System*, 152; "*E Unibus Pluram*: Television and U. S. Fiction," 171; *Infinite Jest*, 131–32, 143, 155, 172; influence on Anderson, 133; *The Pale King*, 152; Salinger's influence on, 133; "This Is Water," 152. *See also* "Little Expressionless Animals"
Watkins, Peter, *The Gladiators*, 178, *196–97*, 197–200

Weber, Myles, 139
Wernblad, Annette, 30
Wheel of Fortune, 13
White Men Can't Jump (Shelton), 32, 99, *100*, 101–3, *102*, 111, 113, 128
Whitfield, Stephen J., 41, 72
Who Wants to Be a Millionaire?, 5–6, 13, 18–19, 63
Who Wants to be an Erotic Billionaire?, 112–14, 122
Win, Lose, or Draw, 16
Wire, The, 5–6
"Wise Up," 165–66, 173
Wittgenstein, Ludwig, 36, 169

You Don't Know Jack, 13
You Too Can Have a Body Like Mine (Kleeman), 32, 110, 115–24, 127

Zuckerman Unbound (Roth), 32, 73–78

ABOUT THE AUTHOR

Photo by Nick Ramey

Mike Miley teaches literature at Metairie Park Country Day School and film studies at Loyola University New Orleans. His work has appeared in *TheAtlantic.com*, *Bright Lights Film Journal*, *Critique*, *Music and the Moving Image*, *The Smart Set*, and elsewhere. While he has never appeared on a game show, he has dominated many a trivia night.

www.ingramcontent.com/pod-product-compliance
Lightning Source LLC
Chambersburg PA
CBHW050438240426
43661CB00055B/2432